MW00678241

Component-Based Software Engineering

Selected Papers from the Software Engineering Institute

MW00678241

Component-Based Software Engineering

Selected Papers from the Software Engineering Institute

edited by Alan W. Brown

IEEE Computer Society Press
Los Alamitos, California

Washington • Brussels • Tokyo

IEEE Computer Society Press
10662 Los Vaqueros Circle
P.O. Box 3014
Los Alamitos, CA 90720-1314

Copyright © 1996 by The Institute of Electrical and electronics Engineers, Inc.
All rights reserved

Copyright and Reprint Permissions: Abstracting is permitted with credit to the source. Libraries may photocopy beyond the limits of US copyright law, for private use of patrons, those articles in this volume that carry a code at the bottom of the first page, provided that the per-copy fee indicated in the code is paid through the Copyright Clearance Center, 222 Rosewood Drive, Danvers, MA 01923.

Other copying, reprint, or republication requests should be addressed to: IEEE Copyrights Manager, IEEE Service Center, 445 Hoes Lane, P.O. Box 1331, Piscataway, MJ 08855-1331.

IEEE Computer Society Press Order Number BP07718
ISBN 0-8186-7718-X
Library of Congress Number 96-77860

Additional copies may be ordered from:

IEEE Computer Society Press
Customer Service Center
10662 Los Vaqueros Circle
P.O. Box 3014
Los Alamitos, CA 90720-1314
Tel: + 1-714-821-8380
Fax: + 1-714-821-4641
E-mail: cs.books@computer.org

IEEE Service Center
445 Hoes Lane
P.O. Box 1331
Piscataway, NJ 08855-1331
Tel: + 1-908-981-1393
Fax: + 1-908-981-9667
mis.custserv@computer.org

IEEE Computer Society
13, Avenue de l'Aquilon
B-1200 Brussels
BELGIUM
Tel: + 32-2-770-2198
Fax: + 32-2-770-8505
euro.ofc@computer.org

IEEE Computer Society
Ooshima Building
2-19-1 Minami-Aoyama
Minato-ku, Tokyo 107
JJAPAN
Tel: + 81-3-3408-3118
Fax: + 81-3-3408-3553
tokyo.ofc@computer.org

Assistant Publisher: Matt Loeb
Editor-in-Chief: Jon Butler
Acquisitions Editor: Bill Sanders
Acquisitions Assistant: Cheryl Smith
Advertising/Promotions: Tom Fink
Production Editor: Lisa O'Conner
Cover Design: Alex Torres

Printed in the United States of America by BookCrafters

 The Institute of Electrical and Electronics Engineers, Inc.

CONTENTS

PART IV. SOFTWARE UNDERSTANDING AND EVOLUTION

Preface:
Foundations for Component-Based Software Engineering

Alan W. Brown

Software Engineering Institute
Carnegie Mellon University
Pittsburgh, PA, 15213, USA
awb@sei.cmu.edu

1. Introduction

Major changes are taking place in the way large-scale software-intensive systems are being developed, fielded, and updated. During the past few years a range of technical, economic, and social factors have come together to encourage a new way of software engineering that is often referred to as *component-based software engineering*.

The concept of designing and implementing software systems as a set of components is nothing new. Such approaches have gained popularity for at least three decades. What is new, however, is that large-scale software development is increasingly achieved through component selection, evaluation, and assembly processes where the components are acquired from sources external to the system building organization. A number of factors are driving this approach:

- The development of the world wide web (WWW) and the internet have increased understanding and awareness of distributed computing. The WWW encourages users to consider systems to be loosely coordinated services that reside "somewhere in hyperspacc". In accessing information it becomes unimportant to know where the the information physically resides, what underlying engines are being used to query and analyze the data, and so on.

- Both the use of object-oriented software design techniques and languages, and the move from mainframe-based systems toward client/server computing, lead developers to consider application systems not as monolithic, but rather as separable, interacting components. In some applications, for example, compute-intensive storage and search engines are separated from visualization and display services.

- The rapid pace of change in technology has brought many advantages, but also a number of problems. Organizations are struggling in their attempts to build systems in such a way that they can incrementally take advantage of technology improvements over the system's lifetime.

Such flexibility to accept technology upgrades is seen as a key to gaining competitive advantage.

- The economic realities of the 1990's have led to downsizing, restructuring, and rescoping of many organizations. In many situations it is infeasible to consider constructing each new system from scratch. To stay in business organizations must learn to reuse existing practices and products, and when appropriate to build upon commercial packages in as many parts of a system as possible.

- The latest thinking in industry is having its impact in government. During the past few years government strategy and policy are attempting to address the need for flexibility, portability, and interoperability in its software systems. Most often such needs are expressed in terms of open systems and greater use of commercial products.

However, in pursuing a component-based approach there are many obstacles to be overcome. While many of these are non-technical in nature (e.g. legal liability issues, business case justification), significant *technical* issues must also be faced. Typical questions to be addressed include: How are components evaluated and selected? How is a component-based system assembled to ensure it has appropriate qualities? What factors inhibit communication and data sharing among components? How are existing legacy systems evolved toward a component-based approach? Such questions must be answered to make component-based software engineering a reality.

1.1 The Role of the SEI

The Software Engineering Institute (SEI) is a Federally Funded Research and Development Center (FFRDC) sponsored by the U.S. Department of Defense. The role of the SEI is to provide advice and assistance to its customers in transitioning the best of the state-of-the-art in software engineering into common practice.

Fundamental to the SEI's role is the need to keep track of the latest advances in software engineering, and to apply appropriate research and development effort to discovering techniques for overcoming technical barriers to successful technology transition. In the case of component-based software engineering the SEI is an independent source of advice, investigating advanced techniques and technologies, performing detailed evaluations through application of those technologies, and widely reporting the results in an effort to improve understanding of the technology and its application.

This book contains a set of papers written during 1995 and 1996 by members of the technical staff at the SEI together with collaborators from government, industry, and academe. The papers represent a substantial body of work taking place at the SEI to address the development, deployment, operation, and evolution of component-based systems. The papers explore many issues critical to component-based software engineering, providing the foundations on which this approach to software development can be better understood, applied, and improved.

2. Main Themes of this Book

A number of themes run through the component-based software engineering work being carried out at the SEI, and are reflected in the papers presented in this book. These themes identify the primary considerations in moving from a traditional development approach to a component-based approach: evaluating software components, assembling components within an appropriate software architecture, and introducing and evolving a component-based system.

Software Evaluation

Selection and evaluation of components are critical activities in component-based software engineering. It is vital to have well-developed techniques that allow new technologies and components to be assessed and compared with an existing body of knowledge. Furthermore, once a system has been built, it is important to be able to examine its qualities to ensure it is well-matched to the system's requirements and operating context.

Software Architecture

In building any software system, the architecture of the solution is a determining factor for many of the qualities of that system. In component-based systems, where major pieces of the system are not under the control of the system designer, the architecture plays an even bigger role: it is the blueprint for component integration. While the importance of software architecture is clear, many key aspects remain largely unexplored. Critical areas to be addressed include understanding the role a software architecture plays in a component-based system, creating techniques to analyze resultant architectures, and predicting system qualities based on a given architecture.

Software Understanding and Evolution

Many organizations using commercial software components find themselves just as much locked into their current system as they were using locally-developed software. As well as acquiring commercial components, an organization must also consider the evolution of a component-based system. Many technical challenges must be faced to facilitate disciplined evolution of component-based systems ranging from the need to be able to analyze large amounts of existing legacy code to the difficulties of replacing components in continuous operation mission-critical systems.

However, technical aspects of component-based software engineering cannot be dealt with in isolation. Many organizations find it is non-technical aspects of the problem that predominate. Often this is a result of the practicalities of trying to use someone else's software — such software can never be completely known and understood, thus requiring additional techniques to ensure it is performing as expected. In other cases it is a result of human nature — natural distrust of other people's software. The consequences are a range of social, economic, and legal issues that must be addressed in moving to component-based software engineering. This is reflected in migrating existing legacy applications towards component-based design, and affects the initial introduction of a new system and its ongoing evolution.

3. An Overview of the Papers

The papers in this book are organized into 4 parts. The first is an introduction to component-based software engineering, while the remaining three address the major technical themes identified above: software evaluation, software architecture, and software understanding and evolution. Here we briefly review the papers in the order presented in this book.

Part I. Introduction

- *From Subroutines to Systems: Component-Based Software Development.* This paper discusses the roots of component-based software development, describes some of the key aspects of a component-based approach, and identifies challenges to be faced in acquiring and using commercial components.

- *Engineering of Component-Based Systems.* This paper presents a reference model for the assembly of component-based systems that can be used as the basis for defining a systematic approach to the development of such systems, and for describing major issues to be addressed in moving to a component-based software engineering approach.

Part II. Software Evaluation

- *A Framework for Systematic Evaluation of Software Technologies.* This paper examines the problems of evaluating the impact of a new software technology within an organization, and describes an important component of such an evaluation based on understanding the "deltas" in capability provided by the new technology.

- *Predicting Software Quality by Architecture-Level Evaluation.* This paper presents a method, the Software Architecture Analysis Method (SAAM), for predicting system level quality attributes based upon software architectural evaluation. SAAM makes use of task scenarios derived from the different roles involved in a computer system (administrator, user, maintainer, etc.)

- *Assessing the Quality of Large, Software-Intensive Systems: A Case Study.* This paper presents a case study in carrying out an audit of a large software-intensive system, highlighting quality aspects such as modularity, openness, and evolvability.

Part III. Software Architecture

- *Software Architecture: An Executive Overview.* This paper summarizes the field of software architecture at an executive level. As such it addresses the key question of what is software architecture, and why is it perceived as providing a solution to the inherent difficulty in designing and developing large, complex systems?

- *Toward a Distributed, Mediated Architecture for Workflow Management.* This paper proposes an architecture for a distributed workflow management system based on separable workflow components, and describes reasons for believing it is a viable approach based on early experimental results.

- *A Situated Evaluation of the Object Management Group's (OMG) Object Management Architecture (OMA).* This paper is a case study in the use of the object management architecture to integrate legacy software components into a distributed object system, concentrating on deriving architectural strategies for component-based integration for this class of system.

- *The Gadfly: An Approach to Architectural-Level System Comprehension.* This paper describes the Gadfly, an approach for developing narrowly-focused, reusable domain models that can be integrated and (re)used to aid in the process of architecture-level system comprehension.

Part IV. Software Understanding and Evolution

- *Reengineering: An Engineering Problem.* This paper discusses a conceptual framework for reengineering that is based on a view of reengineering as an engineering problem. Under this view the objective of reengineering is to facilitate the disciplined evolution of a software-intensive system from its current state to a desired state.

- *Coming Attractions in Program Understanding.* This paper identifies a set of emerging technologies in the field of program understanding. Technical capabilities currently under development that may be of significant benefit to practitioners within five years are presented. Three areas of work are explored: investigating cognitive aspects, developing support mechanisms, and maturing the practice.

- *Discovering a System Modernization Decision Framework: A Case Study in Migrating to Distributed Object Technology.* This paper provides an in-depth look at the engineering trade-offs made in modernizing a manufacturing engineering design system to use existing disparate components, and to build on distributed object technology as the underlying infrastructure.

- *Evolving Dependable Real Time Systems.* This paper provides an informal review of the Simplex Architecture, which has been developed to support safe and reliable on-line upgrade of dependable computing systems. In particular, the Simplex architecture addresses the problem of introducing new hardware and software components into deployed systems safely, reliably and easily, in spite of the inevitable bugs in some of the new components.

- *Modernization of Software Maintenance Practices using Computer-Aided Sub-Processes (CASPs).* This paper considers some of the problems of transitioning new practices into a software maintenance organization, focusing on the collection of support material required to transition any software component or tool into long-term effective use.

4. A Look Toward the Future

The work described in this book provides a foundation for component-based software engineering, and forms the basis on which many further investigations must take place. Future work at the SEI (and elsewhere) must be aimed at improving our understanding in a number of areas, requiring a variety of investigations to be performed. These include:

- creating conceptual models of the component-based software engineering approach that direct, inform, and guide exponents of the approach;

- carrying out experiments to verify the validity of the approaches and technologies that form the basis of component-based software engineering;

- performing surveys of end-user organizations to ensure that their needs are fully understood, and that component-based solutions directly address those needs;

- assessing the practical implications of the technologies that have been verified in small-scale studies, but which require improvement and packaging to be ready for large-scale industrial use;

- improving our understanding of the non-technical issues (e.g., acquisition policies, legal aspects, business practices, and organizational structures) as they affect component-based software engineering, and developing technology transition packages which overcome these challenges.

Future plans at the SEI include detailed studies in each of these areas within a number of initiatives in product-line engineering, component-based systems, and dependable system evolution.

5. Acknowledgments

The work of the SEI has greatly benefited from a number of collaborative efforts with other government agencies, industry, and academe. It is our pleasure to recognize the contribution made by a number of people in the development of the work described in this book, including: Gregory Abowd, Rick Kazman, Jock Rader, John Rice, and Evan Wallace.

A number of the papers in this book have previously been published elsewhere. We gratefully acknowledge permission to reprint the following papers in this book:

- *From Subroutines to Subsystems: Component-Based Software Development*, American Programmer, V8 #11, November 1995. Cutter Information Corp.

- *Engineering of Component-Based Systems*, in Proceedings of the 2nd IEEE International Conference on Engineering of Complex Computer Systems, October 1996. IEEE Computer Society Press.

- *Predicting Software Quality by Architecture-Level Evaluation*, in Proceedings of the 5th International Conference on Software Quality. Austin, Tx, October. 1995, pp485-498. American Society for Quality Control.

- *A Framework for Systematic Evaluation of Software Technologies,* IEEE Software, September 1996.

- *Assessing the Quality of Large, Software-Intensive Systems: A Case Study*, in Proceedings of the 5th European Software Engineering Conference, September 1995, Lecure Notes in Computer Science Vol. 989, Spinger-Verlag 1995.

- *Toward a Distributed, Mediated Architecture for Workflow Management,* in Proceedings of the NSF Workshop on Workflow and Process Automation in Information Systems: State-of-the-Art and Future Directions, May 1996, Athens, Ga, NSF.

- *A Situated Evaluation of the Object Management Group's (OMG) Object Management Architecture (OMA)*, in Proceedings of the 11th Annual ACM Conference on Object-Oriented Programming Systems, Languages and Applications (OOPSLA), October 1996, ACM.

- *The Gadfly: An Approach to Architectural-Level System Comprehension,* in Proceedings of the 4th Workshop on Program Comprehension, March 1996, Berlin, Germany, pp178-186. IEEE Computer Society Press.

- *Coming Attractions in Program Understanding*, in Proceedings of CASCON'96, Toronto, Canada, October 1996. IBM Toronto Labs.

- *Discovering a System Modernization Decision Framework: A Case Study in Migrating to Distributed Object Technology*, in Proceedings of the International Conference on Software Maintenance (ICSM), November 1996, IEEE Computer Society Press.

- *Evolving Dependable Real Time Systems*, in Proceedings of the IEEE Aerospace Applications Conference, February 1996. IEEE Computer Society Press.

The Software Engineering Institute is sponsored by the U.S. Department of Defense.

Part I. Introduction

From Subroutines to Subsystems: Component-Based Software Development

Paul C. Clements

Software Engineering Institute
Carnegie Mellon University
Pittsburgh, PA, 15213, USA
pclement@sei.cmu.edu

1. Subroutines and Software Engineering

In the early days of programming, when machines were hard-wired and every byte of storage was precious, subroutines were invented to conserve memory. Their function was to allow programmers to execute code segments more than once, and under different (parameterized) circumstances, without having to duplicate that code in each physical location where it was needed. Software reuse was born. However, this was a different breed of reuse than we know today: This was reuse to serve the machine, to conserve mechanical resources. Reuse to save human resources was yet to come.

Soon, programmers observed that they could insert subroutines extracted from their previous programs, or even written by other programmers, and take advantage of the functionality without having to concern themselves with the details of coding. Generally-useful subroutines were collected into libraries, and soon very few people would ever again have to worry about how to implement, for example, a numerically-well-behaved double-precision cosine routine.

This phenomenon represented a powerful and fundamental paradigm shift in how we regarded software. Invoking a subroutine from a library became indistinguishable from writing any other statement that was built in to the programming language being used. Conceptually, this was a great unburdening. We viewed the subroutine as an atomic statement -- a *component* -- and could be blissfully unconcerned with its implementation, its development history, its storage management, and so forth.

Over the last few decades, most of what we now think of as software engineering blossomed into existence as a direct result of this phenomenon. In 1968, Edsger Dijkstra pointed out that how a program was structured was as important as making it produce the correct answer [2]. Teaching the principle of separation of concerns, Dijkstra showed that pieces of programs could be developed independently. Soon after, David Parnas introduced the concept of information-hiding [6] as the design discipline by which to divide a system into parts such that the whole system was easily changed by replacing any module with one satisfying the same interface. Design methodologists taught us how to craft our components so that they could live up to their promise. Prohibiting side effects, carefully specifying interfaces that guard implementation details, providing predictable behavior in the face of incorrect usage, and other design rules all contributed to components that could be plugged into existing systems. Object-oriented development was a direct, rather recent result of this trend.

2. Software engineering for components

Today, much of software engineering is still devoted to exploring and growing and applying this paradigm. *Software reuse* is about methods and techniques to enhance the reusability of software, including the management of repositories of components. *Domain engineering* is about finding commonalities among systems to identify components that can be applied to many systems, and to identify program families that are positioned to take fullest advantage of those components. *Software architecture* studies ways to structure systems so that they can be built from reusable components, evolved quickly, and analyzed reliably. Software architecture also concerns itself with the ways in which components are interconnected, so that we can move beyond the humble subroutine call as the primary mechanism for sending data to and initiating the execution of a component. Mechanisms from the process world, such as event signalling or time-based invocation, are examples. Some approaches can "wrap" stand-alone systems in software to make them behave as components, or wrap components to make them behave as stand-alone systems. The *open systems* community is working to produce and adopt standards so that components of a particular type (e.g., operating systems developed by different vendors) can be seamlessly interchanged. That community is also working on how to structure systems so they are positioned to take advantage of open standards (e.g., eschewing non-standard

Originally published in *American Programmer*, Vol. 8, No. 11, Nov. 1995, Published by Cutter Information Corp., Arlington, MA (617) 648-1950, http://www.cutter.com. Reprinted with permission.

3

operating system features, which would make the system dependent on a single vendor's product). The emerging *design patterns* community is trying to codify solutions to recurring application problems, a precursor for producing general components that implement those solutions.

3. CBSD: Buy, Don't Build

This paradigm has now been anointed with the name "Component-based software development" (CBSD). CBSD is changing the way large software systems are developed. CBSD embodies the "buy, don't build" philosophy espoused by Fred Brooks [1] and others. In the same way that early subroutines liberated the programmer from thinking about details, CBSD shifts the emphasis from *programming software* to *composing software systems*. Implementation has given way to integration as the focus. At its foundation is the assumption that there is sufficient commonality in many large software systems to justify developing reusable components to exploit and satisfy that commonality.

4. What's New?

In some ways, there is little new about CBSD; it is just a re-iteration of decades-old ideas coming to fruition. There are, however, some exciting new aspects.

Increasing component size and complexity. Today, available off-the-shelf components occupy a wide range of functionality. They include operating systems, compilers, network managers, database systems, CASE tools, and domain-specific varieties such as aircraft navigation algorithms, or banking system transaction handlers. As they grow in functionality, so does the challenge to make them generally useful across a broad variety of systems. Math subroutines are conceptually simple; they produce a result that is an easily-specified function of their inputs. Even databases, which can have breathtakingly complex implementations, have conceptually simple functionality: data goes in, and data comes out via any of several well-understood search or composition strategies. This conceptual simplicity leads to interface simplicity, making such components easy to integrate with existing software. But what if the component has many interfaces, with information flowing across each one that cannot be simply described? What if, for example, the component is an avionics system for a warplane that takes input from a myriad of sensors and manages the aircraft's flight controls, weapons systems, and navigation displays? From one point of view, this software is a stand-alone system; however, from the point of view of, say, an air battle simulator, the avionics software for each of the participating aircraft is just a component. The simulator must stimulate the avionics with simulated sensor readings, and absorb its flight control and weapons commands in order to represent the behavior of the aircraft in the overall simulation. Is it possible to make a plug-in component from such a complex entity? The Department of Defense is working on standards for just such a purpose, to make sure that simulators developed completely independently can interoperate with each other in massive new distributed simulation programs, in which the individual vehicle simulators are simply plug-in components.

Coordination among components. Classically, components are plugged into a skeletal software infrastructure that invokes each component appropriately and handles communication and coordination among components. Recently, however, the coordination infrastructure itself is being acknowledged as a component that is potentially available in pre-packaged form. David Garlan and Mary Shaw have laid the groundwork for studying these infrastructures in their work that catalogues *architectural styles* [3]. An architectural style is determined by a set of component types (such as a data repository or a component that computes a mathematical function), a topological layout of these components indicating their interrelationships, and a set of interaction mechanisms (e.g., subroutine call, event-subscriber blackboard) that determine how they coordinate. The Common Object Request Broker Architecture (CORBA) is an embodiment of one such style, complete with software that implements the coordination infrastructure, and standards that define what components can be plugged into it.

Nontechnical issues. Organizations are discovering that more than technical issues must be solved in order to make a CBSD approach work. While the right architecture (roughly speaking, a system structure and allocation of functionality to components) is critical, there are also organizational, process, and economic and marketing issues that must be addressed before CBSD is a viable approach. Personnel issues include deciding on the best training, and shifting the expertise in the work force from implementation to integration and domain knowledge. For organizations building reusable components for sale, customer interaction is quite different than when building one-at-a-time customized systems. It is to the organization's advantage if the component that the customer needs is most like the component the organization has on the shelf. This suggests a different style of negotiation. Also, customers can form user groups to collectively drive the organization to evolve their components in a particular direction, and the organization must be able to deal effectively with and be responsive to such groups. The organization must structure itself to efficiently produce the reusable components, while still being able to offer variations to important customers. And the organization must stay productive while it is first developing the reusable components. Finally, there are a host of legal issues that are beyond the scope of this paper and beyond the imagination (let alone the expertise) of the author.

5. Buying or Selling?

Different organizations may view CBSD from different viewpoints. A single organization might be a component supplier, a component consumer, or both. The combination case arises when an organization consumes components in order to produce a product that is but a component in some larger system.

Suppose an organization is producing a *product line*, which is a family of related systems positioned to take advantage of a market niche via reusable production assets. In this case, one part of the organization might be producing components that are generic (generally useful) across all members of the product line; the organization may be buying some of the components from outside vendors. Other parts of the organization integrate the components into different products, adapting them if necessary to meet the needs of specific customers. From a component vendor's point of view, product line development is often a viable approach to CBSD because it amortizes the cost of the components (whether purchased or developed internally) across more than one system.

6. Structuring a System to Accept Components

From a consumer's perspective, CBSD requires a planned and disciplined approach to the architecture of the system being built. Purchasing components at random will result in a collection of mis-matched parts that will have no hope of working in unison. Even a carefully-considered set of components may be unlikely to successfully operate with each other, as David Garlan has pointed out in his paper on architectural mis-match [4. The reason is that designers of software components make assumptions that are often subtle and undocumented about the ways in which the components will interact with other components, or the expectations about services or behaviors of those other components. These assumptions are embodied in the designs. Specific and precise interface specifications can attack this problem, but are hard to produce for complicated components. Still harder is achieving consensus on an interface that applies across an entire set of components built by different suppliers.

An architectural approach to building systems that are positioned to take advantage of the CBSD approach is the layered system. Software components are divided into groups (layers) based on the separation of concerns principle. Some components that are conceptually "close" to the underlying computing platform (i.e., would have to be replaced if the computer were switched) form the lowest layer. However, these components are required to be independent of the particular application. Conversely, components that are application-sensitive (i.e., would have to be switched if the details of the application requirements changed) constitute another layer. These components are not allowed to be sensitive to the underlying computing or communications platform. Other components occupy different layers depending on whether

they are more closely tied to the computing infrastructure or the details of the application. The unifying principle of the layered approach is that a component at a particular layer is allowed to make use only of components at the same or next lower layer. Thus, components at each layer are insulated from change when components at distant layers are replaced or modified.

Figure 1 is an example of a layered scheme proposed by Patricia Oberndorf, an open systems expert at the Software Engineering Institute. In this scheme, computer-specific software components compose the lowest layer and are independent of the application domain. Above that lie components that would be generally useful across most application domains. Above that are components belonging to domains related to the application being built. Above that are components specific to the domain at hand, and finally special-purpose components for the system being built.

For example, suppose the system being built is the avionics software for the F-22 fighter aircraft. The domain is avionics software. Related domains are real-time systems, embedded systems, and human-in-the-loop systems. Figure 1 shows components that might reside at each layer in the diagram.

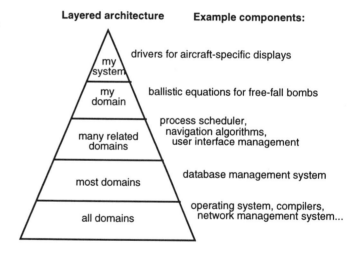

Figure 1. A domain-sensitive layered software architecture

The triangle reflects the relative abundance or scarcity of components at each level. A system developer should not expect to find many components that exist that are specific to the system under construction. It will be easier to find and choose from components that are less domain-specific. For mid-level components, adopting data format and data interchange standards may aid in the search for components that can interoperate with each other.

Domain analysis techniques such as Feature-Oriented Domain Analysis (FODA) [5] can be of assistance in iden-

5

tifying the domain of the system, identifying related domains, and understanding the commonality and variation among programs in the domain of interest.

7. The Payoff and the Pitfalls

The potential advantages to successful CBSD are compelling. They include

- **Reduced development time.** It takes a lot less time to buy a component than it does to design it, code it, test it, debug it, and document it -- assuming that the search for a suitable component does not consume inordinate time.

- **Increased reliability of systems.** An off-the-shelf component will have been used in many other systems, and should therefore have had more bugs shaken out of it -- unless you happen to be an early customer, or the supplier of the component has low quality standards.

- **Increased flexibility.** Positioning a system to accommodate off-the-shelf components means that the system has been built to be immune from the details of the implementation of those components. This in turn means that any component satisfying the requirements will do the job, so there are more components from which to choose, which means that competitive market forces should drive the price down -- unless your system occupies a market too small to attract the attention of competing suppliers, or there has been no consensus reached on a common interface for those components.

Obviously, the road to CBSD success features a few deep potholes. Consider the questions that a consumer must face when building a system from off-the-shelf components:

- If the primary supplier goes out of business or stops making the component, will others step in to fill the gap?

- What happens if the vendor stops supporting the current version of the component, and the new versions are incompatible with the old?

- If the system demands high reliability or high availability, how can the consumer be sure that the component will allow the satisfaction of those requirements?

These and other concerns make CBSD a trap for the naive developer. It requires careful preparation and planning to achieve success. Interface standards, open architectures, market analysis, personnel issues, and organizational concerns all must be addressed. However, the benefits of CBSD are real and are being demonstrated on real projects of significant size. CBSD may be the most important paradigm shift in software development in decades -- or at least since the invention of the subroutine.

8. References

[1] Brooks, F. P. Jr., "No Silver Bullet: Essence and Accidents of Software Engineerig," *Computer*, vol. 20, no. 4, pp. 10-19, April 1987.

[2] Dijkstra, E. W.; "The structure of the 'T.H.E.' multiprogramming system," *CACM*, vol. 11, no. 5, pp. 453-457, May 1968.

[3] Garlan, D., and Shaw, M.; "An introduction to software architecture," in *Advances in Software Engineering and Knowledge Engineering,* vol. I, World Scientific Publishing Company,1993.

[4] Garlan, D., R. Allen, and J. Ockerbloom; "Architectural Mismatch (Why its hard to build systems out of existing parts)", *Proceedings, International Conference on Software Engineering*, Seattle, April 1995.

[5] K. Kang, S. Cohen, J. Hess, R. Novak, and S. Peterson; *Feature-Oriented Domain Analysis Feasibility Study: Interim Report*; technical report CMU/SEI-90-TR-21 ESD-90-TR-222, August 1990.

[6] Parnas, D.; "On the criteria for decomposing systems into modules," *CACM*, vol. 15, no. 12, pp. 1053-1058, December 1972.

Engineering of Component-Based Systems

Alan W. Brown & Kurt C. Wallnau

Software Engineering Institute
Carnegie Mellon University
Pittsburgh, PA, 15213, USA
{awb, kcw}@sei.cmu.edu

Abstract

Many organizations are moving toward greater use of commercial off-the-shelf (COTS) components in the development of application systems. The development of component-based systems introduces fundamental changes in the way systems are acquired, integrated, deployed and evolved. In this paper we present a reference model for the assembly of component-based systems that can be used as the basis for defining a systematic approach to the development of such systems. This reference model is described, and used to explore a number of fundamental development issues.

1. Introduction

For more than a decade good software development practice has been based on a "divide and conquer" approach to software design and implementation. Whether they are called "modules", "packages", "units", or "computer software configuration items", the approach has been to decompose a software system into manageable components based on maximizing cohesion within a component and minimizing coupling among components [13].

However, recently there has been a renaissance in the component-based approach to software development spurred on by two recent advances;

- the object-oriented development approach which is based on the development of an application system through the extension of existing libraries of self-contained operating units;

- the economic reality that large-scale software development must take greater advantage of existing commercial software, reducing the amount of new code that is required for each application system.

Both of these advances, object-oriented development and greater use of commercial off-the-shelf (COTS) software, raise the profile of software components as the basic building blocks of a software system. The development and maintenance of component-based systems, however, introduces fundamental changes in the way systems are acquired, integrated, deployed and evolved. Rather than the classic waterfall approach to software development, systems are designed by examining existing components to see how they meet the system requirements. This is followed by an iterative process of refining the requirements to match the existing components, and deciding how those components can best be integrated to provide the necessary functionality. Finally, the system is engineered by assembling the selected components using locally-developed code.

While many organizations are attempting to understand and take advantage of component-based software development, they lack a basic conceptual framework in which they can describe and discuss their needs, understand different methods and tools, and express issues and concerns. Without this conceptual framework confusion and misunderstandings often occur among engineers and managers, and decisions made cannot easily be rationalized or understood. A number of existing papers (e.g., [11][24]) describe various problems associated with the use of component-based systems, but without presenting a conceptual framework for organizing and categorizing the issues that must be addressed. Such a conceptual framework is a foundation on which further analyses and investigations can take place.

In this paper we present a reference model that can be used as the basis for defining a systematic approach to the development of component-based systems. The model is deliberately simple in its form in order to enable its use as a communication vehicle within and among different organizations. Despite the fact that the model concentrates primarily on technical aspects of the component assembly process and does not address many business and economic issues, we are finding that the model is invaluable as a means of describing and communicating between managers and engineers, for relating and focusing formerly disparate work, and as the basis for planning future tasks.

The remainder of this paper is organized as follows. Section 2 discusses the scope of component-based systems as they form the domain of our work in general, and this paper

0-8186-7718-X/96 $5.00 © 1996 IEEE

in particular. Section 3 describes the stages of the reference model in detail. Section 4 focuses on the transitions between states in the reference model and uses this to explore a number of fundamental issues with respect to the development of component-based systems. Section 5 summarizes the paper, and points to future work that is required to expand the model and its application.

2. Component-based Software Development

While all (real) systems are composed of components, in our usage *component-based* systems are comprised of multiple software components that:

- are ready "off-the-shelf," whether from a commercial source (COTS) or re-used from another system;
- have significant aggregate functionality and complexity;
- are self-contained and possibly execute independently;
- will be used "as is" rather than modified;
- must be integrated with other components to achieve required system functionality.

Examples of component-based systems can be drawn from many domains, including: computer-aided software engineering (CASE), design engineering (CADE) and manufacturing engineering (CAME); office automation; workflow management; command and control, and many others.

From a component-based perspective the process of system design involves the selection of components, together with an analysis of which components can be acquired from external sources (e.g., COTS) and which ones must be developed from scratch. In contrast to the development of other kinds of systems where system integration is often the tail-end of an implementation effort, in component-based systems determining how to integrate components is often the primary task performed by designers. As a result, component integration needs are vital to the component selection process, and a major consideration in the decision to acquire or build the components.

The importance of the integration process has been illustrated in a number of application domains. For example, in the CASE domain the study of component integration is well-established (e.g., see [3][2]). In this domain a number of conceptual models of the integration issues have been developed, and mechanisms specifically targeted at CASE tool integration have been produced. From this work it has been found that an understanding of the component integration process is vital to enable:

- component vendors to develop components that can more easily be integrated with others;
- component integrators to develop efficient engineering techniques that produce coherent systems with acceptable functional and afunctional properties;
- system acquirers to evaluate alternative system engineering solutions for their suitability within a given context;
- system users to understand the implications of requested changes and enhancements to operational component-based systems.

The key to the reference model that follows is a recognition of the central role played by integration in the engineering of component-based systems, and the help this recognition provides in understanding many of the challenges being faced in making component-based system development both efficient and effective.

3. A Reference Model for Component-Based Systems

As suggested in the previous section, the engineering of component-based systems can be considered to be primarily an assembly and integration process. This suggests a reference model for describing the engineering practices involved in assembling component-based systems, as depicted in Figure 1..

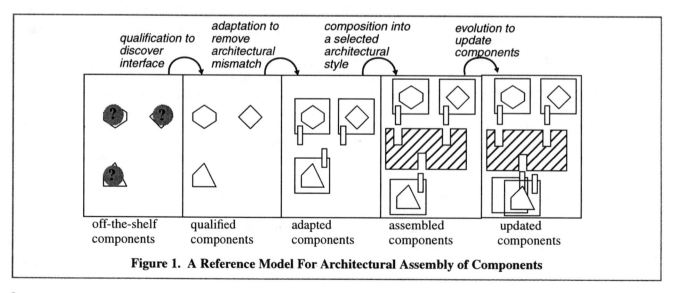

Figure 1. A Reference Model For Architectural Assembly of Components

The vertical partitions depicted in Figure 1. describe the central artifact of component-based systems—the components—in various states. Briefly stated, these partitions are as follows:

- *Off-the-shelf components* have hidden interfaces (using a definition of interface that encompasses all potential interactions among components, not just an application programming interface[18]).

- *Qualified components* have discovered interfaces so that possible sources of conflict and overlap have been identified. This is (by the definition of interface) a partial discovery: only those interfaces important to effective component assembly and evolution are identified.

- *Adapted components* have been amended to address potential sources of conflict. The figure implies a kind of component "wrapping," but other approaches are possible (e.g., the use of mediators and translators).

- *Assembled components* have been integrated into an architectural infrastructure. This infrastructure will support component assembly and coordination, and differentiates architectural assembly from ad hoc "glue."

- *Updated components* have been replaced by newer versions, or by different components with similar behavior and interfaces. Often this requires wrappers to be re-written, and for well-defined component interfaces to reduce the extensive testing needed to ensure operation of unchanged components is not adversely effected.

Having briefly described the main panels of Figure 1, we now discuss each panel in more detail.

3.1 Off-the-shelf Components

Components come from a variety of sources, some developed in-house (perhaps used in a previous project), others specifically purchased from a commercial vendor (typically packages such as database management systems and network monitors). This variety of sources is both a major strength of the component-based approach, and a major challenge, since the components have varied pedigree, many unknown attributes, and are of varied quality.

Selection and evaluation of components are the key activities that take place early in the life cycle of a component-based system. Typically, once the broad functional requirements for a system are known, an organization makes an inventory of known local and external components that may provide elements of that functionality. How the organization proceeds from this point in evaluating the available components depends upon the individual organization.

Many organizations have relatively mature evaluation techniques for selecting from among a group of peer products, and this is reflected in the literature. For example, a number of papers describe general product evaluation criteria (e.g., [10]), while others describe specialized techniques which take into account the particular needs of specific appli-

cation domains (e.g., CASE tools [9] or testing tools [19]). These evaluation approaches typically involve a combination of paper-based studies of the components, discussion with other users of those components, and hands-on benchmarking and prototyping. The complexity of component selection has already been recognized in software engineering literature—a decision framework that supports multi-variable component selection analysis has been developed in order to address some of this complexity [11].

A recent trend in some organizations is toward a "product-line" approach to software development based on a reusable set of components that appear in a range of software products [15]. This approach is based on the premise that similar products (e.g., most radar systems) have a similar software architecture, and a majority of the required functionality is the same from one product to the next. The common functionality can be provided by the same set of components, simplifying the development and maintenance life-cycle.

3.2 Qualified Components

Typically, a component is described in terms of an interface that provides access to component functionality. In many cases this interface is the main source of information about a component: the user manual is often simply a step-by-step guide to the operations available at this interface. However, in a much broader interpretation the interface to a component includes far more than the functionality it provides. To make use of a component one must also understand aspects of the components performance, reliability, usability, and so on.

As a result, for most components there are many unknowns. While much information about a component and its operation can be found through hands-on evaluation, a number of gaps will remain. For example, in real-time safety-critical domains certification of software systems relies on gaining information about mean time between failures, performing timing analysis using techniques such as rate monotonic analysis, and bounding resource usage by ensuring that livelocks and deadlocks cannot occur. In assembling systems from components information on each component is required to complete the analyses. This information includes failure rates, performance models, and detailed software design data. Such information is rarely provided with COTS components, and is frequently missing from in-house component libraries.

There is little established work on how to carry out qualification of software components. In fact, there is little agreement on which attributes of a component are critical to its use in a component-based system. Perhaps the most useful recent work that begins to address this issue is the work on describing quality attributes of software systems. For example, Bass et al. [1] have developed a software architecture analysis method (SAAM) that distinguishes

9

between intrinsic and extrinsic properties of a component, and investigates the influences of those properties on a software architecture. However, much further work remains in this area.

Qualification of a component can also extend to a qualification of the development process used to create and maintain a component. Again, this is most obvious in safety-critical applications (for example, ensuring algorithms have been validated, and that rigorous code inspections have taken place). However, the concept is extending beyond the safety-critical domain. For example, many organizations now insist that contractors are ISO 9000 certified [20], or that they have reached a certain level on the SEI's Capability Maturity Model (CMM) [12]. This ensures that the software components they produce have been developed using well-defined practices and procedures.

3.3 Adapted Components

The variety of sources for components leads to a number of problems. These arise because stand-alone components are being used to construct a system where the components must cooperate. The result is a number of conflicts with respect to concerns such as:

- sharing resources such as memory, swap space, and printers;
- carrying out common activities such as data management, screen management, and version control;
- environment set-up using environment variables, temporary files, and common naming policies.

These conflicts are symptoms of a more pervasive problem in engineering component-based systems: architectural mismatch of components [7]. That is, the wide variety of conflicting operating assumptions made by each component. (This issue is examined in much more detail in the next section.)

As a consequence of these conflicts, components must be adapted based on a common notion of component "citizenship" (i.e., based on rules that ensure conflicts among components are minimized). This usually involves some form of component wrapping — locally developed code that provides an encapsulation of the component to mask unwanted and incompatible behavior. Different forms of wrapping exist based on how much access is provided to the internal structure of a component. The approaches can be classified as white box, where access to source code allows a component to be significantly re-written to operate with other components, grey box, where source code of a component is not modified but the component provides its own extension language or application programming interface (API), and black box, where only a binary executable form of the component is available and there is no extension language or API [23].

Wrapping is not the only approach to overcoming component incompatibilities. Another approach is through the use of mediators. Informally, we can view a mediator as an active agent that coordinates between different interpretations of the same system property. For example, a mediator may translate between different data formats, establish common events, or define common administrative policies (e.g., for security and access control).

3.4 Assembled Components

The assembled components are integrated through some well-defined infrastructure. This infrastructure provides the binding that forms a system from the disparate components.

It is useful to consider at least three different levels at which the infrastructure must operate:

- At the highest abstract level the infrastructure embodies a coordination model that defines how the different components will interact to carry out the required end-user functionality. It is the role of the infrastructure to allow this coordination model to be readily described, validated, and enacted.
- At a lower level the infrastructure provides services that will be used by the components to interact and to carry out common tasks. The interface to these services must be complete and consistent.
- At the most practical level the infrastructure is itself a software component that implements the necessary coordination services required. It must be well-written so that it is easily understood, perform effectively, and be readily updated to new modes of component interaction.

There is a long history of developing infrastructure capabilities based on three classes of technology: operating systems, database management systems, and messaging systems. Each has their particular strengths and weaknesses. Currently, most active research is taking place with the use of messaging systems as infrastructure providers, particularly using object request brokers (ORBs) conforming to the Common Object Request Broker Architecture (CORBA). While use of ORBs is immature, initial reports cite a number of advantages to their use in building component-based systems [25][17].

3.5 Updated Components

As with any system, a component-based system must evolve over time to fix errors and to add new functionality. Here again, component-based systems bring their own strengths and weaknesses.

On the surface a component-based approach brings advantages in terms of its ease of evolution: components are the unit of change. Hence, to repair an error an updated component is swapped for its defective equivalent treating components as plug-replaceable units. Similarly, when additional functionality is required it is embodied in a new component which is added to the system.

However, this is too simplistic a view of component upgrade. Replacement of one component with another is often a time-consuming and arduous task since the new component must be thoroughly tested in isolation and in combination with the rest of the system. Wrappers must typically be re-written, and side effects from changes must be found and assessed.

Compounding this upgrade problem is that component producers frequently upgrade their components based on error reports, perceived market needs, and product aesthetics. New component releases require a decision from the component-based system developer on whether or not to include the new component in the system. To answer" yes" implies facing an unknown amount of re-writing of wrapper code and system testing. To answer "no" implies relying on older versions of components that may be behind the current state-of-the-art and may not be adequately supported by the component supplier.

As an illustration of the impact of component upgrades consider a system consisting of 12 COTS components, each of which is released as a new version every 6 months. To keep up with the latest version of each component requires on average a system upgrade every two weeks. If new releases are not installed, analysis of which component versions are compatible become more and more difficult, leading to a system administrator's nightmare.

In safety-critical systems the problems of system upgrades are even more acute. Not only is the testing and analysis of new components a critical yet time-consuming endeavor, it is usually unacceptable to have long periods of time in which the system is unavailable. In such cases complex techniques for dependable upgrade of highly-available systems must be employed (e.g., using approaches such as the Simplex architecture [21]).

3.6 Summary

In this section a reference model for the engineering of component-based systems has been described. The model highlights the component assembly process and the various activities that must take place in building a component-based system.

In the next section we make use of the reference model as a framework for describing a number of issues that distinguish the engineering of component-based systems from traditional development approaches.

4. Component Integration Issues

Using the concepts of the reference model presented in Section 2, we describe what we believe are four key issues that must be addressed in the engineering of component-based systems. We begin with a discussion of system life-cycle issues peculiar to component-based systems, then focus more narrowly on the technical issues that arise as a consequence of transitioning between key states (panels) of the architectural assembly reference model depicted in Figure 1.

4.1 Understanding the Component-Based Systems Life-cycle

The traditional software engineering life-cycle is not applicable when engineering systems from components. The typical waterfall phases of requirements, design, implementation, test, and maintenance clearly still apply. However, due to extensive use of existing components, the activities involved in each phase and the relationships among phases are often significantly changed from current approaches.

We can characterize the component-based approach as essentially one of negotiating a set of engineering trade-offs for the integration of a set of existing components to satisfy a particular set of requirements. The key to the engineering of component-based systems is to understand what trade-offs are being made, to record the rationale used in making trade-off decisions, and to evaluate how those trade-offs affect the resultant product in practice. This provides the necessary basis for improving the system as requirements or operating conditions evolve over time.

Here we consider 2 key engineering trade-offs involved in assembling and evolving component-based systems.

System requirements vs. available components

The initial stages of developing a component-based system involve the selection of components that are likely to satisfy the main system requirements. However, most organizations restrict selection of components to a small number in recognition that the organization can be more efficient if it does not manage too diverse a set of components. Thus, scanning the complete marketplace for every possible component that may be of interest is typically not carried out: an organization uses those components with which it is familiar.

As a result of initial component selection, the typical "80/20" rule often applies — 80% of the system functionality can be provided relatively easily with the selected components, while the remaining 20% can only be provided with much more difficulty. At this point the system engineers may consider what changes to the system requirements may make the use of selected components more effective. Once identified, these can be discussed with the users of the system to understand the priority of these requirements, and make decisions concerning which requirements can be amended.[1]

---

1. In fact, recently proposed changes in U.S. DoD policy state that where greater use of COTS components is possible, the system requirements should be changed to facilitate this.

In component-based system development, system designers must address a number of important buy versus build decisions with respect to many parts of the system. Such decisions are faced in all application domains, but are particularly important in safety-critical systems where reliability, availability, and predictability are essential. Often the majority of the system is developed in-house to ensure the organization has complete understanding and control of the system operation and evolution. In spite of any savings that may accrue, using commercial components in such situations is frequently considered too high a risk.

System architecture vs. component interfaces

The architecture of a system defines the basic components of the system and their connections [8]. Many alternatives exist in designing the architecture of a system, each with its own strengths and weaknesses in terms of how that architecture provides the key attributes of the system. A primary task of a system engineer is to evaluate the architectural alternatives by prioritizing system attributes based on perceived end-user needs. Components must then be assembled to provide those attributes.

Such an approach raises a number of challenges. First, it is unclear what are the attributes of a system that most contribute to a system's efficiency and effectiveness, and how such attributes can practically be assessed. Second, the relationships among afunctional attributes (e.g., performance, dependability, usability, maintainability, etc.) is poorly understood. While practical experience has identified a number of trade-offs between afunctional attributes of a system (e.g., between performance and maintainability), analytical techniques for examining these trade-offs are still lacking. Finally, it has been found in practice that there are characteristics of a component interface that facilitate some kinds of system architecture while precluding others [16]. For example, the granularity of access to component data often influences the rate at which data synchronization among components can practically occur. Further work is required to more fully understand how component interfaces influence the component assembly process.

While attempts have taken place to address these challenges by classifying system architectures in terms of their key attributes, currently system engineers primarily base their system architectures on past experience in building similar systems. Particular models of system behavior are reused from one system to another, modifying the architecture to meet the particular characteristics of the specific components being used.

4.2 Interface Discovery and Analysis

Obviously, a pre-condition for successful integration of components is that their interfaces are known. Borrowing a phrase from the hardware domain (always a risky proposition in the software domain), component integrators need to discover the *function and form* of software components—the

services provided, and the means by which consumers access these services, respectively.

Different degrees of sophistication can be found in techniques used to discover the form and function of software components. At one extreme a few key functions may be of such high priority as to obviate the need for exhaustive component analysis. The discovery process in these cases can be as simple as browsing vender literature, examining programmer documentation, etc. At the other extreme component classes (e.g., database, geographic information system, network management, spreadsheet) can be modeled in terms of features. Then, particular components can be described via functional profiles against these component-domain models, much like *Consumer Reports* might describe different brands of televisions or food processors. This more robust discovery approach has been adopted by COTS-focused efforts that espouse a product-line approach to component-based systems [4].

However, even a complete understanding of component functionality and the interfaces to this functionality is insufficient for anything but trivial system integration problems. In fact, the *complete* interface of a component includes more than just the mechanisms that a component uses to make its functionality available to clients: it includes all of the assumptions made by a component about integration-time and run-time uses of the component. For example, each of the following might be considered part of a component interface:

- application programming interface (API);
- required development and integration tools;
- secondary storage requirements (run-time), processor requirements (performance) and network requirements (capacity);
- required software services (operating system, or from other components);
- security assumptions (access control, user roles, authentication);
- embedded design assumptions, such as the use of specific polling techniques;
- exception detection and processing.

This list—which is by no means exhaustive—illustrates that implementation decisions normally thought to be "hidden" by abstract interfaces play a crucial role in determining whether, and how easily, components can be integrated. Further, these assumptions are not easily detected from vendor literature or functional interface specifications.

To this list we can also add an additional class of component properties sometimes referred to as "quality attributes" [10]. Assumptions about the run-time environment may impinge upon quality attributes such as reliability; for example, a component may not be designed for continuous operation, or operation in environments that may experience varying degrees of degraded performance.

The essential problem we are describing is that our current interface specification techniques do not adequately address all of the properties exhibited by components that will determine, ultimately, the integrability of the component. Nor do we yet know all of the different kinds of assumptions that components can make that may result in architectural mismatch. Thus, we are hampered from discovering the interface of a component because we are not always sure what we need to look for. Worse, we do not have well-defined notations or theories for describing and measuring all interface properties, especially those relating to quality attributes. All of this is compounded, of course, when we are confronted with components that are "black boxes" as is the case with COTS components: we are groping in the dark to discover the features of a component that lies on the other side of a locked door.

4.3 Removal of Architectural Mismatches

Assuming that we can discover the *complete* interface of a component, the next step is to repair any mismatches that have been detected among components[2]. Given the difficulty of discovering complete interfaces, however, this would seem to be a glib prescription.

At this juncture the role of *software architecture* can be asserted. Software architecture deals with high-level design patterns, often expressed as components, connectors and coordination [8]. Components[3] refer to units of functionality, connectors with the integration of components, and coordination as the manner in which components interact at run-time. One role of software architecture (in component-based systems) is to restrict the classes of potential mismatches that might arise among component interfaces, and thus offer useful constraints for the interface discovery process. For example, by prescribing a specific coordination model, a software architecture in effect identifies and prioritizes the *key* run time interfaces a component must exhibit either natively or via adaptation.

The topic of component adaptation has received even less attention than interface discovery. The consensus seems to be that this process is inherently ad hoc, low-level and very messy. Various euphemisms for adaptation such as "glue" and "chewing gum" are revealing in themselves. A euphemism with more sanitary connotations is "wrapper." Nevertheless, considering the important role that component adaptation code will play in large-scale component-based systems— especially those with safety or security requirements—it seems necessary to gain a firmer grasp of this topic.

---

2. Many of the latent "bugs" in component-based systems arise because of undetected, and hence un-repaired, architectural mismatch.

3. The component-based definition of this term is more restrictive than its use in software architecture literature.

A first step along this road is to classify the different adaptation techniques that are possible, and to understand when their uses are required. For example, glue and wrapper are evocative of different component adaptation approaches. Wrappers suggest that a component is adapted by encasing it within a virtual component that presents an alternative, translated interface; glue suggests a somewhat less contained approach, with code oozed between components, for example a collection of shell scripts and filters.

More generally, integration involves a relationship between entities[22]. Adaptation can occur at one or all endpoints of a relationship, or on the relationship itself, for example through the introduction of an intermediary component (a.k.a. "mediator"). The software architecture may provide mechanisms to facilitate component adaptation; alternatively, adaptation mechanisms may lie outside of the scope of the architecture. Examples of both have appeared in practice.

4.4 Architecture Selection & System Composition

The selection of a particular architectural style, or the invention of a custom style, is perhaps the most important design decision of all. The functionality of a component-based system will be found in the components; the quality attributes (e.g., security, maintainability) will be found in the architecture. Beyond this, the architecture will drive the integration effort: as discussed in the previous section, architecture defines the integration-time and run-time contexts into which components must be adapted.

For example, in developing a command and control system from COTS components it may be possible to select from a number of architectural styles:

- database, in which centralized control of all operation data is the key to all information sharing among components in the system;

- blackboard, in which data sharing among components is opportunistic involving reduced levels of system overhead;

- message bus, in which components have separate data stores coordinated through messages announcing changes among components.

Each architectural style has its own strengths and weaknesses in terms of overall system qualities, and requires different considerations in the selection of components.

Despite the importance of this early design decision, our understanding of architectural styles, the combination of different styles, and the use of one or more styles to achieve targeted quality attributes, is still very immature. Moreover, little work has been focused directly upon the question of which architectural styles are best-suited to component-based systems. To be sure, canonical architectural styles have emerged from application domains that exhibit component-based properties, e.g., integrated computer-aided software engineering (CASE) [3]. Nevertheless, the CASE experience has been a mixed success at best; in any event, different application domains have different needs and hence will require different architectural approaches than found in CASE.

To illustrate the still-unsettled nature of our understanding of architectures for component-based systems, consider the fundamental dichotomy between function-oriented and structure-oriented architectural approaches. The function-oriented approach is by far the predominant approach to component-based systems. It defines components to match available off-the-shelf components, and defines interfaces in terms of component functionality. Greater abstraction is sometimes obtained by generalizing component-specific interfaces, thus encapsulating some technology and vendor dependencies. A good illustration of a function-oriented approach has been defined in the command and control domain [14]. Function-oriented architectures are good for describing system functionality and for integrating specific functionality but are weak for addressing the run-time properties of a design, e.g., throughput, latency and reliability.

The structure-oriented approach has emerged as the study of software architecture has intensified. Rather than defining component interfaces in terms of functionality, structural styles define interfaces in terms of the role a component plays in a *coordination model*—a model that describes how the components interact. A simple illustration of a structural style is UNIX pipes and filters; more sophisticated illustrations include structural models for flight simulators [5], the Simplex architecture for evolvable dependable real-time systems [21], and prototype architectures for distributed workflow management [6] and distributed manufacturing design engineering [25]. The structural approach yields architectures that support analysis of dynamic system properties, but are not optimized to support access to component-specific functionality.

Which of these approaches should be adopted? What about approaches that merge some aspects of both—a structural approach to describe how components interoperate, with functional extensions as common infrastructure facilities? Such a hybrid is found in an emerging, standard high-level architecture for interoperable simulations [5]. Whatever approach is taken will have a profound effect on the integrability of a component-based system. In addition, better design heuristics are needed to select among these (and many other) architectural trade-offs.

4.5 Predictable Component Update

Systems in operational use must periodically be updated. Typically, this involves developing an updated system, performing extensive testing, and then switching over to the new system in the field. A number of potential problems arise in doing this:

- identifying and bounding the changes that are required to the system;
- testing the system sufficiently to ensure that the updates do not have undesirable consequences on the rest of the system;
- ensuring that the old system can be put back on-line should the behavior of the new system be unacceptable,

In mission-critical application domains (e.g., avionics or health care patient monitoring) the consequences of poorly planned and implemented system upgrades are sufficient that often systems are not upgraded. This occurs despite the availability of improved algorithms, techniques, and technology that could improve the system's overall effectiveness.

Engineering systems from components further complicates the upgrade problems, since many of the components are maintained by third party organizations. As a result, changes to those components are often not well-understood by system integrators and end-users, and often not documented in sufficient detail. This leaves system integrators with the challenge of evolving component-based systems in a predictable, dependable way in the face of incomplete information about the components to be upgraded.

A number of approaches have been taken to try to address these problems. One of the most interesting involves the design of a layer of software that supports reliable and safe upgrade of on-line systems [21]. This layer of software, known as the Simplex Architecture, is based on three key ideas: components as replaceable system units, controlled replacement transactions, and a real-time publish and subscription facility. The Simplex Architecture also supports the use of analytic redundancy through a fault-tolerant protocol known as the Simple Leadership Protocol (SLP). In addition to supporting system evolution, model-based voting used by SLP allows the tolerance of combined hardware and software failures.

A number of demonstrations of this approach have been built. In one of these based on a triplicated computer fault tolerant group utilizing SLP, it was shown that safe on-line upgrade of application software, operating systems, and hardware components are all feasible using this approach. While many issues remain to be addressed with this approach (e.g., scaleability issues when applied to large systems), it provides an very useful illustration of how dependable evolution of component-based systems may be possible in the future.

5. Summary and Conclusions

The trend towards greater reliance on off-the-shelf components for even the most complex software systems is increasingly clear. Numerous large system acquisitions in the US DoD and Government agencies in very demanding application domains—air traffic control, real-time simulators, and command and control to name just a few—are pushing the limits of our ability to develop systems with predictable properties.

Unfortunately, engineering practices have not been keeping pace with the changing nature of system building. Our ability to describe the key properties of software components to enable their rapid and error-free integration is inadequate; our techniques for discovering the interfaces of previously-developed, possibly COTS components is significantly hampered; and our understanding of architectural patterns best suited for component-based systems, and the techniques best suited for adapting components to these patterns is still quite immature.

However, much work is in progress to try to address these challenges. Interface discovery techniques are being developed by extracting experiences from system integrators; understanding of software architectures is maturing; and system evolution techniques are emerging which allow safe on-line upgrade of component-based systems.

In this paper we have explored the challenges to engineering of component-based systems by presenting a reference model of the key activities in the constructive phases of component-based systems development (assembly and re-assembly/evolution). Although we briefly touched on other aspects of component-based systems, such as requirements acquisition processes sensitive to off-the-shelf component reuse, our focus has been on the technical aspects of integrating component-based systems. The reference model we presented, while not complete or detailed, provides a good foundation for discussing key component integration issues and for relating different trends in software engineering (notably, software architecture and component-based systems).

Acknowledgments

We are grateful to David Carney and Ed Morris for their valuable comments on earlier drafts of this paper.

The SEI is sponsored by the U.S. Department of Defense.

6. References

[1] Abowd, G., Bass, L., Kazman, R., Webb, M., "SAAM: A Method for Analyzing the Properties of Software Architecture," in proceedings of the 16th International Conference on Software Engineering, Sorrento, Italy, pp. 81-90, May 1994.

[2] Brown, A.W. and Penedo, M.H., "An Annotated Bibliography of Software Engineering Environment Integration", ACM Software Engineering Notes V17 #3, pp47-55, July 1992.

[3] Brown, A.W., Carney, D.J., Morris, E.J., Smith, D.B., Zarella,P.F., *Principles of CASE Tool Integration*, Oxford University Press, 1994.

[4] Comprehensive Approach to Reusable Defense Software (CARDS) Home Page, http://www.cards.com

[5] Defense Modeling and Simulation Organization, High-Level Architecture, http://www.dmso.mil/project/hla

[6] Earl, A., Long, F., and Wallnau, K., "Towards a distributed, mediated architecture for workflow management," To appear in proceedings of NSF Workshop on Workflow Management:

State of the Art and Beyond, Athens, GA, May 8-10, 1996.

[7] Garlan, D., Allen, R., Ockerbloom, J., "Architecture Mismatch: Why Reuse is so Hard", IEEE Software V12, #6, pp17-26, November 1995.

[8] Garlan, D. and Shaw, M., "An Introduction to Software Architecture," in Advances in Software Engineering and Knowledge Engineering, vol. I, World Scientific Publishing Company,1993

[9] IEEE Recommended Practice on the Selection and Evaluation of CASE Tools, P1209, 1994.

[10] Information Technology — Software Product Evaluation — Quality Characteristics and Guidelines for their Use, International Standards Organisation (ISO), ISO/IEC 9126:1991, 1991.

[11] Kontio, J., "A case study in applying a systematic method for COTS selection" proceedings of the 18th International Conference on Software Engineering (ICSE), pp. 201-209, March 1996.

[12] Paulk, M.C., Curtis, B., & Chrissis, M.B. *Capability Maturity Model for Software*. Technical Report CMU/SEI-91-TR-24, ADA240603, Software Engineering Institute, Carnegie Mellon University, Pittsburgh, PA, August 1991.

[13] Parnas, D.L., "On the criteria to be used in decomposing systems into modules," Communications of the ACM, Vol. 15, No. 2, pp. 1053-1058, 1972.

[14] PRISM Generic Command Center Architecture, http://www.cards.com/PRISM/prism_gcca.html

[15] MBSE Home Page, http://www.sei.cmu.edu/technology/mbse/mbse.html

[16] Nejmeh, B., *Characteristics of Integrable Tools*. Technical Report INTEG_S/W_TOOLS-89036-N Version 1.0, Software Productivity Consortium, May 1989.

[17] Orfali, R., Harkey D., and Edwards, J., "The Essential Distributed Objects Survival Guide", John Wiley and Sons, Inc., 1996.

[18] Parnas, D.L., "Information distribution aspects of design methodology," in proceedings of IFIP conference, 1971, North Holland Publishing Co.

[19] Poston R.M., and Sexton M.P., "Evaluating and Selecting Testing Tools", IEEE Software,V9, #3, pp33-42, May 1992.

[20] Schumauch C.H., *ISO 9000 for Software Developers*, ASQC Quality Press, 1994.

[21] Sha, L., Rajkumar, R., and Gagliardi, M., *A Software Architecture for Dependable and Evolvable Industrial Computing Systems*, Technical Report CMU/SEI-95-TR-005, Software Engineering Institute, Carnegie Mellon University, Pittsburgh, PA, July 1995.

[22] Thomas, I. and Nejmeh. B., "Definitions of Tool Integration for Environments" IEEE Software, Vol 9, No.3, pp. 29-35, March 1992.

[23] Valetto, G. and Kaiser, G.E., "Enveloping Sophisticated Tools into Computer-Aided Software Engineering Environments", Proceedings of 7th IEEE International Workshop on CASE, July 1995.

[24] Vidger, M.R., Gentleman, W.M., and Dean, J., "COTS Software Integration: State-of-the-art", Technical Report, National Research Council Canada, January 1996. http://wwwsel.iit.nrc.ca/abstracts/NRC39198.abs

[25] Wallnau, K., and Wallace, E., "A Robust Evaluation of the Object Management Architecture: A Focused Case Study in Legacy Systems Migration" submitted to OOPLSA'96.

15

Part II.   Software Evaluation

Predicting Software Quality by Architecture-Level Evaluation

Paul Clements & Len Bass

Software Engineering Institute
Carnegie Mellon University
Pittsburgh, PA, 15213, USA

Rick Kazman

Department of Computer Science
University of Waterloo
Waterloo, Ont., N2L 3G1, Canada

Gregory Abowd

College of Computing
Georgia Institute of Technology
Atlanta, GA 30332, USA

Abstract

The importance of evaluating a software design for fitness and achievement of quality as early as possible in the software development life cycle is discussed. An architectural description of a proposed system is an early opportunity for determining the quality trade-offs, the priorities implicit in the design, and the feasibility of achieving the desired functionality within the specified design. We present a method, the Software Architecture Analysis Method (SAAM), for predicting system level quality attributes based upon software architectural evaluation. SAAM makes use of task scenarios derived from the different roles involved in a computer system (administrator, user, maintainer, etc.) in order to evaluate competing architectures. We illustrate SAAM in the context of a simple but classic software architecture example, a key-word-in-context system.

1. Introduction

In order to achieve a predictable, repeatable process for engineering high-quality software systems, it is clear that quality must be introduced and evaluated at the earliest phases of design. From a developer's point of view, it is not acceptable to proceed through detailed design and implementation phases only to discover that the decisions made early in the process, at the architectural level, did not turn out to promote the desired quality attributes to be achieved. Perhaps the decomposition into components was inappropriate to accommodate likely life-cycle modifications; perhaps the inter-component communication protocols were too complex to permit the required performance, or not complex enough to provide the necessary security and protection from intrusion.

In fact, there are at least two reasons for wanting to evaluate a system from the perspective of its architecture. First, from a customer's point of view, it is not acceptable to be forced to take a vendor's word that a system under development will meet its quality requirements (particularly with respect to long-term quality needs and the system's response to change) without being able to independently evaluate the vendor's architectural decisions. The customer should be able to perform independent evaluations based upon the design of the vendor's system. Second, from a developer's point of view, design decisions should be evaluated as early as possible in the software development life cycle.

This paper describes an attempt to reduce the problematic nature of high-level evaluation of a design with respect to software quality attributes. The method focuses attention on architectural features which reveal design biases and flaws early in the life cycle. From a customer perspective, this technique provides a framework for deciding among competing products at an architectural level.

This paper is divided into two logical components:

1. We discuss the role of architectural evaluation in the achievement of system quality.

2. We summarize the Software Architecture Analysis Method, or SAAM, which provides a way to achieve early insight into the quality attributes offered (or prohibited) by a software architecture. SAAM has been tested on actual architectures in the user interface software [4], Internet information systems [5], air traffic control [1], and CASE tool domains, and is currently undergoing refinement, expansion, and formalizing in order to expand its domain of applicability.

Section 2 lays some conceptual groundwork for the method. An overview of SAAM is presented in Section 3. Section 4 uses the key-word-in-context (KWIC) example to demonstrate how the evaluation works. This is an example of interest, since it has been used by several authors as a simple case study for comparing different architectural solutions. Section 5 discusses the applicability of SAAM and suggests directions for future research.

2. Evaluating a Software Architecture

2.1 The Roles of Software Architecture

By software architecture, we mean the components into which a system is divided at a gross level of system organi-

Reprinted from *Proc. 5th Int'l Conf. Software Quality*, 1995, pp. 485-498.
The American Society for Quality Control, Inc., 1995. Reprinted with permission.

19

zation, and the ways in which those components behave, communicate, interact, and coordinate with each other [2, 6]. Examples of components include modules, processes or tasks, subsystems, Ada packages, or Unix filters. Examples of coordination mechanisms include procedure call (remote or otherwise), synchronization (e.g., rendezvous), data sharing, message passing, event broadcast, subscription schemes, and Unix pipes [8]. An architectural view of a system[1] separates the concerns of components' functionality (computation) from the ways in which they interact to cooperatively perform the system's job (coordination).

An architecture plays several roles in project development, all of them key. They include

- **Basis for communication**. Project team members, managers, and customers all turn to the architecture as the basis for understanding the system and its development.

- **Project blueprint**. The choice of components is institutionalized in the developing organization's team structure, work assignments, management units, schedule and work breakdown structures, integration plans, test plans, and maintenance processes. Once it is made, an architectural decision has an extremely long lifetime and survives even outside of the software that it describes.

- **Embodiment of earliest design decisions**. The architecture represents the first mapping from requirements to computational components. The selection of components and connections, as well as the allocation of functionality to each component, is a codification of the earliest design decisions about a project. As such, they are the decisions that are the hardest to change, have the most far-reaching consequences, and deserve the most scrutiny.

- **First order approach to achieving quality attributes.** An architecture can either allow or preclude the achievement of most of a system's targeted quality attributes. Modifiability, for example, depends extensively on the system's modularization, which reflects the encapsulation strategies. Reusability of components depends on how strongly coupled they are with other components in the system. Performance depends largely upon the volume and complexity of the inter-component communication and coordination, especially if the components are physically distributed processes. Thus, an architecture embodies decisions about quality priorities and tradeoffs and represents the earliest opportunity for evaluating those decisions and tradeoffs.

- **Blueprint for product line development.** An architecture may be reused on other systems for which it is appropriate. If managed carefully, an entire product family may be produced using a single architecture. In this case, the importance of an appropriate architecture is magnified across all the projects it will serve.

---

1. There may be more than one such view for a given system.

2.2 The Role of Architectural Evaluation

Because of the importance of architectural decisions, it is fitting that they receive tight scrutiny. In particular, few will argue that it is more cost-effective to evaluate software quality as early as possible in the life cycle, assuming the quality evaluation is correct, because software quality cannot be appended late in a project; it must be inherent from the beginning. It is in the project's best interest for design candidates to be evaluated (and rejected, if necessary) during the design phase, before long-term institutionalization occurs.

Therefore, a technique to assess a candidate architecture—*before* it becomes the project's engraved blueprint—has great value.

On the other hand, it should be noted that an architecture cannot guarantee the functionality or quality required of a system. Poor downstream design or implementation decisions can always undermine an architectural framework. Decisions at all stages of the life cycle—from high level design to coding and implementation—will impact on quality. Therefore, quality cannot be completely assessed on the basis of an architectural description. An architecture-based quality assessment provides only one dimension of a system's quality characteristics and is a necessary, but not sufficient, component of evaluating the overall quality of a system.

Associated with the large variance of an assessment of quality based on architectural analysis is the granularity of the system description necessary to perform an evaluation and the types of tests that can be performed. In our analysis method, we use gross divisions of functionality and minimally detailed scenarios to perform the analysis. The output of the evaluation is a relative ranking of the candidate architectures, but not absolute numbers of architectural quality. This reflects the inherent variance of performing architectural analysis at a very coarse grain. We justify this coarse analysis by noting that we can perform it at a relatively low cost and very early in the software development life cycle.

2.3 Evaluating Qualities with Scenarios

Most software quality attributes are too complex and amorphous to be evaluated on a simple scale, in spite of our persistence in describing them that way. Consider

- Suppose a system can accommodate a new computing platform merely by being re-compiled, but that same system requires a manual change to dozens of programs in order to accommodate a new data storage layout. Do we say this system is or is not *modifiable*?

- Suppose the user interface to a system is carefully thought out so that a novice user can exercise the system with a minimum of training, but the experienced user finds it so tedious as to be inhibiting. Do we say this system is *usable* or not?

The point, of course, is that quality attributes do not exist in isolation, but rather only have meaning within a context. A system is modifiable (or not) with respect to certain classes of changes, secure (or not) with respect to specific threats, usable (or not) with respect to specific user classes, efficient (or not) with respect to specific resources, and so forth. Statements of the form "This system is highly maintainable" are, in our opinion, without operational meaning.

This notion of context-based evaluation of quality attributes has led us to adopt *scenarios* as the descriptive means of specifying and evaluating quality attributes. SAAM is a scenario-based method for evaluating architectures; it provides a means to characterize how well a particular architectural design responds to the demands placed on it by a particular set of scenarios, where a scenario is a specified sequence of steps involving the use or modification of the system. It is thus easy to imagine a set of scenarios that would test what we normally call modifiability (by proposing a set of specific changes to be made to the system), security (by proposing a specific set of threat actions), performance (by proposing a specific set of usage profiles), etc.

A particular scenario actually serves as a representative for many different scenarios. For example, the scenario "change the background color on all windows to blue" is essentially equivalent to the scenario "change the window border decorations on all windows". We use the clustering of scenarios as one of our evaluation criteria. As a consequence, judgment needs to be exercised as to whether the clustered scenarios represent variations on a similar theme or whether they are substantially different. In the first case, the clustering is a good thing; in the second, it is bad. In other words, if a group of scenarios are determined to be similar, and they all affect the same component or components in an architecture (i.e., they cluster), we deem that to be a good thing, because it means that the system's functionality has been modularized in a way that properly reflects the modification tasks. If, on the other hand, a group of similar scenarios affect many different components throughout an architecture, we deem that to be bad.

As an aid to creating and organizing scenarios, we appeal to the concept of *roles* related to the system. Examples of roles include: the person responsible for upgrading the software—the end user; the person responsible for managing the data repositories used by the system—the system administrator; the person responsible for modifying the run-time functions of the system—the developer; the person responsible for approving new requirements for the system, etc. The concept of roles matches the difference between runtime qualities and non-runtime qualities, i.e., those qualities that are a function of the system's execution (such as performance), and those that reflect operations performed offline in a development environment (such as modifiability). Scenarios of the former variety would be performed by roles such as end user; the latter by developers or maintainers.

3.   Overview of the Analysis Method

In this section we present our analysis method. In broad brush strokes, it has three stages:

1. define a collection of scenarios that represent important usages of a system in the domain including the points of views of all of the roles involved in the system

2. perform an evaluation with respect to how the individual scenarios impact the candidate architectures

3. perform an evaluation with respect to how the scenarios interact with each other

The analysis will provide, for each scenario, a ranking of the architectures being evaluated (the so-called *candidate* architectures). It is the responsibility of the evaluator to determine the weighting of the scenarios with respect to each other and, hence, an overall rating of the candidates.

3.1 SAAM

For the purposes of exposition, here we assume that we are comparing two architectures (and hence the rankings can be given as +/-, but the generalization to more architectures should be obvious). For N scenarios, we generate N+1 rankings: one for each scenario plus one measuring scenario contention.

The steps of the method are

1. Develop task scenarios that illustrate the kinds of activities the system must support. These will reflect the non-functional qualities of interest, but the explicit connection between scenario and qualities is not necessary. These scenarios will also present interactions from different roles, such as end user, system administrator, maintainer, and developer. This task should be undertaken by a domain expert. These scenarios should reflect all roles relevant to the system.

2. Express the candidate architectures in a common syntactic architectural notation and with a common granularity.

3. For each task scenario, determine whether each candidate architecture supports this task without modification (i.e., can the system carry out this scenario without human intervention), or whether the candidate architectures needs to be modified in order to support the task.

   If both candidate architectures support this task, we rank them as equal with respect to this scenario, and we need do no further analysis with respect to this scenario.

   If one candidate architecture supports this task directly and the other does not, the candidate architecture that supports the task directly is ranked + and the other is ranked -, and we do no further analysis with respect to this scenario.

If neither candidate architecture supports this task, we need to continue with the steps below.

4. For each remaining scenario and for each architecture, indicate what computational components are affected by that scenario. This requires in-depth knowledge of the architecture which would typically be provided either by the developer or by a complete set of system specifications. Where such information is not available, this method may suggest areas which require more complete specifications and may suggest what design decisions to make.

5. For each architecture and for each scenario, determine the number of computational components affected.

   If the number is equal in both architectures, rank them equally with respect to this scenario.

   Otherwise, rank the architecture with the smaller number of components affected as a +; rank the one with the larger number of components affected as a -.

6. For those scenarios and candidate architectures where the computational components affected by the scenario were indicated, determine how many components within each architecture were affected by multiple (different in kind) scenarios. Give the candidate architecture with the fewest contentions among scenarios a + and the other -.

7. Finally, weight each scenario and the contention among scenarios, and use that weighting to determine the overall ranking.

Some of these steps may be iterative. For example, the choice of scenarios will be influenced by the systems in the domain to be analyzed. All of these choices can be made by reiterating through the appropriate steps of the method.

3.2 Discussion of Method

The evaluation method depends on counting the number of computational components affected by a scenario or by scenario contention. There are a number of uncertainties associated with this step:

- granularity of representation. If two different representations for the same system were compared, the one with the coarser granularity would score better on the individual scenarios and the one with the finer granularity would score better on the scenario contention step. Because multiple scenarios are necessary to determine contention, the use of this method with a single scenario makes the results very dependent on the granularity of representation.

- minor versus major modification to a component. There is not a distinction in the method between making a simple one-line change to a component and making major structural modifications to that component.

- scenarios as representative of a class. We mentioned above that it is a good thing for closely related scenarios to cluster

and a bad thing for disparate scenarios to cluster. This is manifest in the step of evaluating scenario contention. If the scenarios that contend are closely related, then the clustering is, in fact, a good thing.

Because of these uncertainties, the application of this method requires some design experience and judgement. We are currently conducting experiments to determine how repeatable the method is with a variety of different designers.

The concept of clustering of scenarios is, in fact, a stage toward turning this method into a generative method where the scenarios are used to drive the design. This is what has happened in more mature domains, such as databases, compilers, or user interfaces, where an existing, widely agreed-upon *functional partitioning* is available for use. In such cases, this functional partitioning may be used instead of purely basing the evaluation upon scenarios, as has been demonstrated [4]. Such distinctions represent refinements of the method presented here.

4. A Simple Example

In this section, we apply SAAM to an example application, KWIC (key-word-in-context), that has been used previously by others to illustrate points about software engineering and software architecture. This example, due to Parnas [7], is small, easily understandable, and familiar. Thus, it makes a good example to illustrate our method. This example has also been used elsewhere [2, 3] to illustrate the powers of architectural analysis, and so provides an interesting benchmark for comparing techniques for software architectural analysis.

On the other hand, because of its small size and technical limitations, some of the discussions about possibilities become contrived within the context of the example. We assume the reader will understand that the contrived portions are intended to be illustrative and not to be taken seriously as extensions to the KWIC problem.

The message of Parnas' paper in 1972 was the virtue of information hiding as the abstraction around which to organize a system's functionality. We take many of the ideas which are implicit in that paper and make them explicit through our evaluative method. This is the single most important contribution of SAAM—the explicit statement of a method for evaluation—not the use of scenarios nor the comparison of candidate architectures by means of scenarios.

The initial functional description for the KWIC program is to take as input a list of sentences where each sentence is an ordered set of words. The program outputs a listing of all circular shifts of all sentences in alphabetical order. So, for example, if the following sentences were given as input:

predicting software quality

architecture level evaluation

The KWIC program would produce, as output:

architecture level evaluation

evaluation architecture level

level evaluation architecture

predicting software quality

quality predicting software

software quality predicting

4.1 Defining Roles and Scenarios

The KWIC example has two roles of interest: the *end user* who wishes to produce the KWIC index and the *developer* who produces or modifies the code that produces the KWIC index.

Two of the scenarios we use that have been discussed by various authors involve the end user:

1. Modify the KWIC program to operate in an incremental rather than a batch fashion. This version of the program would work by accepting one sentence at a time, and producing an alphabetical list of all permutations of all sentences input to date.

2. Modify the KWIC program to eliminate entries beginning with "noise" words (articles, prepositions, pronouns, conjunctions, etc.).

The other two scenarios we will use involve the developer but are not apparent to the end user:

3. Change the internal representation of the sentences (e.g., compressed or uncompressed).

4. Change the internal representation of intermediate data structures (e.g., either store the shifted sentences directly or store an index to the shifted words).

4.2 Describing Candidate Architectures

The next step of the method is to represent the candidate architectures in a common notation. This is done in order to ease the evaluation process so that the evaluator knows exactly what a box or arrow means in the architectural diagram.

Shared memory solution

In the first candidate architecture, there is a global storage area, called *Sentences*, where all of the input sentences are stored. The input sentences are: read by the *Input* routine; stored in *Sentences*; shifted by the *Circular Shift* routine (which builds a *Shift Index* of the starting locations of each of the shifted permutations of the original input sentence, rather than storing the sentences themselves in shifted form); alphabetized by the *Alphabetize* routine (which stores an alphabetized version of the *Shift Index*); and then output. *Master Control* passes control to the various routines as required.

Figure 1. is annotated with the evaluations from the scenarios (the numbers in the various computational components). In this step we can simply ignore the annotations.

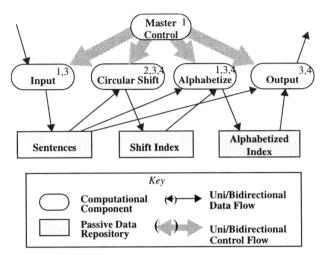

Figure 1.   KWIC—shared memory solution

Abstract data type solution

The second architecture, represented in Figure 2., uses an abstract data type (ADT) where each function hides and protects its internal data representation and provides specialized access functions as the only way to store, retrieve, and query the data. The *Sentence* ADT has access functions *set* and *getNext* to add and retrieve a sentence. The *Shifted Sentences* ADT provides the *setup* access function to set up its circular shifts of the sentences,[2] and the *getNext* function to retrieve the shifted sentences.

The *Shifted Sentences* ADT makes use of the *getNext* function from the *Sentence* ADT to retrieve stored input sentences. The *Alphabetized Sentences* ADT provides a *setup* function and an *i-th* function. The *setup* function calls *Shifted Sentences'* *getNext* function repeatedly to retrieve all the lines to be sorted and sorts them. The *i-th* function, called specifying some integer parameter *i*, returns the ith sentence from the sorted list of *Shifted Sentences*.

---

2. As both Parnas [7] and Garlan and Shaw [2] point out, the ADT solution admits of other possibilities. For example, the *setup* function in the *Shifted Sentences* ADT may in fact do nothing when it is called, and all shifts are done "on demand." That is, whenever the *Shifted Sentence getNext* function is called, the ADT gets another sentence from the *Sentences* ADT and shifts it. However, for the purposes of architectural analysis, some assumptions must be made about how the functions will work together. SAAM assumes that each function is accompanied by a specification, so that when doing an architectural analysis, these decisions are known.

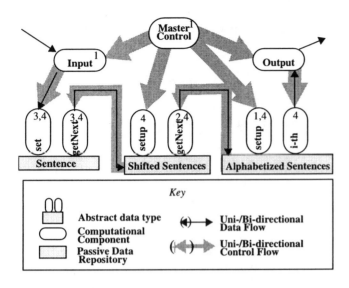

Figure 2. KWIC—ADT solution

4.3 Evaluating the Candidate Architectures

Now that we have specified the candidate architectures in a common notation, the next step in the method is to evaluate the architectures against the scenarios. The evaluation proceeds by considering each of the scenarios in turn. Each of the scenarios which we have chosen for evaluation of the KWIC architectures are indirect. That is, they can not be directly executed by the candidate architecture so that all of the evaluation is dependent upon some modification to the architecture.

Scenario 1

The first scenario is to move from a batch mode to an incremental mode. That is, operate on one sentence at a time rather than inputting all of the sentences and operating on the total input.

For the shared memory solution, this requires a modification of the *Input* routine, so that it yields control after each sentence. *Master Control* must be modified because the sequencing among the subordinate routines is going to be repetitive rather than calling each routine only once. The *Circular Shift* will need to be modified because an incremental algorithm, such as insertion sort, must be used rather than one that sorts all of the sentences at once. Presumably, the *Circular Shift* routine operates on one sentence at a time and the output function outputs whatever is available whenever it is called.

Note the assumptions we are making about the specification of the routines in the shared memory solution. In general, the accuracy of the judgments are dependent on knowledge of the internal workings of the various computational components. That is why we expect the evaluation to be performed by individuals either with general knowledge of the computa-

tional components or with access to the specification of the components.

For the ADT solution, shown in Figure 2., the *Input* function needs to be changed so that only one line at a time is input each time it is called. The *Sentence* abstraction is assumed to be implemented to relinquish control when it has stored its input. Since it receives input one sentence at a time, this need not be changed. The *Shifted Sentences* abstraction is also assumed to be implemented to request and shift all available sentences when it is invoked. Thus, this routine also does not need to be modified. The *Alphabetized Sentences* abstraction must be modified as in the shared memory example.

For this scenario, since both candidate architectures have been affected equally, we rate the two architectures neutral.

Scenario 2

The second scenario is the elimination of noise words. This change is most easily performed by modifying the shifter function in both architectures (*Circular Shift* in the shared memory architecture and *Shifted Sentences* in the ADT architecture) to eliminate those shifted sentences beginning with noise words. Since the shifter function is localized in both architectures, and since noise word elimination does not affect the internal representation of the sentences, the difficulty of making this modification is equivalent for the two architectures.

Scenario 3

The third scenario is the modification of the internal representation of an input sentence, e.g., moving from an uncompressed representation to a compressed representation.

In the shared memory architecture all functions share a common representation, and so all of the functions are affected by this scenario, except for the *Master Control*. In the ADT architecture, the input sentence internal representation is buffered by the *Sentence* abstraction. Thus, the ADT architecture is better than the shared memory architecture for this scenario.

Scenario 4

In this scenario—changing the representation of the intermediate data structures—we observe that the shifting and alphabetizing functions maintain indices to the input sentences and only one copy of the input sentence exists.

For the shared memory example, this requires a modification of the *Circular Shift*, the *Alphabetizer* and the *Output* routines.

For the ADT solution, this requires a modification of the *Shifted Sentences* and the *Alphabetized Sentences* ADTs. Thus the ADT solution affects fewer components and is superior for this example.

Contention Analysis

Both figures have been annotated to reflect the impact of each scenario. For example, the "1" inside the *Master Control* component in Figure 1 reflects the change to that component required to support Scenario 1. Examining the candidate architectures to determine which one has more contention of scenarios (components with more than one scenario annotation) we see that the ADT is superior in this regard. While both architectures show scenario contention in four components, in the shared memory solution the contention is among three of the task scenarios in two components (*Circular Shift* and *Alphabetize*), whereas no component in the ADT solution has contention from more than two tasks.

Summary of evaluation

Table 1 summarizes the results of our evaluation. A 0 indicates that neither architecture is superior with respect to this task scenario. In a real evaluation, the evaluation would conclude by weighting the scenarios to represent the organization's priorities. For example, if the addition of functions was the primary concern (as represented by scenario 2) then the two architectures would be ranked closely, since they do not differ with respect to this task.

If, on the other hand, a change in the internal representation of sentences (as represented by scenario 3) was of primary concern to the organization, then the ADT solution would be clearly superior.

Table 1. Summary of Evaluation

	Scenario 1	Scenario 2	Scenario 3	Scenario 4	Contention
Shared Memory	0	0	-	-	-
Abstract Data Types	0	0	+	+	+

5. Summary

SAAM is a method for early, coarse-grained evaluation of architectures with respect to stated concerns about quality attributes expressed in the context of specific circumstances (scenarios). It provides a conceptually straightforward vehicle for performing what is a necessary, but not sufficient, step in evaluating an architecture-level design for a software system. In particular, it provides a way to compare competing architectures against a common quality standard. Passing the SAAM test (or any architecture evaluation) does not guarantee a system that will meet its requirements; downstream design and implementation decisions can always undermine the best architectures. However, SAAM does provide an early "sanity check" during a development phase in which precious little analysis is possible.

Currently, SAAM is not well-suited for predicting performance qualities. Given a scenario that captures what is important to achieve about performance, a SAAM user would then perform a thought experiment that conceptually executes the scenario and conceptually measures the results. Conceptually measuring performance is not particularly reliable, although the procedure of defining the scenarios is a necessary step before one can predict performance by more analytic means. The incorporation of performance evaluation into SAAM at the same coarse-grained level is an on-going area of investigation.

In the future, we would like to render SAAM more repeatable. That is, it should be likely that two different evaluators, given the same set of scenarios, should derive the same functional partitioning and the same evaluation results. Our approach to this problem will be through attempting to further formalize the method as well as through field studies and empirical evaluations.

6. References

[1] Brown, A; Carney, D.; & Clements, P. "A Case Study in Assessing the Maintainability of a Large, Software-Intensive System." *Proceedings of the International Symposium on Software Engineering of Computer Based Systems*. Tucson. IEEE Computer Society, March 1995.

[2] Garlan, D. & Shaw, M. "An Introduction to Software Architecture." *Advances in Software Engineering and Knowledge Engineering*. Volume I. World Scientific Publishing, 1993.

[3] Garlan, D.; Kaiser, G.; & Notkin, D. "Using Tool Abstraction to Compose Systems." *IEEE Computer 25*, 6 (June 1992): 30-38.

[4] Kazman, R.; Bass, L.; Abowd, G.; & Webb, M. "SAAM: A Method for Analyzing the Properties Software Architectures," 81-90. *Proceedings of the 16th International Conference on Software Engineering*. Sorrento, Italy, May 1994.

[5] Kazman, R.; Bass, L.; Abowd, G.; & Clements, P. "An Architectural Analysis Case Study: Internet Information Systems." *Proceedings, First International Workshop on Architectures for Software Systems*. Seattle, April 1995.

[6] Perry, D. & Wolf, A. "Foundations for the Study of Software Architecture." *Software Engineering Notes 17*, 4 (October 1992): 40–52.

[7] Parnas, D. L. "On the Criteria To Be Used in Decomposing Systems into Modules." *Communications of the ACM 15*, 12 (1972): 1053-1058.

[8] Shaw, M.; DeLine, R.; Klein, D.; Ross, T.; Young, D.; & Zelesnik, G. "Abstractions for Software Architecture and Tools to Support Them." *IEEE Transactions on Software Engineering 21*, 4 (April 1995).

A Framework for Systematic Evaluation of Software Technologies

Alan W. Brown & Kurt C. Wallnau

Software Engineering Institute
Carnegie Mellon University
Pittsburgh, PA 15213

(awb, kcw@sei.cmu.edu)

Abstract

Many organizations struggle to make informed decisions when investing in new software technologies. This paper examines the problems of evaluating the likely impact of a new software technology within an organization, and describes an important component of such an evaluation based on understanding the "deltas" provided by the new technology. The main contribution of this paper is a framework for organizing software technology evaluations that highlights technology deltas. That is, the framework centers on the premise that new technologies must be positioned within the context of their contemporaries, and analyzed from the point of view of what they contribute in relation to those existing technologies.

The technology delta framework is described, and is illustrated through its application to the Object Management Group's Object Management Architecture (OMA). Strengths and weaknesses of the approach are then analyzed, and required future work in this area discussed.

1. Introduction

All organizations developing or using software-intensive systems must continually make decisions regarding the selection, application, and introduction of new software technologies. Some technology decisions are made explicitly following a detailed examination of the alternatives (e.g., deciding on a standard word processor within the organization), while others are made implicitly with little detailed study of the potential impact of the decision (e.g., deciding to ignore a new product line from an operating system vendor). In all of these cases the organization is attempting to understand and balance a number of competing concerns regarding the new technology. These concerns include:

- the initial cost of acquiring the new technology;
- the long term effect on quality, time to market, and overall cost of the organization's products and services when using the new technology;
- the impact of introducing the new technology into the organization in terms of training, and other necessary support services;
- the relationship of this new technology in the organization's overall future technology plans;
- the attitude and actions of direct competitor organizations with respect to this new technology.

Based on these and other factors the organization develops an assessment of the likely return on investment (ROI) of using this new technology. While in many domains ROI has a well-defined meaning and is calculated using established techniques and formulas, this is not the case in the software technology domain. In fact, while highly desirable, attempts at developing a general, repeatable approach to the calculation of software technology ROI have been unsuccessful. There are many reasons for this, foremost among them being the difficulty in establishing cause and effect when assessing the impact of new software technologies within an organization.

Unable to generate a concrete prediction of ROI for a new technology, most organizations must instead obtain an informed view of the technology based on applying a collection of techniques. While these techniques are mostly informal in nature (e.g., attending trade shows, pilot application, case studies) they nevertheless lead to an "informed intuition" about the technology that can be used to make a decision.

Performing technology evaluations is an important component of the role of Software Engineering Institute (SEI). The SEI provides advice to its customers on current software engineering best practices, helps to transition promising technologies, and raises awareness of future technology trends. One particular effort underway at the SEI, called **STEIM** (Software Technology, Evaluation, Integration and Measurement), focuses on developing evaluation techniques and measures which are particularly applicable to technologies that support integration of systems comprised

A shorter version of this paper appears in *IEEE Software*, September 1996.
Copyright © 1996 by The Institute of Electrical and Electronics Engineers, Inc. All rights reserved.

of off-the-shelf components. Our experiences with examining a range of system integration technologies highlighted the need for greater rigor in the way in which our evaluation data was collected and analyzed, and for a more systematic approach to planning, executing, and interpreting evaluation results. To address these problems we have developed a conceptual framework that can be used to categorize the different software technology evaluations that are possible, and suggest a method for carrying out a systematic evaluation based on populating the framework with the results of specific experiments that reveal information about a software technology.

Briefly stated, the premise of our evaluation framework is that one key piece of evidence needed by an organization is qualitative and quantitative reports on technology "deltas", i.e., descriptions of the impact of the new features introduced by a technology as differentiated from features found in existing technologies. Hence, in this paper we describe a framework that highlights techniques for identifying and describing these technology deltas, and for defining focused application-oriented experiments to estimate the costs and benefits of these deltas in particular usage scenarios.

The remainder of this paper is organized as follows. Section 2 reviews existing techniques that are used to evaluate and compare different software technologies. Section 3 describes the technology delta framework and its use in performing software technology evaluations. Section 4 provides a detailed case study of the use of the technology delta framework. Section 5 summarizes the main points of the paper and briefly describes future work we plan to carry out in this area.

2. Current Approaches to Technology Evaluation

Most organizations recognize the importance of technology refreshment to improve the quality of their products and services, to be competitive with other organizations providing similar products and services, and to remain attractive to investors in the organization and to a technology-oriented workforce. To stay in business an organization must invest in appropriate new technologies.

Hence, careful decision making on new technologies is essential to an organization. Given the release of an update to an existing technology, or the availability of a new competing technology, an organization must initiate an evaluation process that provides timely, balanced information on which an informed decision can be made. As a result, a number of approaches and techniques for technology evaluation are in use, and a number have been described in the software engineering literature. In this section we review the approaches commonly in use in practice, and those described in the literature.

2.1 Technology Evaluation in Practice

Today technology evaluations are typically carried out in an ad hoc way, heavily reliant on the skills and intuition of the staff carrying out the evaluation. By examining current industrial practice, and through surveying existing experience reports we can identify a number of approaches that are being employed by an organization. These approaches include:

- obtaining objective data on the technology by documenting case studies at other organizations;
- gathering subjective opinions and experiences with the new technology by attending trade shows, and by conducting interviews or by sending out questionnaires to vendors and users of the technology;
- conducting focused experiments to mitigate high-risk aspects of a new technology;
- demonstrating the feasibility of a new technology by executing a pilot project;
- comparing a new technology to existing practices by conducting a shadow project and examining the results of both approaches;
- phased exposure to a new technology by initiating demonstrator projects within a small part of the organization.

Sometimes an organization focuses on one of these approaches, while at other times some combination of approaches is employed.

Regardless of the approaches used we find that what is missing is a well-developed conceptual framework for technology evaluation that allows the results of the evaluation to be considered in terms of what this new technology adds to the existing technology base. Rather, a typical organization carries out one or more of the approaches above, gathers any resultant data, and forms an intuition concerning the value of that technology. It is our assertion that much of the informality in interpreting the results of any evaluation is due to the absence of:

1. well-defined goals before starting on the evaluation;

2. controlled, rigorous techniques for data gathering when carrying out the evaluation;

3. a conceptual framework for analyzing the data that is produced in the context of existing technologies.

While similar observations have been made [1], most attention has been concentrated on the second of these issues, exploring the need for rigorous data gathering and the use of quantitative software evaluation techniques (e.g., [2][3][4]). In this paper we address the remaining two items by developing a conceptual framework that allows evaluation goals to be defined and the resultant data to be analyzed in context.

2.2 Technology Evaluation in the Literature

A number of interesting papers on technology evaluation have appeared in the software engineering literature over the past few years. In analyzing these papers it is useful to distinguish between two classes of evaluation which we can refer to as product-oriented and process-oriented:

- *Product-oriented*: selecting among a set of products that provide similar functionality (e.g., a new operating system, design tool, or workstation);

- *Process-oriented*: assessing the impact of a new technology on existing practices to understand how it will improve performance or increase quality (e.g., a new design methodology, programming language, or software configuration management technique).

Many organizations have relatively mature evaluation techniques for the product-oriented decisions, and this is reflected in the literature. For example, a number of papers describe general product evaluation criteria (e.g., [5]), while others describe specialized techniques which take into account the particular needs of specific application domains (e.g., CASE tools [6] or testing tools [7]).

Process-oriented evaluation approaches address a more difficult decision faced by an organization which is trying to assess the potential impact of a new technology approach as a whole, and to estimate the impact of that technology approach on the organization's practices, products, and services. Documented approaches in the literature tend to focus on process improvement first (often based around the SEI's Capability Maturity Model (CMM) [8] or ISO 9000 standards [9]), with technology support a secondary consideration.

There are two interesting exceptions to this approach. First, a paper by Boloix and Robillard describes a system evaluation framework that provides high-level information to managers about the characteristics of a software system [10]. The strength of the approach is that it provides a broad snapshot of a system by considering a number of different perspectives (end-user, developer, and operators). However, it aims at providing a rapid high-level review (for example, a complete review of a system takes about an hour and a half). Little detailed insight into the strengths and weaknesses of a technology in comparison with its peers are either sought or revealed.

Second, in work by Bruckhaus a technology impact model is defined and applied to a large CASE tool development [11][12]. The method provides quantitative data on the impact of various CASE tool alternatives based on assessing the number of steps that are required when carrying out a particular scenario. While the approach is valuable, it concentrates on impact purely as a measure of increasing or decreasing the number of process steps, ignoring the intrinsic value of the technology itself, and avoiding any attempt to compare peer technologies for their relative value-added.

2.3 Summary

The problem of evaluating software technology has been addressed with a wide range of methods and techniques that address different aspects of the problem. Our examination of this work has found a number of limitations with respect to its lack of a clear framework for defining goals and analyzing results, and its focus on single product instances. Our work has been aimed at overcoming these limitations to provide a conceptual framework that facilitates:

- setting of technology evaluation goals based on understanding the value-added of a new technology approach;

- use of a range of evaluation techniques within an overall framework for synthesizing the disparate results obtained;

- individual product evaluations that concentrate on their distinguishing characteristics in relation to their technology precursors and product peers.

3. The Feature Delta Framework: Principles and Techniques

In order to determine the value-added of a technology, it is necessary to identify the features which differentiate a candidate technology from other technologies, and to evaluate these differential features (the *feature delta*) in a specific and well-defined application context. But how does one identify and then assess feature deltas in a disciplined way? Figure 1. provides a high-level depiction of the tech-

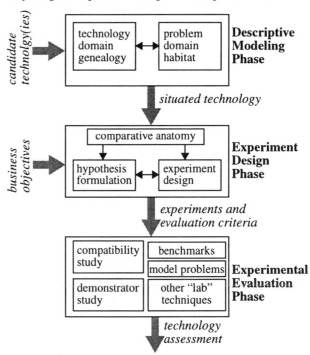

Figure 1. Technology Delta Evaluation Framework

29

nology delta framework, an approach we have developed to answer this question.

3.1 Technology Delta Principles

The framework embodies a number of important principles. First, of course, is the notion that the potential impact of a technology is best understood in terms of its feature delta. That is, while all of the features of a technology are relevant to understand the technology and how to apply it, to understand the value-added of a new technology it is essential to focus attention on its distinctive features, i.e., to discover its value-added *with respect to some other technologies*.

Second, it is not sufficient to simply describe the distinctive features of a technology; it is also essential to evaluate these features in a well-defined and sharply-focused usage context. The technology delta framework exhibits a strong bias towards the use of rigorous experimental techniques for evaluating feature deltas. Specifically, hypotheses are formed about how a feature delta supports a defined usage context, and experimental techniques are then used to confirm or refute these hypotheses.

Third, the framework reflects and embraces the inherent complexity, ambiguity and dynamism of the technology marketplace. Technologies are not static; nor do they exist in isolation. A technology's feature set is a function of the way it is intended to be used, and a function of what competing technologies provide, and both change over time. The use of descriptive modeling to analyze and document the interdependencies between technologies, and between technologies and their usage contexts, is crucial to a disciplined technology evaluation.

Last, the framework reflects a limited but well-defined objective. There are many factors to consider when evaluating a technology, for example installation costs, market forecasting, organizational resistance, and other non-technical considerations. We view the technology delta framework as addressing a necessary but not sufficient aspect of technology evaluation. Our desire is to robustly address the technical aspects of determining valued-added, and leave questions pertaining to, e.g., technology transition and return on investment, to disciplines better equipped to deal with such issues.

In the following sections we describe the techniques we have used in each of the evaluation phases depicted in Figure 1.

3.2 Descriptive Modeling Phase

The descriptive modeling phase addresses feature discovery and impact prediction through the development of *technology genealogies* and *problem habitats*, respectively. The output of this phase is a *situated technology*: models which describe how a technology is related to other technologies, and the usage contexts in which it can be evaluated. Situating a technology in a technology marketplace and in a problem domain provides a basis for identifying feature deltas.

The technology genealogy reflects the fact that new technologies are most often minor improvements of existing technologies (in fact, this assertion represents a capsule summary of the history of technology). As a consequence, if we want to understand a technology in terms of its features, we need to understand the historical and technological antecedents which led to the evolution of the technology. For example, to understand the unique contribution of object-oriented programming technology it is essential to understand its heritage in programming language theory (data abstraction, polymorphism), design theory (information hiding), and simulation and human-computer interaction (modeling real-world entities in software).

However, the features of a technology alone are insufficient to understand value-added; for this, it is necessary to understand how these features will be used and what benefits will accrue from their use—this is the role of the problem habitat. For example, the world-wide web is essentially an integration of several pre-existing technologies (internet, graphical user interface, scripting language, protocols, and hypertext), and can be described largely in terms of the features of these constituents. The potential impact of the web, however, is enormous despite its modest lineage. To predict this impact, the web must be understood in terms of its potential use in electronic publishing, entertainment, and direct sales to name a few.

Our choice of terminology for denoting these models is significant. There is an interesting analogy between the task of describing technology features and usage contexts and the task of describing biological species and habitats. In both cases we define species and technologies through externally visible characteristics: morphology for species and features for technology. Further, the characteristics we use for descriptive purposes, while not arbitrary, are selected because they are easy to use and are sufficient to distinguish species and assign individuals to species. Finally, for Darwinians, there is a strong correlation between these characteristics and habitat, both of which change over time.

The important point to note is that descriptive models are just that—they are descriptions of assumptions made by the technology evaluator concerning the kinds of features that are of interest, and their relationship to usage contexts that will later form the basis of experimental evaluation. There are no formal tests for the completeness or consistency of these models, nor should we expect there to be. Instead, we should view the descriptive models as a foundation for a rigorous approach to describing technologies, for achieving community consensus on the key features needed to distinguish technologies, and for documenting the evaluation process itself.

Descriptive modeling has analogues in the field of domain analysis [13]. Concepts have been borrowed from feature-oriented domain analysis methods, in particular ODM [14]. From ODM, notions of descriptive modeling, domain genealogy and comparative feature analysis are borrowed whole cloth. Unlike domain analysis, however, the descriptive models generated for technology deltas are not end-products, but are instead used as guides for structuring evaluation experiments and for interpreting the results of these experiments. Thus, we are less concerned with formalizing the notation or the specific form of the work products produced for descriptive modeling than are practitioners of domain analysis.

Genealogies and habitats can be modeled as semantic networks. While we have not yet defined a rigorous ontology for constructing such networks—and believe that it is premature to do so—several different node and link types have proven useful, and these are summarized[1] in Table 1.

Table 1. Primitives for Genealogy and Habit Models

Ontology	Form	Interpretation
Technology	Node	A class of functionality, analogous in meaning to "species."
Specification	Node	A description of a technology for its producers/consumers.
Product	Node	An implementation of a technology or specification.
Peer	Link	Nodes (of any type) that have similar features.
Competitor	Link	Products or specifications that compete in marketplace.
Problem Context	Link	Class of problems addressed by a node (of any type).
Is-A	Link	Product or specification is an instance of a technology.
Part-Of	Link	Bundled and/or separable products or specifications.

Nodes in these models represent different ways of thinking about technology, while the links help establish relationships between these views of technology, and form a basis for making assertions about feature deltas. To this end it is also useful to annotate the links with feature lists. For example, consider

---

1. Technology analysts should freely extend this ontology, but should be guided by the principle that each element of the ontology should serve to relate technologies, and ultimately yield feature deltas.

a hypothetical genealogy of middleware technologies. In such a genealogy it would be plausible to describe SoftBench [15] and FIELD [16] as *peers*; this link could be annotated with the features that distinguish SoftBench from FIELD.

Examples of genealogy and habitat models are provided in Section 4. We note here, however, that these models are co-dependent (as is illustrated in Figure 1.). That is, it is often necessary to develop these models iteratively, as the problem-domain habitat suggests technologies to consider, while the technology-domain genealogy conditions our ideas about which problems can be addressed.

3.3 Experiment Design Phase

The experiment design phase is essentially a planning activity. The output of this phase is a set of hypotheses about the value-added of a technology that can be substantiated or refuted through experimentally-acquired evidence, and a set of defined experiments that can generate this evidence and that are of sufficient breadth and depth to support sound conclusions regarding value-added. As illustrated in Figure 1., three activities are involved in this planning: *comparative anatomy*, *hypothesis formulation* and *experiment design*.

Comparative anatomy involves a more detailed investigation of features deltas. We have found that as hypotheses are formed and experiments are designed questions arise that require a more detailed examination of technology features; conversely, these examinations often suggest hypotheses and experimental approaches. It might appear that comparative anatomy should be undertaken in the descriptive modeling phase as just another kind of feature study. However, we placed comparative anatomy in the experimental design phase because we have empirical rather than purely descriptive techniques for conducting comparative anatomy:

- reference model benchmarking for qualitative feature descriptions using an *a priori* feature vocabulary; and,
- feature benchmarking for quantitative feature descriptions.

There is no precise definition for what constitutes a reference model; in our usage we consider a reference model to be an annotated feature list. In some domains reference models have already been developed [17], often exhibiting considerably more internal structure than mere feature lists. A reference model provides a ready to hand vocabulary of features and, sometimes, their inter-relationships. By mapping peer technologies to these reference models using profiling techniques [18], feature descriptions can be normalized to a common vocabulary, and surprising questions are sometimes surfaced. For example, two competing technologies may be found to provide complementary rather than wholly-overlapping services; this, in turn, may suggest compatibility experiments that address their combined use in a particular problem setting.

Feature benchmarks are quantitative measures of features in a context-neutral setting: they quantify features in terms that make sense for the feature and the technology, but in a way that is independent of any problem domain. To illustrate, for middleware products we might measure message throughput under various load conditions. Such benchmarks may represent weak hypotheses, i.e., the kinds of load factors that will influence performance, but these hypotheses need not be explicit nor tied to the problem domain habitat. As with reference model benchmarking, feature benchmarking may reveal properties of a technology that suggest hypotheses about its use in a particular problem setting.

Examples of reference model benchmarking and feature benchmarking are provided in Section 4. At the risk of over-extending the biological metaphor, reference modeling and feature benchmarking can be thought of as *in vitro* analysis— "in an artificial environment, outside the living organism."[2] In contrast, the experimentally-based evaluation phase can be thought of as involving *in vivo* benchmarking—"within a living organism" (i.e., in actual problem settings).

There is not much to say about hypothesis formulation and experimental design other than to note that a hypothesis needs to be carefully crafted to ensure that:

- it is refutable from experimental evidence;
- suitable experimental techniques exist to address it; and,
- the set of hypotheses are sufficient to form a basis for evaluating value-added.

The first item above requires nothing more than discipline and precision on the part of the evaluator. The third item is inherently difficult to validate, and perhaps the best that can be done to ensure completeness is to establish traceability links from hypotheses to problem domain habitat (which incidentally suggests a fairly detailed model of the habitat). The second item requires a familiarity with various evaluation techniques (referred to as "lab techniques" in Figure 1.). This topic is addressed in the following section.

3.4 Experimental Evaluation Phase

The evaluation phase is where experiments are conducted, experimental evidence is gathered and analyzed, and hypotheses are confirmed or refuted. We have begun to catalogue different experimental techniques that may be useful given certain kinds of hypotheses, requirements for precision, and budget considerations. These are described, below.

Before describing these techniques, we note that there are collateral benefits to employing a hands-on, problem-domain-situated evaluation of a technology beyond the rigorous accumulation of data. Foremost among these benefits is that the evaluation produces as a side-effect a competence in the use of the technology. Moreover, we have found that hypotheses often focus on critical usage issues, e.g., design and implementation issues, and that experiments yield not just confirmation or refutation of hypotheses, but also yield insights into the optimal use of a technology to address these underlying critical issues.

Model Problems

Model problems are narrowly-defined problems that the technology can address, and that can be extracted from, and to some extent understood in isolation of, broader considerations of an application domain. Examples of model problems might include determining schedulability in real time and manufacturing domains; and integrating applications with independent control loops in the component integration domain. The virtues of using model problems is that they provide a narrow evaluation context, and that they allow a direct comparison of alternative technologies in a way that might be too expensive to do in a broader setting (e.g., through demonstrators).

Compatibility Studies

Compatibility experiments are the complement of model problems: rather than determining how a single technology behaves in a narrow problem context, compatibility experiments are intended to determine whether technologies interfere with each other or, optimally, whether they can be effectively used together. Compatibility experiments are particularly useful if a technology might be inserted into an established technology baseline where interactions between the new and established technologies are suspected. Compatibility experiments can also be useful if competing technologies provide disjoint features in addition to overlapping features: it might be useful to determine whether the disjoint features can be used without having overlapping features interfere.

Demonstrator Studies

Although narrowly-focused experiments may reveal many interesting characteristics of a technology, there is no substitute for trial applications of a technology in a real-life, scaled-up application setting. Although full-scale demonstrator applications can be expensive, a properly designed demonstrator can achieve some of the scale factors needed to stress-test a technology under investigation, while excluding other factors. For example, system documentation could be dispensed with; reliability and performance might be down-played (assuming these were not crucial to any hypothesis). Nevertheless, demonstrators may require a substantial commitment of resources by an organization, and this phase of an evaluation will probably be deferred until it is determined that a technology has a reasonable likelihood of success.

---

2. From the American Heritage Dictionary.

An important point to note is that we distinguish a demonstrator study from what is commonly referred to as a *pilot project*. In our view, pilot projects are intended to be initial full-deployments of a technology. In contrast, demonstrators, as noted above, may elide some otherwise essential engineering efforts. A further distinction between demonstrators and pilots is that demonstrators (at least in the technology delta parlance) remain focused on the distinguishing features of a technology. In other words, a demonstrator may deliberately exaggerate the use of some features of a technology in a problem setting in order to expose its strengths and deficiencies. In contrast, pilot efforts will be driven instead by optimal engineering trade-offs.

Synthetic Benchmarks

Synthetic benchmarks may only be useful to a narrow range of problem domains. Synthetic benchmarks are primarily useful in examining technologies that have run-time aspects, and where the problem domain can be simulated. For example, in evaluating a middleware technology, test messages can be injected into a command and control system to simulate system operation in normal and crisis modes. Synthetic benchmarks may be difficult to conduct without a pre-existing application that permits such instrumentation. Also, considerable effort may be required to acquire valid synthetic loads—again, this could require instrumentation of existing applications. Synthetic benchmarks are different from feature benchmarks precisely in the degree to which such problem-domain specific factors are included in the experiment.

3.5 Summary of Key Points

The key idea behind the technology delta framework is that the evaluation of a technology depends upon two factors:

1. understanding how the evaluated technology differs from other technologies; and

2. understanding how these differences address the needs of specific usage contexts for the technology.

Our emphasis is on developing rigorous techniques to address both. These techniques include a range of informal descriptive modeling techniques for documenting assertions about the nature of a technology and its usage context, and more empirical techniques for conducting experiments.

The main virtue of the technology delta approach is that it provides a framework for analyzing and describing inherently subjective aspects of technology evaluation, and for linking subjective assertions to objective data. A secondary virtue is that the experimental methodology also yields a competence in the technology and its use in sharply-focused application settings.

4. Application of the Technology Delta Framework to OMA and CORBA

To illustrate the technology delta framework we describe its application to one technology that has direct bearing on

software systems integration[3], and that has also been the subject of considerable media attention and speculation: the Object Management Group's Object Management Architecture (OMA) [19]. Within recent months implementations of the OMA and its more widely-known component, the Common Object Request Broker Architecture (CORBA) [20], have begun to appear in the marketplace. However, there are many competing claims in the literature and among experts in object-oriented technology, middleware technology, and operating systems, about what is unique about the OMA, and how effective it will be in various problem domains. It was, in part, to answer such questions that we began to systematically investigate the OMA technology delta.

In the following discussion we describe how the technology delta framework has guided our evaluation of the OMA and CORBA. We highlight aspects of the application of the framework that resulted in a new or clearer understanding of the OMA. The description concentrates on how the framework has been used and omits many of the results of the evaluations themselves. These details are provided elsewhere [21][22][23].

4.1 OMA/CORBA Descriptive Models[4]

The key elements of the OMA are depicted in Figure 2..

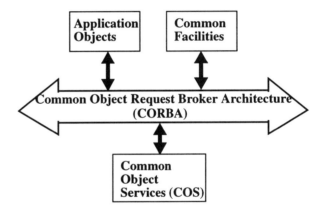

Figure 2. The Object Management Architecture

CORBA is a communication infrastructure that enables clients to locate and make requests of (possibly remote) objects. There are different classes of objects within the OMA. Common Object Services (COS) are objects that provide widely applicable services, e.g., transactions, event management, and persistence. Common Facilities are objects that provide useful but less widely-used services,

---

3. Our project is centered on software component integration as a topic of investigation.

4. In the following discussion we provide a very brief overview of the OMA and CORBA. Readers wishing further details on either should consult [19][20].

e.g., electronic mail. Finally, application objects are application-specific, and are not (at this time) a subject for standardization within the Object Management Group. Note that in the following discussion, the OMA acronym will be used to refer to all of the elements depicted in Figure 2., while the CORBA acronym always refers only to the communications infrastructure of the OMA.

OMA/CORBA Genealogy

Figure 3. depicts the OMA genealogy. The most significant

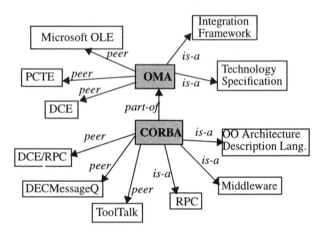

Figure 3. OMA/CORBA Genealogy

point made by the genealogy is that CORBA and the OMA are, to some extent, separable technologies. To those familiar with these technologies, this point is neither subtle nor profound; yet, in our experience, even enlightened technologists confuse the details of the OMA and CORBA as well as the role each can play in a system integration effort.

A number of more subtle points are made by the genealogy. The concepts relating to OMA via "is-a" relationships are not necessarily technologies, but rather are evocative of properties that may be significant in evaluating the OMA. To illustrate, the *"OMA is-a technology specification"* relationship implies, minimally, that implementations of the OMA need to conform to an authoritative specification[5]. The *"PCTE is-a technology specification"*[6] also implies conformance rules. However, while both OMA and PCTE [24] specifications define notions of conformance, both do so in different ways. Both the common features of technology specifications and their variant interpretations by peer technologies (e.g., PCTE) are revealing about the OMA.

Another point worth noting concerns peer relationships, and what these relationships imply, and do not imply. First, an assertion that Microsoft's OLE [25] is a peer technology to

OMA implies that there are some features in common between both technologies.[7] The relationship does not imply, however, that there is a substitutability relationship between OLE and OMA—that is an entirely different assertion. This serves as a warning to analysts: the open-ended nature of genealogy and habitat models does not imply a lack of precision in the models; the relationships should be documented and used in a consistent fashion. This is essential if the models are to serve a role in providing a rational foundation for experimentation.

OMA/CORBA Habitat

Figure 4. illustrates a portion of the OMA habitat. In general a habitat will be more complex than a genealogy, and care must be taken to balance thoroughness against complexity. With this in mind the concepts that are missing

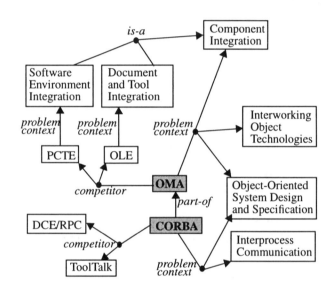

Figure 4. Elements of the OMA/CORBA

from the habitat are just as significant as the concepts that appear: the habitat is an assertion by the analyst about the features of a technology that are of interest. Thus, although it can be argued that the OMA addresses a problem context concerned with developing object-oriented patterns and frameworks [27], this problem context was not of interest for our investigations. Instead, our interests were in the use of the OMA to support component integration, interworking object technologies, and object-oriented systems development.

The OMA habitat also illustrates that it is often useful to extend the model beyond the immediate technologies of

---

5. Other properties, such as the manner in which specifications are defined and evolve, may also be significant and are relevant to this illustration.

6. Some relationships are not shown in the interest of clarity.

---

7. More accurately, there are common features between both technology specifications. As with the PCTE illustration, understanding how OMA specifications differ from Microsoft's specifications can be revealing.

interest in order to obtain a deeper understanding of the technology being evaluated. For example, it is often thought that the OMA and Microsoft's OLE are competing technologies; in fact, there is some truth to this. However, upon a deeper investigation of both (driven by the need to substantiate this assertion in the habitat), it emerged that the OMA addresses component integration in general, while OLE addresses a more limited form of component integration centered on document management. The OMA habitat asserts an "is-a" link between the OLE and OMA problem contexts to capture this subset relationship. The consequence of this observation on our evaluation was to defer experiments relating to the OMA/OLE feature delta until such time as a sufficient range of OMA common facilities for document management have been defined and are implemented.

On the other hand, if document management architectures were our concern rather than component integration, we might find it useful to conduct a comparative feature study of the OLE component object model and the CORBA object model. This might lead to a better understanding of the strengths and weaknesses that the OMA might experience if it were to form the basis of a document management architecture. Although we did not undertake this more detailed comparison of OLE with the OMA, we did use the genealogy and habitat models to develop more detailed feature comparisons between the OMA and PCTE, ToolTalk [26] and remote procedure call (RPC). Some of these studies are highlighted below.

4.2 OMA/CORBA Experiment Design

We conducted an extensive comparative anatomy of the OMA and several technologies identified in the OMA genealogy and habitat. A sampling of our efforts, and their influence on the evaluation, are described below. For fluency of exposition, discussion of concrete hypotheses and experiment designs is deferred to Section 4.3, where actual experiments are described.

Reference Models

We developed a number of feature-level reference models that described the OMA in terms of related technologies. Although each technology that appears as either a peer or a competitor in the genealogy and habitat should also appear in a reference model, for practical considerations our investigations focused primarily on feature comparisons of the OMA with PCTE, ToolTalk, and Sun/RPC[8].

We constructed one form of reference model by mapping CORBA to a reference model of software environment integration framework technologies [17]. We employed a two-step mapping process of first mapping features found in the reference model to CORBA, and then mapping CORBA features to the reference model. The first step identifies the fea-

---

8. We did not have an implementation of DCE/RPC available to us.

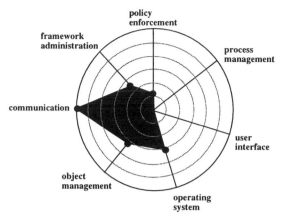

Figure 5. CORBA Mapping to NIST Software Environment Framework Reference Model

tures CORBA shares with software development environment integration frameworks, while the second step highlights features of CORBA not found in environment framework technology. A summary of the reference model-to-CORBA mapping is illustrated in Figure 5. (with the outer rings corresponding to "greater correlation"). Full details of this mapping are provided in [28].

This kind of rough survey can be very useful in focusing analysis efforts to particular classes of features; the mapping illustrated in Figure 5. led us towards more detailed comparisons of CORBA with communications mechanisms (ToolTalk and RPC, for instance) and object management mechanisms (PCTE, for instance). It is also useful for conducting comparative descriptions of technologies. Consider the feature mapping illustrated in Figure 6., which superimposes a mapping of PCTE onto the CORBA mapping.

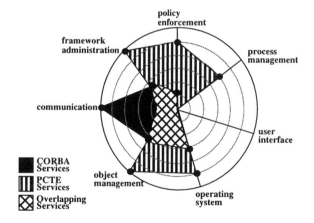

Figure 6. Overlapping and Disjoint Services

From this mapping an analyst can postulate that a system might make use of PCTE services for policy enforcement (e.g., security policy) while using CORBA services for inter-object communication. Conversely, the analyst might postulate that there is sufficient overlap between object management services that a hybrid PCTE/CORBA system would need to defer all object management functions to either PCTE or CORBA in order to avoid feature collision.

However, neither the reference model nor mappings derived from it are sufficiently rich in semantics to support or refute these conjectures. This suggests the design of experiments (in the form of compatibility studies) that are focused on determining the kinds of feature interactions that might arise between the technologies in a hybrid CORBA/PCTE system (e.g., resource contention), or experiments for determining how features might be effectively combined. Determining how features of the OMA and PCTE can be combined might have practical importance in a large-scale applications that has to satisfy a wide-range of sometimes competing requirements (real time vs. distributed processing, interactiveness vs. fault tolerance, etc.). In such cases, knowledge of how and when to delegate features among a range of overlapping technologies can be crucial to meeting application requirements. For example, a real-time or highly secure application might use an ORB to broker communication links that make use of specialized communications hardware and software that are not managed by the ORB.

Feature Benchmarks

We found feature benchmarks to be useful for understanding performance variations among different vendor implementations of the CORBA specification, and also for understanding factors in the implementation of object request brokers (ORBS) that influence performance. We also found it extremely useful to compare the performance characteristics of these CORBA implementations with a commercial implementation of RPC, in order to test our assertion that RPC and CORBA are both peers and competitors. Details of these benchmarks and an analysis of the results can be found in [21]. Figure 7. illustrates one such feature benchmark, where we compared the performance of three CORBA implementations and Sun/RPC. Several other performance-oriented benchmarks were created that varied the number of objects, the size of messages, etc. In still other benchmarks, additional interprocess communication technology was introduced, such as Sun/Sockets.

We also note that there are some practical benefits to writing feature benchmarks quite apart from the quantifiable data produced by the benchmarks. The most significant of these benefits is that feature benchmarks can be viewed as very simple applications (in terms of structure and algorithms). As such, they provide a relatively low-cost means for the analyst to acquire "hands-on" experience with a technology. We found these simple benchmark programs to be quite revealing of several dimensions of the CORBA specification, including code portability, inconsistent concepts visible to client writers and object service providers, deficient administrative and security aspects of ORBs, and issues of the robustness of the ORB and ORB-based applications, interactions between the

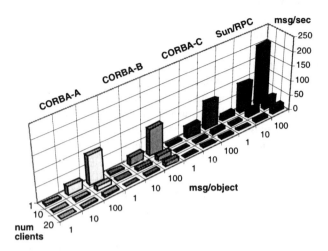

Figure 7. Sample Feature Benchmarks
ORB and the host platform and operating system, associated software development tools, and so on.

4.3 OMA/CORBA Experimental Evaluation

The descriptive models and comparative anatomies provided us with a good idea of the OMA feature delta: those features that distinguished OMA and CORBA from PCTE, ToolTalk and RPC (to name a few). In addition, we also had formulated several hypotheses concerning how this technology delta would behave in our selected problem domain (i.e., integration of large-scale, off-the-shelf software components). The next step was to define experimental scenarios that would allow us to apply the OMA feature delta under controlled circumstances, and to test our hypotheses. These experiments and their results are described in high-level terms in the following paragraphs.

Before proceeding we note two points. First, we designed quite a few more experiments than we had the resources to ultimately carry out. We suspect we are not alone in having resource constraints—however, the experiment design process is useful in and of itself, and even those experiments not conducted were revealing. Second, in the interest of space we do not describe all of the experiments we conducted, only a sampling that we believe are revealing of the technology delta method.

Model problems

Model problems can be derived from a number of sources identified in the genealogy and habitat. For example, the CORBA genealogy asserts that CORBA *is-a* architecture description language (ADL). A pre-existing set of model problems for software architecture is available [29]; similarly, a set of model problems for software architecture description languages[9] is also available [30]. Problem contexts are also a ready source of model problems: interprocess communication and distributed systems problem contexts have many known model problems. For our investigations the model problems of interest were derived from the tool and software component integration problem context.

Experiment Overview

The model problem we describe here concerns *architectural mismatch* [31]. The essential problem is that reused, off-the-shelf components embed many integration-time and run-time assumptions about their usage contexts, and often the assumptions made by one component are inconsistent with assumptions made by others. One common manifestation of architectural mismatch concerns the locus of control in an application comprised of many different large-scale components, i.e., who is in charge? There are many more kinds of manifestations.

Hypotheses

Architectural mismatch comprises a wide-range of experimental scenarios and hypotheses, and this is still an active area of experimentation within our project—for example, to classify and catalogue techniques for removing architectural mismatches. From past experience, we knew that removing architectural mismatches often requires intricate, low-level code. Given the claims that CORBA could be used to encapsulate and integrate legacy applications, we wished to examine the effect of CORBA on this code. In particular, we wished to determine the sensitivity of architectural mismatch solutions to ORB-vendor features. Our hypothesis was that vendor-specific features would have a minor effect on implementation strategies to architectural mismatch. Supporting or refuting this hypothesis is important for our project so that we can determine to what extent our documented techniques for architectural mismatch-removal are vendor-specific.

Experiment Design

Our experiment design involved the integration of a CORBA object implementation with a graphical user interface (GUI) into a single executing process. [10] CORBA object implementations typically have event loops that accept requests for services from arbitrary clients; GUI components have event loops that manage display events. For our experiments we used *Tk/wish* [32] as the GUI component; the object service integrated with the GUI was a simple two-dimensional array that allowed clients to put and get values at specified locations. We used two different commercially available ORBs, and developed a model solution using one ORB and attempted to "port" this solution to the second ORB. This experiment illustrates the essential characteristics of the problem without introducing extraneous details—the functionality of the final integrated application is trivial while the

integration requirements are not trivial and are a valid representation of a potentially challenging integration problem.

Experiment Results

In brief, the experiment convincingly refuted the hypothesis. We discovered that component integration within a single address space exposed a wide range of ORB vendor-specific idiosyncracies, and the solutions we selected for one ORB were not implementable in the other. Although we knew that the OMA does not support source code portability for object implementations, the extent of the variation between our two model solutions was more dramatic than we had anticipated. In postmortem analysis of the experiment, we determined that it would have been possible to implement a model solution that, with some minor re-programming, would work on both ORBs. However, this uniform solution would be considerably more complex than either ORB-specific solution, and we would only have low confidence that the uniform solution would be applicable to a third ORB with a different set of vendor features.

Regardless of the specific interpretations of our experimental results, a great deal of information about the OMA and its exemplar implementations were derived with modest cost and development effort (on the order of 200 source lines of C++ for each model solution). This level of effort is probably an indicator of a well-constructed model problem.

Demonstrators

Ultimately, the impact of a technology is felt over the full range of issues related to application development. Experienced software engineering practitioners are well acquainted with technologies that provide leverage early in a software life cycle only to introduce more compelling problems later in the development cycle. The model problem just described was intended to focus on relatively narrow aspects of the OMA. In contrast, demonstrators are intended to reveal the broader characteristics of a technology when it is applied to a representative "complete" problem in an application domain.

We have developed two OMA demonstrators: (1) integration and wide-area distribution of a collection of legacy software components, and (2) an open, distributed-object-based workflow process definition and enaction framework. For reasons of space limitation only the first is described here; details of the second are documented elsewhere [23].

Experiment Overview

This experiment was conducted collaboratively by the National Institute of Standards and Technology (NIST) Manufacturing Engineering Laboratory (MEL), Sandia National Laboratories, and the SEI. NIST/MEL has long-standing interest in improving the state of manufacturing

---

9. The OMA Interface Definition Language (IDL) is sometimes referred to as an architecture description language—this is the meaning of the placement of ADL's in the OMA/CORBA genealogy.

10. Other experiments were performed where the components did not share a process address space.

technology, in particular involving the use and integration of manufacturing-related software technologies. Sandia is involved in the design and manufacture of high-performance materials, and thus has similar interests from the consumer-side.

The manufacturing processes required to move a product from concept to realization are many and varied, often requiring highly-specialized computing resources. In many cases these resources are independent of the underlying application domain—manufacturability analysis for automotive parts and washing machine parts are quite similar. Some believe that a breakthrough in manufacturing efficiency can be achieved if these "horizontal" resources are freed from their existing "vertical" market confinements, and allowed to develop in the free-market. The challenge is how to re-assemble these horizontal specialties into *virtual enterprises*—specialty companies collaborating in a vertical manufacturing enterprise. Among other things, virtual enterprises require technology infrastructure to support:

- the integration of separately-developed, specialized, computer-aided manufacturing technologies;
- geographical distribution of computing resources, and support for heterogeneous computing environments; and,
- fee-for-service brokering of computer-based services to enable competition for specialized tools and skills.

In short, virtual enterprises will rely increasingly upon information technology such as distributed object technology. This experiment focused on the use of the OMA to support flexible integration and wide-area-distribution of legacy manufacturing engineering design components.

Hypotheses

In contrast to the model problem described above, our concern in this experiment was less on ORB vendor-specific issues and more on how OMA-defined features supported a specific class of integration problems. Our hypothesis was that, as compared to RPC-based approaches, the OMA feature delta would result in an integration framework that would:

- be more abstract and thus easier to maintain, evolve and standardize;
- be more flexible with respect to component location, coordination, and other run-time concerns;
- better address system-level issues such as data management, persistence, and transactions.

We also were concerned that ORB-vendors did not uniformly implement OMA features beyond CORBA, i.e., CORBA products need not be bundled with implementations of common object services or common facilities (refer to Figure 2.). Therefore, our hypothesis further stipulated that OMA services not provided by an ORB vendor could be either partially- or fully-implemented by application develop-

ers with only a modest increase in application development effort[11].

Experiment Design

Our experiment design involved the integration of several Sandia-provided manufacturing engineering design tools. The integration experiment focused on the use of advanced OMA features, rather than a more primitive RPC-like use of CORBA, thus:

- an object model for the engineering design activities comprised by the tools was modeled in CORBA IDL;
- OMA services such as persistence and relationships were used for the object model to support long-running, wide-area distributed design sessions;
- the Sandia tools were "wrapped" to fit into the distributed object model, rather than wrapped to export tool-specific functionality, and distributed across different sites (at the SEI and NIST); and,
- an end-user virtual interface was implemented to make the location and identity of the Sandia tools transparent.

We sketched a paper design of this system using simple RPC primitives to establish a comparative (if hypothetical) baseline; we went so far to give RPC the "benefit of the doubt" that we used CORBA/IDL as an RPC interface specification language, rather than the more primitive specification languages supported by most existing RPC implementations.

As a whole, the experiment design addressed the hypothesis as well as the underlying application domain (virtual enterprises for manufacturing). The total effort devoted to the main design and implementation phase of the demonstrator was approximately six person months, applied by two software engineers over a period of three months. This was substantial enough to construct a non-trivial demonstrator.

Experiment Results

The major elements of the OMA feature delta—object services and an object-oriented interface description—provided an excellent foundation for designing and implementing distributed component-based systems; in large measure, the first part of our hypothesis was sustained. However, we discovered that in practice developers will require an even richer set of object services than currently defined; it remains to be seen whether vendors will as a rule provide implementations of these services. We were also able to convincingly refute the second part of our hypothesis: we demonstrated that custom implementation of OMA services such as relationship management is impractical, and the use of non-standard services, such as vendor-specific persistence mechanisms, introduces additional prob-

---

11. We did not actually believe this, but it is often more useful to state a hypothesis in an affirmative tone and then falsify it, rather than the stating a negative hypothesis and attempt to prove it.

lems, such as coding complexity and non-orthogonality with OMA concepts.

As with all of our experiments, a wide-range of practical results beyond the immediate hypotheses were established. From this experiment we discovered a variety of software-architecture related facets of the OMA. In particular, we discovered the affinity of OMA concepts, when applied to wide-area component integration, to a hybrid repository-style [35] and structural style [36]. We were able to demonstrate how this hybrid style addressed many of the technical requirements for flexible, evolvable wide-area component integration; and, further, how it addressed the sometimes ambiguous, inconsistent or incompletely-specified run-time semantics of OMA specifications.

4.4 Summary of Key Points

The OMA is an interesting example of a new class of technologies that many believe will have a major impact on the design and implementation of distributed systems. In order to investigate this technology we have carried out a wide range of studies and experiments that help us to gain insight into the technology's strengths and weaknesses.

The technology delta framework played an important role in this technology investigation by:

- separating the different evaluation tasks into manageable pieces;

- suggesting an ordering, or methodology, for carrying out different kinds of evaluations;

- allowing the information collected to be considered as part of a larger picture that provides a more complete understanding of the technology.

5. Conclusions and Future Work

While the evaluation of software technologies is seen as a vital task in many organizations, most organizations carry out those evaluations without clearly defining their goals and expectations, and are heavily reliant on the intuition and experience of personnel performing the work. In this paper we have presented the basis for a systematic approach to software technology evaluation focused on establishing the contribution of that technology in relation to it peers and predecessors. This approach has been illustrated through its application to the Object Management Group's OMA and CORBA technologies.

A number of limitations and weaknesses of the current framework remain to be addressed. Specifically, we recognize the need for further development of the technology delta framework in the at least the following areas:

- *Additional rigor in the modeling of genealogies and habitats.* The current semantic nets approach provides great flexibility, but at the cost of some precision and repeatability. We hope to further define the modeling language in these areas through further application of the framework.

- *Improved integration of metrics techniques.* The ultimate goal of any evaluation is to define and apply appropriate quantitative techniques that yield objective data on which to base a decision. We hope to examine the technology delta framework as an opportunity for facilitating greater use of quantitative metrics within technology evaluations.

- *Application to a wider set of technologies.* Currently the technology delta framework has only been applied to system integration technologies. While we expect the concepts to be readily transferable to other domains, this assertion must be validated through its application to candidate technologies.

The technology delta framework was created through analyzing the methods that we had been using for a range of technology evaluations in the area of systems integration, culminating with our evaluation of OMA and CORBA. Currently planned is further application of this framework for the evaluation of other classes of system integration technologies (e.g., scripting languages such as Java [37], Python [38], TCL [32]), and for the use of the OMA in domains other than component integration (e.g., real-time, reliable systems). It is expected that these future applications will lead to a more robust framework and evaluation methodology, applicable to a wide range of software technologies.

Acknowledgments

The SEI is sponsored by the U.S. Department of Defense.

NIST/MEL sponsored the SEI participation in the demonstrator experiment described in this paper.

6. References

[1] Basili V., Selby R.W., and Hutchens D.H., "Experimentation in Software Engineering", IEEE Transactions on Software Engineering V12, #7, pp733-743, July 1986.

[2] Fenton, N.E., "Software Metrics: A Rigorous Approach", Chapman and Hall, London, UK., 1991.

[3] Tichy W.F., Lukowicz P., Prechelt L., and Heinz E.A., "Experimental Evaluation in Computer Science: A Quantitative Study", Journal of Systems & Software V28, #1, pp9-18, January 1995.

[4] Welzel D., and Hausen H.-L., "A Method for Software Evaluation", Computer Standards & Interfaces V17, #1, pp121-129, January 1995.

[5] Information Technology — Software Product Evaluation — Quality Characteristics and Guidelines for their Use, International Standards Organisation (ISO), ISO/IEC 9126:1991, 1991.

[6] IEEE Recommended Practice on the Selection and Evaluation of CASE Tools, P1209, 1994.

[7] Poston R.M., and Sexton M.P., "Evaluating and Selecting Testing Tools", IEEE Software, V9, #3, pp33-42, May 1992.

[8] Paulk, M.C., Curtis, B., & Chrissis, M.B. *Capability*

Maturity Model for Software. Technical Report CMU/SEI-91-TR-24, ADA240603, Software Engineering Institute, Carnegie Mellon University, Pittsburgh, PA, August 1991.

[9] Schumauch C.H., *ISO 9000 for Software Developers*, ASQC Quality Press, 1994.

[10] Boloix, G., and Robillard, P.N., "A Software System Evaluation Framework", IEEE Computer, pp17-26, December 1995.

[11] Bruckhaus, T., "The Impact of Inserting a Tool into a Software Process", in Proceedings of the 1993 CASCON Conference, pp 250-264, IBM Toronto, October 1993.

[12] Bruckhaus, T., "TIM: A Tool Insertion Method", in Proceedings of the 1994 CASCON Conference, on CD-ROM, IBM Toronto, November 1994.

[13] Iiscoe, N., Williams, G., Arango, G., "Domain modeling for software engineering," in proceedings of the 13th International Conference on Software Engineering, Austin TX, 1991.

[14] Simos, M., "Organizational Domain Modeling", STARS Informal Technical Report CDRL 05156, July 1993.

[15] Cagan, M.R., "The HP SoftBench Environment: An Architecture for a New Generation of Software Tools", Hewlett-Packard Journal, V41, #3, June 1990.

[16] Reiss, S.P., "Connecting Tools Using Message Passing in the FIELD Environment", IEEE Software. pp57-99, June 1990.

[17] NIST, "Next Generation Computing Resources: Reference Model for Project Support Environments (Version 2.0)", NIST Special Publication 500-213, November 1993.

[18] Carney, D.J., "Guidelines for Mapping to the Reference Model for Software Engineering Environments", SEI Special Report, CMU/SEI-93-SR-21, 1995, Software Engineering Institute, Carnegie-Mellon University, Pittsburgh, PA.

[19] Object Management Architecture Guide, Revision 3.0, Third Edition, Soley, R. (ed), Stone, C., John Wiley & Sons, Inc., ISBN 0-471-14193-3.

[20] The Common Object Request Broker: Architecture and Specification, Revision 2.0, July 1995, Object Management Group, 492 Old Connecticut Path, Framingham, MA, 01701.

[21] Wallnau, K., Rice, J., "ORBS In the Midst: Studying a New Species of Integration Mechanism", in Proceedings of International Conference on Computer-Aided Software Engineering (CASE-95), Toronto, CA, July 1995.

[22] Wallnau, K.C. and Wallace, E., "A Robust Evaluation of the OMA: An Experimental Case Study in Legacy System Migration", submitted to OOPLSA'96, SEI and NIST technical reports in preparation.

[23] Wallnau, K., Long, F., Earl, A., "Toward a Distributed, Mediated Architecture for Workflow Management," in proceedings of NSF Workshop on Workflow and Process Automation in Information Systems: State-of-the-Art and Future Directions, May 8-10, see also http://lsdis.cs.uga.edu/activities/NSF-workflow.

[24] Wakeman, L. and Jowett, J., "PCTE: The Standards for Open Repositories", Prentice-Hall, 1993.

[25] OLE Management Backgrounder, Part No. 098-56456, June 1994, Microsoft Corp., One Microsoft Way, Redmond, WA 98052-6399.

[26] Frankel, R., "Introduction to the ToolTalk Service", Sun Microsystems Inc., Mountain View, CA., 1991.

[27] Gamma, E., Helm, R., Johnson, R., Vlissides, J., "Design Patterns, Elements of Object-Oriented Software", Addison Wesley, 1995.

[28] Wallnau, K., "Mapping of CORBA 1.1 to the NIST Reference Model for Frameworks of Software Engineering Environments", Draft SEI Special Report SEI-95-SR-022, Software Engineering Institute, Carnegie Mellon University, September 1995.

[29] Shaw, M., Garlan, D., Allen, R., Klein, D., Ockerbloom, J., Scott, C., Schumaker, M., "Candidate Model Problems in Software Architecture", Draft Technical Report 15-675, the Software Architecture Group, Computer Science Department, Carnegie Mellon University, 1995.

[30] Kogut, P., Clements, P., "Features of Architecture Description Languages", Draft Technical Report, Software Engineering Institute, Carnegie Mellon University, November 1995.

[31] Garlan, D., Allen, R., Ockerbloom, J., "Architecture Mismatch: Why Reuse is so Hard", IEEE Software V12, #6, pp17-26, November 1995.

[32] Ousterhout, J., "Tcl and the Tk Toolkit", Addison Wesley, 1994.

[33] Christie, A., "Software Process Automation: The Technology and its Adoption", Springer Verlag, 1995.

[34] Hollingsworth, D., "Workflow Reference Model", Workflow Management Coalition Specification TC00-1003, Jan. 1995 (email: d.hollingsworth@wsr0104.wins.icl.co.uk)

[35] Garlan, D. and Shaw, M., "An Introduction to Software Architecture," in Advances in Software Engineering and Knowledge Engineering, vol. I, World Scientific Publishing Company,1993

[36] Abowd, G., Bass, L., Howard, L., and Northrup, L., "Structural Modeling: An Application Framework and Development Process for Flight Simulators," SEI Technical Report, CMU/SEI-93-TR-14, 1993, Software Engineering Institute, Carnegie-Mellon University, Pittsburgh, PA.

[37] Java Home Page, http://java.sun.com.

[38] Python Home Page, http://www.python.org.

Assessing the Quality of Large, Software-Intensive Systems: A Case Study

Alan W. Brown, David J. Carney, Paul C. Clements,B. Craig Meyers,
Dennis B. Smith, Nelson H. Weiderman, and William G. Wood

Software Engineering Institute
Carnegie Mellon University
Pittsburgh, PA, 15213, USA

Abstract

This paper presents a case study in carrying out an audit of a large, software-intensive system. We discuss our experience in structuring the team for obtaining maximum effectiveness under a short deadline. We also discuss the goals of an audit, the methods of gathering and assimilating information, and specific lines of inquiry to be followed. We present observations on our approach in light of our experience and feedback from the customer.

1. Introduction

In the past decade, as engineers have attempted to build software-intensive systems of a scale not dreamed of heretofore, there have been extraordinary successes and failures. Those projects that have failed have often been spectacular and highly visible [3], particularly those commissioned with public money. Such failures do not happen all at once; like Brooks' admonition that schedules slip one day at a time [2], failures happen incrementally. The symptoms of a failing project range from the subtle (a customer's vague feelings of uneasiness) to the ridiculous (the vendor slips the schedule for the eighth time and promises that another $30 million will fix everything). A project that has passed the "failure in progress" stage and gone on to full-fledged meltdown can be spotted by one sure symptom: the funding authority curtails payment and severely slows development. When that happens, the obvious question is asked by every involved party: "What now?" The answer is often an audit.

This paper summarizes the experience of an audit undertaken by the Software Engineering Institute (SEI) in the summer of 1994 to examine a large, highly visible development effort exhibiting the meltdown symptom suggested above. The customer was a government agency in the process of procuring a large software-intensive system from a major contractor. The audit team included the authors of this paper, as well as members from other organizations. Members of the team had extensive backgrounds and expertise in software engineering, in large systems development, and in the relevant application domain, but few had experience in conducting a thorough software audit. The deadlines of this one were inflexible, giving the team only 90 days to audit an extremely large system, and our struggle to come to terms with issues of basic approach, logistics, execution, and coordination consumed valuable time. It is the purpose of this paper to share our experiences, in the hopes that others finding themselves in a similar situation may benefit by having to spend less valuable time learning to do the job.

Section 2 of the paper provides the background of the audit, including a description of the system under development and the goals of and circumstances surrounding the audit. Section 3 describes the procedures that our audit team followed in order to meet its mandate. Section 4 presents a summary and commentary on our results, suggesting what worked well and identifying weaknesses in the approach.

2. Overview of the Audit

2.1 Goals

An audit may have many goals, and it is essential to articulate them carefully. Not all will be explicitly mentioned when the work begins. In our case, the goals (some of which only became clear after the audit was launched) were as follows, in approximate decreasing order of importance:

- Assessment of status. The customer had lost the ability to perform effective oversight, and hence could not judge whether the project was headed for fruition (albeit late and costly) or disaster.

- Assessment of salvageability. The customer needed to know whether, in order to field a high-quality system, it would be more cost-effective to perform a massive mid-course correction and press onward with the current effort, or abandon the development, write off the (quite significant) money already spent, and begin afresh.

- Satisfaction of funding authority. The funding agency (in this case, the United States Congress) was demanding that the customer produce a viable plan to bring the project to a successful conclusion; our audit was a significant part of that plan.

- Relation to a previous audit. The customer had received conflicting and incomplete information from a previous audit; our audit was to resolve some of the inconsistencies of that audit.

- Education. The customer desired to understand what went wrong in order to avoid repeating mistakes in future efforts.

- Gaining credibility. The customer had the implicit goal of adding credibility and objectivity to the development effort by employing a team of independent experts to conduct an evaluation. The development effort, were it allowed to continue, would thus receive the blessing of an outside, objective body.

- Protection of reputation: The contractor had the implicit and understandable goal of demonstrating value and quality in the existing (incomplete) work products.

2.2 General Description of the System under Audit

The target of the audit was a large, complex, real-time system of a command and control nature. The requirements of the system were stringent, having extremely precise hard real-time deadlines, with human safety being the critical basis for most timing requirements. The complexity of the system was also affected by the requirements for distribution, availability, and multi-site installation and site-specific customization. The availability requirements were very severe; to a large degree, these requirements drove the key decisions about architecture, test plans, modeling requirements, and many other aspects of the system. The system included both hardware and software, and was intended to replace an existing system.

The architecture of the system had a number of characteristics that distinguished it as inherently complex and largely unprecedented. The architecture was distributed and multiprocessor, using message-oriented and primarily client-server paradigms. In addition, the architecture featured redundancy in both hardware and software aspects. The system used table-driven data, with configuration of each site done through adaptation data that is read in and initialized during installation.

The audit focussed on the software components of the system, not the hardware aspects. The project was at a very late stage of development: software had been designed and developed over several years, and extensive testing had been performed and was in progress both at the development site and at a remote testing facility.

By the time of the audit the system development was several years late, millions of dollars over budget, and although close to final acceptance testing, many people at the user organization had severe doubts about the quality of the design and implementation of the system.

2.3 General Description of the Audit Process

The audit was conducted over a period of three months. The audit team included personnel drawn from two *independent* organizations as well as from the customer's staff. One independent organization had extensive background and expertise in the particular domain of the target system, and the other provided broad expertise in the areas of software engineering, fault-tolerant systems, and real-time software.

Organization of Team

The team included thirteen persons. One member from each independent agency performed administrative duties (although authority was always shared, neither choosing to assume full authority). The opening days of the audit provided evidence that the complexity of the system, and therefore of the audit, was such that it was not feasible for the team to function as a single entity throughout the course of the audit. The team therefore chose to divide into subteams. While there was no clear indication of the optimal partitioning into subteams, the decision was made to divide into three broad subject areas: operational system (the system under audit); infrastructure (the set of facilities, tools, and processes that were used to build and maintain the system); and management (the practices used to monitor and control system development). There was a general agreement that the division into subteams was a convenient structuring device and nothing more. When some aspect of the audit suggested a different partitioning, then we would accommodate whatever different structure was necessary.[1]

Since the project had been monitored by various independent contractors over the course of several years, the audit team had access to some of their data and expertise. The system's contractor was also an active participant in the audit process. The contractor expressed full intention to cooperate in every way with the requests and needs of the audit team, and also expressed a deep interest in seeing that the outcome of the audit was a full and objective examination of the target system.[2]

Information Gathering

The audit team used a six-stage process to learn about the system and guide its investigation. These stages were: get information, clarify information, digest information, formulate questions, feed tentative conclusions back (to the customer and the contractor), and get additional clarification.

To establish the background and general concepts initially, we attended extensive briefings. Some of these were designed and presented by the contractor, and others by the

---

1. This in fact occurred when the team performed a detailed examination of the code.

2. This intention was fulfilled: the audit team was given access to any requested records or documents.

government agency. These briefings provided the audit team with an overview of the system, its development, and its current state of readiness. We also read the overview design documents, and spot-reviewed detailed design documents.

To clarify areas where a particular sub-team lacked understanding, the team conducted follow-up meetings with the contractor, as well as interviews with persons from several other independent sources, including the customer, the testing personnel from the remote testing facility, the independent monitoring agencies, the subcontractor tasked with independent verification and validation (IV&V), and similar other sources. The audit team also interviewed personnel from the different subcontractors that had been participating in the project. As this information was digested, the sub-teams updated their models of the areas of interest to reflect the information gathered.

This process led to formulation of questions and tentative conclusions that were fed back to the customer and contractor. The process was iterated until the understanding of the issues was clear. Thus, to verify an assertion made about the system, the audit team asked the contractor to perform particular actions or demonstrations, or walk the team in detail through a particular topic. The response to such a request was sometimes a prepared briefing or demonstration, sometimes a one- or two-day technical interchange between auditors and contractor personnel, and sometimes a day-long work session of team members and programmers huddled together over a workstation.

In some sub-teams, outside experts were consulted. This activity helped the team clear up remaining issues, gain perspective, and focus on where further information was needed.

It was not possible to learn all of the details, or read all of the documents, relevant to a particular topic. Some documents, such as the architectural overview documents, were available immediately; others became visible early in the audit; and still others became visible in answer to specific detailed questions.

Logistics and Mechanics

The team worked on a full-time basis throughout the three months. During the early phases of the audit the work tended to take the form of plenary meetings, often for briefings from the contractor or from other parties. During the later phases of the audit, most of the intensive work was conducted in sub-team meetings. For the work of the subteams, there were always at least two persons conversant on any particular technical or programmatic issue under consideration. To prepare the final report, the team again met in full plenary sessions.

The findings of the audit were always the product of team consensus. Where differences of opinion were present, there was full debate on every point. This was often a painful and time-consuming process, but ultimately we found this to be a worthwhile (and perhaps necessary) aspect of the audit process.

3. Description of the Audit

In performing the audit, our point of departure was the three subteams (System, Infrastructure, and Management). The system subteam considered the operational system itself; the infrastructure subteam considered all supporting material used to build, test, and maintain the system; the management subteam considered all elements and activities that governed the creation of the system and its infrastructure. The following are the areas considered.

The system was examined with respect to

- documentation
- code quality
- performance
- fault tolerance
- system maintainability

The infrastructure was examined with respect to

- the development and maintenance environments
- configuration management

Management was considered with respect to

- problem trouble reports (PTRs)
- quality of process definitions and management

The audit of the system occupied the greatest amount of time, and those results occupied the largest part of the final audit report.

In this section, we provide a summary of the major issues that arose in performing the audit. Note that in this paper we are not providing the results of the audit, but rather the issues that arose while conducting it.

3.1 Code Quality of the System

In assessing the code of a large and complex system, there are several issues that are pertinent. The first issue concerns coverage of the audit: can the code be inspected in its entirety? And if not, what is the strategy for performing an audit that will provide a meaningful assessment of the code?

The code of the system approached one million lines, and given the schedule constraints we faced, it was impossible to fully examine all of it. The team therefore adopted a dual strategy. On one hand, we performed some investigations over the entire body of code. On the other we chose a few subsystems for close and deep examination. By mixing global searches with "slicing" the large system in this manner we were able to perform a reasonable code analysis, although in-depth analysis took place on a subset of the system.

A second key issue is that the code must be examined in the context of its requirements and design: does the code do what it is supposed to do? And does it do it in terms of the stated design? The former issue relates to verifying that the system's requirements have been met, while the latter has additional importance for the evolution and maintenance of the code.

In assessing the system with respect to this issue, the team took the stated requirements that applied to a randomly selected subsystem and traced those requirements through the design documents to the code modules. This identified those requirements that were met, those that were not, how they were met, how the actual code conformed to the stated design, and so forth. It also contributed to the audit of the documentation of the system, since this portion of the audit uncovered inconsistences both in style and substance between the requirements documents, the design documents, and the code.

A third issue for a code audit is that the code must be examined with respect to some objective measures of code quality: does the code follow sound software engineering practices? These practices are at both a relatively high level (e.g., Does the code exhibit a good degree of data abstraction?) and a relatively low level (e.g., Have the features of the target programming language been used properly and effectively?). One difficulty in this area is that there is often considerable disagreement about an objective measure of "sound practice" or "effective use." The results of an audit in this area are often a set of observations, and possibly qualitative assertions, rather than an assessment in any hard metric sense.

We therefore examined the code with respect to the aggregate software engineering experience of the audit team. The results of this examination produced a list of observations and assertions about coding practices on many levels: modularization, data abstraction, exception handling, naming conventions, and so forth.

Finally, a related but distinct issue to the previous one is that, presuming that some project-wide style guide and conventions exist, does the code adhere to them? This is a distinct issue inasmuch as the project style guide may embody some questionable practices. Thus, an audit should reveal information on: how the code is (or is not) well-engineered, whether the project style guide has been followed; and whether the style guide itself mandates sound engineering practices.

In this respect the audit team compared the code with the recommended practices and conventions found in the project style guide, and identified the discrepancies between it and the code. At the same time, the audit team evaluated the style guide itself against the team's shared experience in software engineering; this provided not only an assessment of the code's conformance, but also some recommendations concerning revision of the style guide itself.

3.2 Performance of the System

It is beyond the scope or capability of a small, short-lived audit team to verify that performance requirements are sufficient and have been successfully met. Instead, the audit team can assess the developer's treatment of performance during development, to try to establish whether or not sufficient attention has been paid and whether sound engineering practices have been followed. In order to assess these conditions, we addressed the following issues:

- system requirements
- system architecture and design
- performance drivers
- performance modeling activities
- verification of performance requirements

System Requirements

The auditor must understand the system's requirements that affect performance. These include how performance requirements are partitioned onto different system components, the rationale for quantification of performance requirements, and whether performance requirements are critical to the system.

System Architecture and Design

Most significant for an audit is the rationale for the system architecture and design, and the degree to which it has been thought out and evaluated. By a combination of detailed reading of documentation, interviews with designers, and analysis of code samples we were able to assess these aspects. To focus our analysis we posed a number of questions that we then sought to answer. High-level considerations included

- To what degree has performance been a driver of the system architecture and design?
- How have performance considerations driven the system architecture and design?
- Has any prototyping work been done to assess design alternatives that may affect performance?

At a lower design level, the following questions were considered:

- Is the system characterized by independent entities that may be scheduled, or is there a central model for scheduling of activities?
- Do the architecture and design include the use of priorities? If so, what are they and what is the rationale, and how is the problem of priority inversion handled?
- How is the treatment of shared resources handled?
- Where appropriate, have recognized engineering methods (e.g., schedulability analysis) been applied?

Performance Drivers

We considered the following performance drivers as most significant:

- *Hardware.* One key question was the rationale for the selection of each hardware component. Other questions were how performance requirements may have influenced such decisions, and whether prototyping had been performed as part of the selection of hardware components.

- *Compiler and runtime system.* The large body of work related to performance assessment of compilers and runtime systems often embodies benchmarks. Hence, the audit questioned the rationale for the choice of the compiler and runtime system, whether and which benchmarks were used, and whether prototyping had been done in the selection of the compiler and runtime system.

- *Non-developed components.* This refers to hardware or software items that are part of the delivered system, but not developed by the contractor.[3] Examples of non-developed components include databases, networking components, and implementations of interfaces that are based on standards. The key questions for NDI concerned whether management has specified that the system shall incorporate non-developed components and if so, whether processes and criteria exist for making such decisions and what verification procedures exist for such components.

- *Integration.* An integration perspective must evaluate a given performance driver in a particular context. For example, the assessment of the compiler and runtime system are done in a hardware context. So the question asked was why were this compiler *and* this hardware platform chosen?

Performance Modeling Activities

Analytic methods represent one form of modeling activity that may be applied to assess system performance issues; some widely-used techniques in this area include *schedulability analysis* and simulation. These techniques may be particularly useful in considering proposed system modifications. The issues we considered included

- What aspects have been modeled and what was the rationale?

- How many of the performance requirements have been included in the model?

- If a quantitative modeling approach was used, how robust is the model (i.e., how believable are the input parameters) and what level of detail has been included in the model?

- How are the results of the modeling used? For example, are they used to influence the design or implementation?

---

3. Such components are often referred to as NDI (non-developed items). This term is more familiar in government acquisitions than commercial acquisitions. COTS (commercial off-the-shelf) is another familiar term.

Analysis of System Performance With Respect to Requirements

Validation that system performance requirements are being met is achieved through testing (unit, integration, or system). In our audit we considered whether there was a sufficient test for each performance requirement, what testing mechanism were used for each performance requirement, how the performance requirements were found to be satisfied, and whether test generators were used to help generate tests and verify results (especially important in large systems).

3.3 Fault Tolerance

One of the most intrusive requirements of the system was fault tolerance. The availability required was regarded to be so restrictive that conventional hot-standby approaches would not work, since there was the possibility of common mode failures, and a likelihood of overloading the network with communications messages during fault recovery. Hence, a standby data management approach was taken, since this was the most likely way to achieve the desired availability. The audit team assessed the developer's approach to fault tolerance from architecture through implementation and testing to try to judge whether or not they would be successful in meeting their very stringent requirements.

The documents that were used as the basis for the investigation are listed below.

- engineering analysis documents written early in the contract to provide rationale that the system would satisfy the high availability requirements. These included documents describing experiments and analysis of the results of these experiments to demonstrate that the design approaches were sufficiently robust to meet the required availability. Too many studies had been produced to enable us to read them all, and therefore spot checking of a few studies was carried out.

- architectural documents and published papers explaining the hardware and software architectures, and the protocols used to achieve high availability. These formed the basis for the fault tolerance in the system; however, many of the important details were missing. These formed the basis for the initial understanding of the system (and follow-up questions).

- descriptions of the architecture of the fault tolerant operating system processes. This included a number of templates for various types of fault tolerant processes, state-machine like definitions of how the processing should be accomplished, and the message types and interfaces involved. Each application program had to conform to one of the design templates, depending on its characteristics.

- descriptions of the interfaces provided by the infrastructure to provide the services required for fault tolerance. These documents were quite lengthy, and were spot checked.

- various white papers written justifying specific design decisions and parameters, and describing the rationale for these decisions. These white papers were usually given to us in response to questions as they arose. The fact that the analysis had been done increased our confidence in the capabilities, and the documents were spot checked also.

- software code listings, and the results of static analysis of the code produced by independent contractors. Some code was inspected by team members, and the contractors walked team member through other parts of the code. The goal of the walkthroughs was to check conformance to the design templates.

At the completion of the process, the fault tolerance issues were organized into categories addressing the fault-tolerant infrastructure of the system, the fault-tolerant services made available to applications, the design and use of fault-tolerance templates, and the appropriate use of the fault-tolerant services by the applications. A list of outstanding risks with the fault-tolerance mechanisms was also developed.

3.4 Maintainability of the System

Years of empirical data have established that in large, long-lived, software-intensive systems, as much as 80% of the overall life-cycle cost can accrue *after* initial deployment (e.g., [4]), and the system we were auditing promised to fall squarely into this class. Therefore, it was important to address the ability of the system to accommodate change and evolution.

We assessed maintainability by investigating several areas, including

- documentation, through which a maintainer learns which parts of the system are (and are not) affected by a proposed modification;

- architecture and high-level design, which embody the major design decisions;

- low-level design (e.g., code modularization strategy), which embodies the majority of the encapsulation and information-hiding decisions;

- implementation, which determines how well the promises made by the documentation are kept, and how well the policies dictated by the design are followed.

Maintainability is also a function of the appropriateness of the maintenance environment, which we addressed elsewhere in our audit (see Section 3.5).

Rather than just try to assign a scalar maintainability metric, which in our opinion is without operational meaning, we assessed maintainability in the context of likely life-cycle evolution scenarios. Our audit procedure took into account the domain-specific, project-specific, and organization-specific aspects of maintainability. It proceeded as follows:

- We enumerated the quality attributes that were important to achieve and maintain. In our example, these included ultra-high availability (accomplished by a sophisticated distributed, fault-tolerant design and implementation scheme), performance, and the ability to extract a functionally useful subset from the system in order to accommodate a contingency plan to field a scaled-down version of the system.

- We enumerated a set of change classes likely to occur to the system over its lifetime. These change classes may come from anticipated requirements for this system, or domain knowledge about changes made to legacy systems of the same genre. The system under audit was an embedded, real-time, reactive, user-in-the-loop, safety-critical system operating at the edge of its performance envelope. Systems of this genre typically undergo the following classes of change:

  - replacement of hardware: computers, display devices, networks, input devices, etc.

  - replacement of system-level software: operating system or network controller upgrades, new compiler releases, etc.

  - incorporation of third-party components: a commercial display driver, employing elements of a reuse library, etc.

  - changing the so-called "quality attribute" requirements: performance, availability, safety, security, etc.

  - adding, deleting, or changing functionality: changing the display symbology, the input language, the layout and/or contents of a display, adding new information to a display, etc.

  - making the system interoperable with new systems in its environment

- We made sure that our list of change classes covered each of the quality attributes listed above (e.g., increase the system's availability requirement), as well as covering the system at the architectural level (i.e., affect its highest-level components), the module level, and the code level.[4]

- For each change class, we defined a specific instance of the change as a *change scenario*. For instance, to test the system's ability to accommodate increased performance, we posited a 50% increase in the maximum number of inputs the system was required to monitor.

---

4. For some systems, there may be no distinction between highest-level components and modules, or between modules and code units.

- For each change scenario, we conducted a *change exercise*, in which the developers were asked to accommodate the change by showing us all components (from architecture-level components, to design-level modules, to low-level code modules) and documentation that would be affected by the change. The result was a set of *active design reviews* [5] in which the participants were pro-active, each in his or her own area.

The purpose of the change scenarios was to assess the system design against likely, rather than arbitrary, changes. During each exercise, we investigated the process to implement each change, and viewed and catalogued the code and documentation that was or would have been produced, accessed, or modified as a result of the change. During some of the exercises, we actually made code changes; for others, the developer had anticipated us by preparing working prototypes with the change installed.

The result of the change exercises was a set of high-confidence metrics, one per class of change, with which project management could project the cost of performing specific maintenance operations to the system.

Finally, since all changes cannot be anticipated, we assessed whether or not generally-accepted software engineering standards had been followed which, in the past, have resulted in systems that were straightforwardly modified with respect to normal life-cycle evolutionary pressures. One aspect of this "unguided" part of the investigation is to inquire after the design rationale to see what information was encapsulated in each component, whether at the system-level, module-level, or package level. This encapsulation implies a set of changes that the designers had in mind, explicitly or implicitly, against which the resulting system is insulated. This step includes the use of standard code quality metrics, as well as traditional documentation inspection and quality assessments.

3.5 Development and Maintenance Environments

Existing approaches to evaluating software development and maintenance environments fall into one of two categories: a technology-oriented view that concentrates on the selection of individual computer-aided software engineering (CASE) tools; and a more process-oriented view that concentrates on assessing the practices used during development and maintenance. We incorporated both of these views in our approach, since we believe that tools, techniques, and processes should not be considered in isolation. Rather, our notion of an "environment" is the combination of all three, each providing context for the others. From this, it follows that an assessment of an environment must also take this view: an assessment must consider tools, techniques, and processes as a whole, and not as separable factors to be evaluated.

We also found it essential to concentrate attention on how the development and maintenance environments specifically apply to the current system being maintained. In particular, this attention included examining the goals of the organization that developed, is maintaining, and is using the system in question. These considerations led us to assess the software development and maintenance environments by performing the following analyses:

- comparing the development and maintenance environments;
- evaluating the plan for transition of responsibility from development to maintenance;
- assessing the key maintenance practices;
- examining the organization's maintenance of other systems.

Comparing the Development and Maintenance Environments

The development environment leaves a legacy of documents, data, and knowledge concerning the system that must be brought forward into maintenance. The accessibility of these artifacts are strongly impacted by the environment through which they came into being; to the extent that the maintenance environment is similar or different, the use of those artifacts will either be facilitated, constrained, or impossible. We therefore compared the two environments by focussing on four key questions:

- When is the maintenance environment instantiated?
- Is the tool makeup consistent between the development and maintenance environments?
- Aside from consistency, what is the intrinsic quality of the tools?
- Is the maintenance environment documentation adequate for the maintenance personnel to carry out their task?

Evaluating the Plan for Transition of Responsibility

For many projects, the development and maintenance organizations are entirely separate. This may be due to the fact that different organizations have been contracted for development and maintenance aspects of the system, or that a single organization is internally structured with separate development and maintenance divisions. In either case, it is inevitable that much valuable information about the system will be lost in transitioning the system from development to maintenance.

To aid transition from development to maintenance, a number of key documents need to be in place, up-to-date, and of high quality. We considered the following documents to be essential:

- a high-level overview of the architecture of the system that establishes the major design requirements for the system, the implementation choices made to meet those requirements, and the typical operation of the system.

- a detailed transition plan for moving the system to maintenance that defines the tools, techniques, and practices to be used in maintenance, the responsibilities and expectations of all participants, and so on.

Assessing the Key Maintenance Practices

The key practices that take place during maintenance parallel the key practices that occur during development. But while most software projects consider these as critical aspects of the development phases, they are often severely neglected when establishing the maintenance environment. We examined a number of key maintenance practices to ensure that the practices were well-defined, adequately documented, and had been agreed to by all relevant organizations. The key process areas that we examined included the code inspection processes, the code bug-fix process, the integration test process, the system build and release practices, and the system change request procedures.

Examining Maintenance of Other Systems

Most organizations simultaneously maintain many large systems. Hence, the maintenance of one large system cannot be considered in isolation; many decisions must take a wider picture of maintenance that provides consistent maintenance practices across the organization as a whole. Of these decisions, we considered four to be paramount.

First, since the system may interface with a number of existing or planned future systems, many decisions (e.g., system interfaces) may have been fixed. This provides substantial design challenges during maintenance. For example, the system we examined interfaced to a wide range of systems constructed over a 25-year period. The continued correct operation of these systems was paramount in any proposed enhancements to the target system.

Second, maintenance engineers have an existing technology base for maintaining systems. The maintenance environment for a new system must harmonize with this existing environment. We examined the planned maintenance environment in the context of the existing maintenance activities of the organization.

Third, the recent climate of systems development toward the use of commercial off-the-shelf (COTS) components provides significant maintenance challenges: large parts of the system are maintained by COTS vendors, access to detailed information on the operation of COTS software is often severely limited, new releases of COTS software occur at the choice of the vendor, and tracing errors can be problematic in systems that include COTS components. In our study we paid particular attention to maintenance activities for COTS components of the system, and examined contingency plans for events such as new releases of COTS software, tracing bugs in COTS software, and actions to be taken if the COTS vendor went out of business.

Fourth, maintenance is required not just for the operational system, but also for all of the software needed for development, testing, maintenance, and release. In comparison with the operational software, the support software in most large systems can be more extensive, in multiple languages, and poorly documented. We attempted to ascertain which support software was essential to the ongoing operation and maintenance of the system (e.g., database systems for data entry and manipulation, assembler code for network support, test scripts written in a high-level scripting language), and to ensure plans were in place to maintain and evolve the information needed to maintain them. This included maintaining large amounts of documentation, data (e.g., test data), and administrative information on support system configurations using during development.

3.6 Documentation

During any large software project there will be a large amount of documentation generated. This is particularly true in projects such as the one discussed in this paper that take place using a variant of the Department of Defense standard development approach, Mil-Std-2167A. In this approach there are a number of points at which detailed documentation is produced that is used as the basis for project reviews.

As part of the audit we spent considerable time examining this and other documentation. Initially, we examined the documentation in order that we ourselves could obtain an understanding of the system. Later our examination was based on the quality of that documentation as it applied to

- others interested in finding out about the system;
- software developers as they sought guidance on technical questions concerning how to implement parts of the system;
- system maintainers as they attempted to fix and evolve the system;
- end users as they tried to operate the system in the field.

For each of these classes of users there are clearly different sets of documents that are of interest, and different document qualities that are of importance. Hence, we attempted to consider the major needs of each of these users and to consider whether the documentation was adequate for those needs.

Additionally, we considered some generic qualities of the documentation that we believe are fundamental to good software engineering practice. Namely, that the documentation be well-written, comprehensive, internally and mutually consistent, and readily accessible. To do this we carried out a number of simple analyses based on realistic scenarios. For example, we selected a number of requirements, tried to find where they were documented, attempted to trace these requirements to documents containing the key design decisions that they influenced, and eventually to pieces of code that implemented them. Such scenarios proved very valuable in revealing whether the documents could be easily navigated, contained accurate information, and captured the information that is needed by practicing software engineers.

3.7 PTR Analysis

Problem Trouble Reports (PTRs) give valuable insight into both the software product and the ongoing software process. In the case of the software product, the problem discovery rates and the problem fix rates give some indication of product volatility and how close the product is to completion. In the case of the software process, the management and control of problem handling is one indication of the overall level of management and control of the entire software process. The PTR process is appealing as an indicator for a software audit because it is discrete and easily analyzed within a well-defined time frame.

Problems are not restricted to "bugs" in the program under construction, but are defined more broadly. PTRs are initiated for performance enhancements, or to accommodate external changes (e.g., in the system's operating environment). They are also opened to report bugs in support software or commercially available software, or to report documentation errors. In the audit conducted by our team, the PTR database contained more than 25,000 records with each record containing over 200 fields of information.

During the course of the audit, the software audit team conducted the following activities:

- interviewed members of the problem management group;
- reviewed PTR process documents and the PTR model;
- reviewed PTR status reports and graphs;
- sat in on a PTR Review Board (PRB) meeting;
- reviewed a random sample of individual PTRs.

The purpose of the initial interviews with the problem management group was to gather information about the definition of PTRs and to gain an understanding of the overall PTR process, including the life cycle of a PTR. Along with initial interviews came documentation of the process that could then be studied off-line. Later we met with this group again when we were in a position to ask more probing questions. We also studied status reports and graphs of PTRs over a several year period showing various metrics including the discovery and closure rates broken down by types of problem, type of module, and severity of problem. We examined the mathematical model for predicting PTR activity based on historical data and life cycle stage.

The PTR Review Board is a group that reviews incoming PTRs and assigns them to be fixed by a certain group by a certain time. By sitting in on a regular meeting, an audit team is less likely to be manipulated by selective information disclosure. In our case we attempted to sit quietly to the side while the meeting was conducted in the usual manner. Finally, we inspected a random sample of actual PTR records in order to discover the integrity, consistency, and completeness of the database.

Among the questions that can be answered during a software audit by a study of PTRs and the PTR process are the following:

- Is sufficient information collected on each PTR, including its status, its history, and its criticality?
- Is the change management process well documented?
- Are the documented change management procedures followed?
- Does the PTR model accurately predict the PTR discovery and fix rates?
- Are PTRs entered during the analysis, design, and implementation stages or only during integration and testing?
- Are the fields in the database complete and consistent so that they produce accurate reports?
- Are PTR reports produced at regular intervals and analyzed consistently based on consistent definitions?
- Is management using PTR data to find the root causes of problems and to identify parts of the software and parts of the organization that are causing high error rates?
- Is the number of outstanding PTRs decreasing or increasing?

It is important to understand that PTRs must be viewed in the context of the current stage of the life cycle. It is normal for PTRs to increase during integration and test. However a sure sign of trouble is when PTR levels stay the same or increase over long periods of time. This is one indication of volatility in requirements. The PTR model used by the contractor in our audit projected that a mere 7% addition of new code from one build to the next would preclude any diminution in the number of outstanding PTRs over time.

3.8 Management Issues

Although the audit focused primarily on the current technical software product, the technical issues often led back to management issues. Deficiencies in the product provided inferences of a chaotic management process on the side of both the government and the contractor. Our approach was a departure from other approaches, which tend to focus exclusively on either the product or the process. By using product deficiencies to point to process and management issues, our conclusions had an empirical grounding, and provided a balance between product and process.

Product-oriented audit investigations revealed major problems in areas of code quality and documentation. The lack of quality in the product led us to investigate how well processes had been defined and management-level enforcement of these defined processes in areas such as code inspections, system testing, and software quality assurance.

Some of these processes had been defined, but their sustained use appeared to have been inconsistent.

In particular, our audit of management practices and procedures of the contractor addressed the following areas of concern:

- Was there a significant attempt to learn from the past through root cause analysis of problems? A symptom of a problem in this area was code that had been developed with errors that should have been caught at earlier stages of development.

- Did the contractor manage shifting requirements effectively? Were requirements changes accepted without sufficient analysis for cost, schedule, and impact on the rest of the system?

- Did management tend to rely on a small group of experts, as opposed to a stable, strong process? If the latter, is it championed by a strong leader?

- Overall, was quality or expediency the more highly valued goal? What are the developer's quality improvement and quality assurance plans and processes?

- Were problems ever addressed frankly by the contractor management in the months before the audit, when trouble was brewing? This might be evidenced by such actions as internal audits, identification of process deficiencies, development of a process improvement plan, etc., and the existence of engineering teams to implement the improvements and dedicated management teams to monitor them.

It must also be recognized that improvement takes time and requires monitoring long after the audit team has disbanded. One result of such an audit may be a list of areas that the customer must monitor in the future. They may include monitoring items such as

- progress in meeting the objectives of the process improvement plan;

- evidence that a viable inspection process has been successful;

- use of the program trouble report database for root cause analysis and management decision making;

- development of an independent quality assurance function;

- verification of successful schedule and project planning;

- initiation of risk mitigation activities;

- establishment of a metrics program for management decision making;

- schedules and milestones for fixing problems addressed in this audit.

On the customer's side, we tried to assess whether their management of the developer and its sub-contractors was strong, reasonable, and consistent. Areas we investigated included

- the number of requirements changes and versions mandated by the customer

- the ability (or inability) of the customer to control the expectations of users;

- degree of visibility into, and monitoring of, contractor work;

- quality control of contractor products

- quality or existence of joint risk management processes;

- whether schedules were driven by management or political needs, rather than technical reality

- degree of effective use of information provided by support contractors (e.g., failure to raise program trouble reports based on information they provide)

4. Comments and Summary

Performing a software audit is typically a stressful task undertaken under great pressure to produce results in a relatively short time. The audit discussed in this paper was typical in this regard: it took place with minimum time for preparation, and using personnel that were largely inexperienced in carrying out such audits. However, we believe that in many regards the audit was successful. We

- documented the current system in a form that highlighted its major characteristics and identified areas of major technical risk.

- provided an assessment of many of the aspects of the system that have a direct relevance to the quality of the overall design of the system.

- examined the major documentation describing the system and its implementation, and provided many suggestions for improvement.

- looked at parts of the system implementation to assess the fidelity of the implementation to the design, and to ensure that the implementation was of high quality.

- considered the engineering environment and practices being used to complete and maintain the system to ensure that they were adequate for the predicted life of the system.

As a result, the information we provided enabled the customer to make appropriate decisions concerning the future of the program being audited. In retrospect, we are able to identify a number of factors that we believe contributed substantially to the success of the audit. These included

- *Personnel.* The audit team consisted of experienced software engineers with a range of technical skills that matched the fundamental characteristics of the system we examined (e.g., experienced in fault-tolerance, performance, and distributed real-time systems).

- *Customer interactions.* We began by negotiating a clear statement of work with the customer that included a well-defined scope and set of objectives for the audit. As the audit progressed, the pressures to amend these goals and objectives had to be rigorously resisted.

- *Contractor interactions.* Early in the audit we established a good relationship with the contractor by demonstrating our technical capabilities, and by being clear that our role was to provide technical data to the customer, and not to offer rash opinions based on little information.

- *Internal organization.* During the period of the audit we received hundreds of documents amounting to many thousands of pages of text, we attended dozens of meetings, and we communicated frequently with the contractor and the customer. A dedicated, responsible support person was essential to the project to manage this information and to organize and distribute relevant material, plan travel and meeting details, and ensure relevant electronic communication mechanisms existed between the team members.

We also recognize a number of criticisms of our audit approach. These include

- *Narrow focus.* Some members of the customer organization were disappointed that we did not address the cost and resource implications of the problems we identified. The customer had a number of support contractors whose role on the project was to plan and monitor such aspects, and our approach was always to refer the customer to these support contractors.

- *Fixed audit scope.* During the audit the customer made decisions concerning the future of the program that led to some of the findings at the end of the audit being irrelevant to the customer. We were also unable to say how some of our findings related to this new strategy, as the strategy was not considered during the audit.

- *Lack of quantitative data.* Wherever possible we justified our comments with facts and data from the system. However, the customer had expected quantitative data that objectively measured many quality attributes of the system. We had to explain that metrics to measure these attributes do not exist.

- *Avoidance of "finger-pointing".* We decided that the outcome of our audit would not focus on assessing blame. This is seldom a useful exercise, since interpretations and excuses can always be found to contradict any assertion of blame. Also, the potential candidates for blame were on all sides of the question; selecting a scapegoat from these possible candidates would not be valuable to anyone.

Apart from the value to the customer, the team itself found the experience of performing a post-mortem software audit to be an interesting and valuable one. Many important lessons were learned concerning the state of the practice in developing large, complex software systems, and the difficulties of project management and monitoring. These have only briefly been discussed in this paper. We are currently in the process of documenting the lessons learned from our audit experiences, and hope to provide a set of more detailed guidelines for audit teams faced with a similar situation to ours.

Acknowledgments

The SEI is sponsored by the U.S. Department of Defense.

While responsibility for this report lies with the stated authors, we gratefully acknowledge the contributions made by other members of the audit team to the design and execution of this audit.

5. References

[1] *IEEE Recommended Practice for the Evaluation and Selection of CASE Tools*, The Institute of Electrical and Electronics Engineers, Inc. (IEEE), 345 East 47th Street, New York, NY 10017, 1992. ANSI/IEEE Std. 1209-1992.

[2] Fred Brooks, *The Mythical Man Month,* Addison Wesley, 1975.

[3] *Scientific American*, "Software's Chronic Crisis," September 1994.

[4] Barry Boehm, *Software Engineering Economics*, Prentice-Hall, Englewood Cliffs, NJ, 1981.

[5] David Weiss and David Parnas, "Active Design Reviews: Principles and Practices," *Proceedings, Eighth International Conference on Software Engineering*, 1985, pp. 132-136.

[6] Alan W. Brown, David J. Carney, Paul C. Clements, "A Case Study in Assessing the Maintainability of a Large, Software-Intensive System," *Proceedings of the International Symposium on Software Engineering of Computer Based Systems*, Tucson, AZ., IEEE Computer Society, March 1995.

Part III. Software Architecture

Software Architecture: An Executive Overview

Paul C. Clements & Linda N. Northrop

Software Engineering Institute
Carnegie Mellon University
Pittsburgh, PA, 15213, USA
{pclement, lmn}@sei.cmu.edu

Abstract

Software architecture is an area of growing importance to practitioners and researchers in government, industry, and academia. Journals and international workshops are devoted to it. Working groups are formed to study it. Textbooks are emerging about it. The government is investing in the development of software architectures as core products in their own right. Industry is marketing architectural frameworks such as CORBA. Why all the interest and investment? What is software architecture, and why is it perceived as providing a solution to the inherent difficulty in designing and developing large, complex systems? This report will attempt to summarize the concept of software architecture for an intended audience of mid to senior level management. The reader is presumed to have some familiarity with common software engineering terms and concepts, but not to have a deep background in the field. This report is not intended to be overly-scholarly, nor is it intended to provide the technical depth necessary for practitioners and technologists. The intent is to distill some of the technical detail and provide a high level overview.

1. Introduction

Software architecture is an area of growing importance to practitioners and researchers in government, industry, and academia. The April 1995 issue of *IEEE Transactions on Software Engineering* and the November 1995 issue of *IEEE Software* were devoted to software architecture. Industry and government working groups on software architecture are becoming more frequent. Workshops and presentations on software architecture are beginning to populate software engineering conferences. There is an emerging software architecture research community, meeting and collaborating at special-purpose workshops such as the February 1995 International Workshop on Software Architectures held in Dagstuhl, Germany, or the April 1995 International Workshop on Architectures for Software Systems held in Seattle, Washington. The October 1996 ACM Symposium on the Foundations of Software Engineering will focus on software

architecture. Textbooks devoted entirely to software architecture are appearing, such as the one by Shaw and Garlan [36]. The government is investing in the development of software architectures as core products in their own right; the Technical Architecture Framework for Information Management (TAFIM) is an example. The Common Object Request Broker Architecture (CORBA) and other computer-assisted software engineering environments with emphasis on architecture-based development are entering the marketplace with profound effect.

Why all the interest and investment? What is software architecture, and why is it perceived as providing a solution to the inherent difficulty in designing and developing large, complex systems?

This report will attempt to summarize the concept of software architecture for an intended audience of mid to senior level management. The reader is presumed to have some familiarity with common software engineering terms and concepts, but not to have a deep background in the field. This report is not intended to be overly-scholarly, nor is it intended to provide the technical depth necessary for practitioners and technologists. Software engineers can refer to the listed references for a more comprehensive and technical presentation. The intent here is to distill some of the technical detail and provide a high level overview.

Because software architecture is still relatively immature from both a research and practice perspective there is little consensus on terminology, representation or methodology. An accurate yet digested portrayal is difficult to achieve. All of the issues and all of the ambiguity in the area of software architecture have yet to be addressed. We have simplified based upon what we believe to be the best current understanding.

While software architecture appears to be an area of great promise, it is also an area ripe for significant investment in order to reach a level of understanding from which significant benefits can be reaped and from which a truly simple overview could be captured.

0-8186-7718-X/96 $5.00 © 1996 IEEE

We invite feedback on the content, presentation, and utility of this report with regard to the intended audience.

The structure of the report is as follows:

- Section 2 discusses the concept of software architecture—its definition(s), its history, and its foundational underpinnings. It also suggests why there has been considerable confusion over the term and why we do not yet have a precise definition.

- Section 3 asks, and attempts to answer, the question "Why is software architecture important?" It discusses the importance of the concept of software architecture in system development from three vantages: as a medium of communication among a project's various stakeholders; as the earliest set of design decisions in a project; and as a high-level abstraction of the system that can be reused in other systems.

- Section 4 discusses the concept of architectural views—the need for different views, a description of some accepted views, and the relationship among views.

- Section 5 explains how the architecture-based model of system development differs from the traditional programming-oriented development paradigms of the past.

- Finally, Section 6 lists some of the most promising research areas in software architecture.

2. What Is Software Architecture?

2.1 Definitions

What do we mean by software architecture? Unfortunately, there is yet no single universally accepted definition. Nor is there a shortage of proposed definition candidates. The term is interpreted and defined in many different ways. At the essence of all the discussion about software architecture, however, is a focus on reasoning about the *structural* issues of a system. And although architecture is sometimes used to mean a certain architectural style, such as client-server, and sometimes used to refer to a field of study, it is most often used to describe structural aspects of a particular system.

These structural issues are design-related—software architecture is, after all, a form of software design that occurs earliest in a system's creation—but at a more abstract level than algorithms and data structures. According to what has come to be regarded as a seminal paper on software architecture, Mary Shaw and David Garlan suggest that these

"Structural issues include gross organization and global control structure; protocols for communication, synchronization, and data access; assignment of functionality to design elements; physical distribution; composition of design elements; scaling and performance; and selection among design alternatives" [19].

Each of the various definitions of software architecture emphasizes certain of these structural issues and corresponding ways to describe them. Each of these positions can usu-

ally be traced to an idea about what the proponent wishes to *do* with the software architecture—analyze it, evolve it, represent it, or develop from it. It is important to understand that though it may seem confusing to have multiple interpretations, these different interpretations do not preclude each other, nor do they represent a fundamental conflict about what software architecture is. We will address these different interpretations or views in Section 3. However, at this point it is important to realize that together they represent a spectrum in the software architecture research community about the emphasis that should be placed on architecture—its constituent parts, the whole entity, the way it behaves once built, or the building of it. Taken together, they form a consensus view of software architecture and afford a more complete picture.

As a sufficiently good compromise to the current technical debate, we offer the definition of software architecture that David Garlan and Dewayne Perry have adopted for their guest editorial in the April 1995 *IEEE Transactions on Software Engineering* devoted to software architecture:

> *The structure of the components of a program/system, their interrelationships, and principles and guidelines governing their design and evolution over time.*

Other definitions can be found in various documents [31, 19, 21, 17, 38]. Diagrams are typically used to illustrate these components and their interrelationships. The choice of diagram is by no means standardized.

The bottom line is that software architecture is about structural properties of a system. Structural properties can be expressed in terms of components, interrelationships, and principles and guidelines about their use. The exact structural properties to consider and the ways to represent them vary depending upon what is of structural interest to the consumer of the architecture.

2.2 Roots of Software Architecture

The study of software architecture is in large part a study of software structure that began in 1968 when Edsger Dijkstra pointed out that it pays to be concerned with how software is partitioned and structured, as opposed to simply programming so as to produce a correct result [15]. Dijkstra was writing about an operating system, and first put forth the notion of a layered structure, in which programs were grouped into layers, and programs in one layer could only communicate with programs in adjoining layers. Dijkstra pointed out the elegant conceptual integrity exhibited by such an organization, with the resulting gains in development and maintenance ease.

David Parnas pressed this line of observation with his contributions concerning information-hiding modules [27], software structures [28], and program families [29].

A program family is a set of programs (not all of which necessarily have been or will ever be constructed) for which it is profitable or useful to consider as a group. This avoids ambiguous concepts such as "similar functionality" that sometimes arise when describing domains. For example, software engineering environments and video games are not usually considered to be in the same domain, although they might be considered members of the same program family in a discussion about tools that help build graphical user interfaces, which both happen to use.[1]

Parnas argued that early design decisions should be ones that will most likely remain constant across members of the program family that one may reasonably expect to produce. In the context of this discussion, an early design decision is the adoption of a particular architecture. Late design decisions should represent trivially-changeable decisions, such as the values of compile-time or even load-time constants.

All of the work in the field of software architecture may be seen as evolving towards a paradigm of software development based on principles of architecture, and for exactly the same reasons given by Dijkstra and Parnas: Structure is important, and getting the structure right carries benefits.

In tandem with this important academic understanding of program and system structure came a long series of practical experiences working with systems in several highly populated domains, such as compilers. Throughout the 1970s and 1980s, compiler design evolved from a series of distinct efforts, each one innovative and unprecedented, into one with standard, codified pieces and interactions. Today, textbooks about how to build a compiler abound, and the domain has matured to the point where no one today would think for a moment of building a compiler from scratch, without re-using and exploiting the codified experience of the hundreds of prior examples.

What exactly is reused and exploited? Those structural necessities that are common to all compilers. Compiler writers can talk meaningfully with each other about lexical scanners, parsers, syntax trees, attribute grammars, target code generators, optimizers, and call graphs even though the languages being compiled may look nothing at all alike. So, for instance, two compilers may have completely different parsers, but what is common is that both compilers *have* a component called a parser, which performs a function in both that (when viewed under at a high level) is exactly the same. Reusing the structural decisions and componentry for a system also allows reusing its work breakdown structures, estimates, team organization, test plans, integration plans, documentation, and many other labor-intensive assets.

Many other domains now exist that, through practice and repetition and sharing among the many early members of the family, now exhibit common structure, interconnection strategies, allocation of functionality to components, component interfaces, and an overall justifying rationale. The current

study of software architecture can be viewed as an *ex post facto* effort to provide a structured storehouse for this type of reusable high level family-wide design information. Work in software architecture can be seen as attempting to codify the structural commonality among members of a program family, so that the high-level design decisions inherent in each member of a program family need not be re-invented, re-validated, and re-described.

2.3 Why Hasn't the Community Converged?

As noted above, the software engineering community has not settled on a universal definition for software architecture. The lack of a definition is perhaps not as significant as the reasons for lack of convergence. We suggest the following reasons for the current ambiguity in the term. We list them as issues to be aware of in any discussion of software architecture.

Advocates Bring Their Methodological Biases with Them

As we have noted, proposed definitions of architecture largely agree at the core, but differ seriously at the fringes. Some require that architecture must include rationale, others hold out for process steps for construction. Some require allocation of functionality to components; others contend that simple topology suffices. Each position depends upon the precise motivation for examining the structural issues in the first place. It is essential to understand that motivation prior to the study of either a definition of software architecture or an architecture artifact.

The Study Is Following Practice, not Leading It

The study of software architecture has evolved by observing the design principles and actions that designers take when working on real systems. It is an attempt to abstract the commonalities inherent in system design, and as such, it must account for a wide range of activities, concepts, methods, approaches, and results. This differs from a more top-down approach that defines software architecture and then maps compliant ongoing activities to the term. What we see happening is that people observe designers' many activities, and try to accommodate those activities by making the term software architecture more broad. Because this study is ongoing, the convergence of the definition hasn't happened.

The Study Is Quite New

Although it possesses long roots, the field of software architecture is really quite new, as judged by the recent flurry of books, conferences, workshops, and literature devoted to it.

The Foundations Have Been Imprecise

Beware: The field has been remarkable for its proliferation of undefined terms that can be land mines for the unsuspecting. For example, architecture defined as "the overall structure of the system" adds to rather than reduces confusion because this implies that a system has but a sin-

---

1. This example illustrates that the members of a program family may include elements of what are usually considered different domains.

gle "overall structure." Figure 1, taken from a system description for an underwater acoustic simulation system, purports to describe the top-level architecture of the system. Exactly what can we tell about the system from this diagram? There are four components, three of which might have more in common with each other (MODP, MODR, and MODN) than with the fourth (CP).

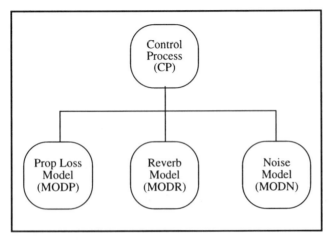

Figure 1. Typical, but Uninformative, Model of a "Top-Level Architecture"

Is this an architecture? Assuming that architecture consists of components (of which we have four) and connections among them (also present), then this would seem to suffice according to many definitions. However, even if we accept the most primitive definition, what can we *not* tell from the diagram?

- What is the nature of the components, and what is the significance of their separation? Do they run on separate processors? Do they run at separate times? Do the components consist of processes, programs, or both? Do the components represent ways in which the project labor will be divided, or do they convey a sense of runtime separation? Are they modules, objects, tasks, functions, processes, distributed programs, or something else?

- What is the significance of the links? Do the links mean the components communicate with each other, control each other, send data to each other, use each other, invoke each other, synchronize with each other, or some combination of these or other relations?

- What is the significance of the layout? Why is CP on a separate (higher) level? Does it call the other three components, and are the others not allowed to call it? Or was there simply not room enough to put all four components on the same row in the diagram?

We *must* raise these questions, for without knowing precisely what the components are, what the links mean, and what significance there is to the position of components and/or direction of links, diagrams are not much help and should be regarded warily.

Consider one more example, a "layered architecture," which is also a commonly-represented architectural paradigm [19]:

> *A layered system is organized hierarchically, each layer providing service to the layer above it and serving as a client to the layer below. In some layered systems inner layers are hidden from all except the adjacent outer layer, except for certain functions carefully selected for export. Thus in these systems the components implement a virtual machine at some layer in the hierarchy... The connectors are defined by the protocols that determine how the layers will interact.*

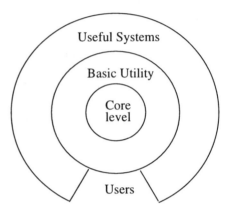

Figure 2. A Layered System [19]

Close examination of this description reveals that it mixes separate concerns. For one thing, "hidden" is a concept that has no meaning at runtime; it is purely a concept that applies at program-write time, and specifies what facilities a particular programmer is or is not allowed to use when writing his or her portion of the system. "Providing service" is the runtime interaction mechanism, but it could reasonably mean any of the following: calls, uses, signals, sends data to. It also fails to capture any notion of concurrency, real or potential. Can software in different layers run simultaneously, or are there mutual exclusion constraints between layers? If we are concerned about the feasibility of fielding our system on a multi-processor environment, shouldn't we be able to discern this information as part of the answer to the question "What is the architecture of a layered system?"

The Term Is Over-Utilized

The meaning of the term architecture as it relates to software engineering is becoming increasingly dilute simply because it seems to be in vogue. It is possible to find references to the following "kinds" of architectures: domain-specific, megaprogramming, target, systems, information, information systems, functional, software, hardware, network, infrastructure, applications, operations, technical, framework, conceptual, reference, enterprise, factory, C4I, manufacturing, building, machine-tool, etc. Often what differs is the nature of the components and connections (e.g., a network architecture specifies connectedness between processors at the endpoints of hardware communication paths); at other times the distinctions are less clear or the term "architecture" is simply an inappropriate reference. Some of these terms will be described in more detail in Section 4.

2.4 The Many Roles of Software Architecture

People often make analogies to other uses of the word architecture about which they have some intuition. They commonly associate architecture with physical structure (building, streets, hardware) and physical arrangement. A building architect has a perspective of architecture that is driven by the need to design a building that as an entity addresses needs and requirements including accessibility, aesthetics, light, maintainability, etc. [3]. A software architect has a perspective that is driven by the need to design a system that addresses needs such as concurrency, portability, evolvability, usability, security, etc. Analogies between buildings and software systems should not be taken literally—they break down fairly soon—but rather used to help understand that perspective is important and structure can have different meanings depending upon the motivation for examining structure. What to glean from this discussion is that a precise definition of software architecture is not nearly as important as the concept and what its investigation allows us to do.

Software architecture usually refers to some combination of structural views of a system, with each view a legitimate abstraction of the system with respect to certain criteria, that facilitates a particular type of planning or analysis. This relatively simple concept has been co-opted by a wide variety of stakeholders and participants in software development; architecture has become a concept that represents many things to many people. In subsequent sections, we will explore some of these views and viewpoints.

3. Why Is Software Architecture Important?

If a project has not achieved a system architecture, including its rationale, the project should not proceed to full-scale system development. Specifying the architecture as a deliverable enables its use throughout the development and maintenance process.

Barry Boehm [6]

What is it about software architecture that warrants all the attention it is receiving? In this section we will suggest some reasons why software architecture is important, and why the practice of architecture-based development is worthwhile.

Fundamentally, there are three reasons:

1. **Mutual communication.** Software architecture represents a common high-level abstraction of the system that most, if not all, of the system's stakeholders can use as a basis for creating mutual understanding, forming consensus, and communicating with each other.

2. **Early design decisions**. Software architecture represents the embodiment of the earliest set of design decisions about a system, and these early bindings carry weight far out of proportion to their individual gravity with respect to the system's remaining development, its service in deployment, and its maintenance life.

3. **Transferable abstraction of a system**. Software architecture embodies a relatively small, intellectually graspable model for how the system is structured and how its components work together; this model is transferable across systems; in particular, it can be applied to other systems exhibiting similar requirements, and can promote large scale reuse.

We will address each in turn.

3.1 Architecture Is the Vehicle for Stakeholder Communication

Each stakeholder of a software system—customer, user, project manager, coder, tester, etc.—is concerned with different aspects of the system for which architecture is an important factor; or, they may be concerned with the same aspects, but from different perspectives. For example, the user is concerned that the system meets its availability and reliability requirements; the customer is concerned that the architecture can be implemented on schedule and to budget; the manager is worried (in addition to cost and schedule) that the architecture will allow teams to work largely independently, interacting in disciplined and controlled ways. The developer is worried about strategies to achieve all of those goals. Architecture provides a common language in which competing concerns can be expressed, negotiated, and resolved at a level that is intellectually manageable even for large, complex systems. Without such a language it is difficult to understand large systems sufficiently to make well informed early decisions that greatly influence their quality and usefulness.

3.2 Architecture Embodies the Earliest Set of Design Decisions About a System

Architecture represents the earliest set of design decisions about a system. These early decisions are the most difficult to get right, are the hardest ones to change, and have the most far-reaching downstream effects, some of which we describe as follows.

Architecture Provides Builders with Constraints on Implementation

An architecture defines a set of constraints on an implementation; an implementation is said to exhibit an architecture if it conforms to the structural design decisions described by the architecture. The implementation must therefore be divided into the prescribed components, the components must interact with each other in the prescribed fashion, and each component must fulfill its responsibility to the other components as dictated by the architecture.

This constraining of the implementation is made on the basis of system- and/or project-wide allocation decisions that are invisible to implementors working on individual components, and permits a separation of concerns that allows management decisions that make best use of personnel. Component builders must be fluent in the specification of their individual components, but not in system trade-off issues; conversely, the architects need not be experts in algorithm design or the intricacies of the programming language.

The Architecture Dictates Organizational Structure for Development and Maintenance Projects

Not only does architecture prescribe the structure of the system being developed, but that structure becomes reflected in the work breakdown structure and hence the inherent development project structure. Teams communicate with each other in terms of the interface specifications to the major components. The maintenance activity, when launched, will also reflect the software structure, with maintenance teams formed to address specific structural components.

An Architecture Permits or Precludes the Achievement of a System's Targeted Quality Attributes

Whether or not a system will be able to exhibit its desired (or required) quality attributes is largely determined by the time the architecture is chosen.

Quality attributes may be divided into two categories. The first includes those that can be measured by running the software and observing its effects; performance, security, reliability, and functionality all fall into this category. The second includes those that cannot be measured by observing the system, but rather by observing the development or maintenance activities. This category includes maintainability in all of its various flavors: adaptability, portability, reusability, and the like.

Modifiability, for example, depends extensively on the system's modularization, which reflects the encapsulation strategies. Reusability of components depends on how strongly coupled they are with other components in the system. Performance depends largely upon the volume and complexity of inter-component communication and coordination, especially if the components are physically distributed processes.

It is important to understand, however, that an architecture alone cannot guarantee the functionality or quality required of a system. Poor downstream design or implementation decisions can always undermine an architectural framework. Decisions at all stages of the life cycle—from high level design to coding and implementation—affect system quality. Therefore, quality is not completely a function of an architectural design. A good architecture is necessary, but not sufficient, to ensure quality.

It Is Possible to Predict Certain Qualities About a System by Studying Its Architecture

If the architecture allows or precludes a system's quality attributes (but cannot ensure them), is it possible to tell that the appropriate architectural decisions have been made without waiting until the system is developed and deployed? If the answer were "no," then choosing an architecture would be a fairly hopeless task. Random architecture selection would perform as well as any other method. Fortunately, it is possible to make quality predictions about a system based solely on an evaluation of its architecture.

Architecture evaluation techniques such as the Software Architecture Analysis Method (SAAM), proposed at the Software Engineering Institute (SEI), obtain top down insight into the attributes of software product quality that are enabled (and constrained) by specific software architectures. SAAM proceeds from construction of a set of domain derived scenarios that reflect qualities of interest in the end-product software. This set includes direct scenarios (which exercise required software functionality) and indirect scenarios (which reflect non functional qualities). Mappings are made between these domain scenarios and candidate architectures, and a score is assigned to the degree by which a candidate architecture satisfies the expectations of each scenario. Candidate architectures can then be contrasted in terms of their fulfillment of scenario-based expectations of them [2, 12, 22].

Architecture Can Be the Basis for Training

The structure, plus a high-level description of how the components interact with each other to carry out the required behavior, often serves as the high-level introduction to the system for new project members.

An Architecture Helps to Reason About and Manage Change

The software development community is finally coming to grips with the fact that roughly 80% of a software system's cost may occur *after* initial deployment, in what is usually called the maintenance phase. Software systems change over their lifetimes; they do so often, and often with difficulty. Change may come from various quarters, including:

• The need to enhance the system's capabilities. Software-intensive systems tend to use software as the means to achieve additional or modified functionality for the system as a whole. Systems such as the Joint Stars battlefield surveillance radar and the MILSTAR network of telecommunication satellites are examples of systems that have achieved enhanced capability through software upgrades. However, with each successive change, the complexity of the system software has increased dramatically.

- The need to incorporate new technology, whose adoption can provide increased efficiency, operational robustness, and maintainability.

Deciding when changes are essential, determining which change paths have least risk, assessing the consequences of proposed changes, and arbitrating sequences and priorities for requested changes all require broad insight into relationships, dependencies, performance, and behavioral aspects of system software components. Reasoning at an architecture level can provide the insight necessary to make decisions and plans related to change.

More fundamentally, however, an architecture partitions possible changes into three categories: local, non-local, and architectural. A local change can be accomplished by modifying a single component. A non-local change requires multiple component modifications, but leaves the underlying architecture intact. An architectural change affects the ways in which the components interact with each other, and will probably require changes all over the system. Obviously, local changes are the most desirable, and so the architecture carries the burden of making sure that the most likely changes are also the easiest to make.

3.3 Architecture as a Transferable Model

Greater benefit can be achieved from reuse the earlier in the life cycle it is applied. While code reuse provides a benefit, reuse at the architectural level provides a tremendous leverage for systems with similar requirements. When architectural decisions can be reused across multiple systems all of the early decision impacts we just described above are also transferred.

Entire Product Lines Share a Common Architecture

Product lines are derived from what Parnas referred to in 1976 as program families [29]. It pays to carefully order the design decisions one makes, so that those most likely to be changed occur latest in the process. In an architecture-based development of a product line, the architecture is in fact the sum of those early design decisions, and one chooses an architecture (or a family of closely-related architectures) that will serve all envisioned members of the product line by making design decisions that apply across the family early, and by making others that apply only to individual members late. The architecture defines what is fixed for all members of the product line and what is variable.

A family-wide design solution may not be optimal for all derived systems, but it is a corporate decision that the quality known to be associated with the architecture and the savings in labor earned through architectural-level reuse compensates for the loss of optimality in particular areas. The architecture for a product line becomes a developing organization's core asset, much the same as other capital investments.

The term *domain-specific software architectures* applies to architectures designed to address the known architectural abstractions specific to given problem domains. Examples of published domain-specific software architectures come from the ARPA Domain-Specific Software Architecture (DSSA) program [22].

Systems Can Be Built by Importing Large Externally-Developed Components That Are Compatible with a Pre-Defined Architecture

Whereas former software paradigms have focused on *programming* as the prime activity, with progress measured in lines of code, architecture-based development often focuses on *composing or assembling components* that are likely to have been developed separately, even independently, from each other. This composition is possible because the architecture defines the set of components that can be incorporated into the system. The architecture constrains possible replacement (or additions) in the way in which they interact with their environment, how they receive and relinquish control, the data that they work on and produce and how they access it, and the protocols they use for communication and resource sharing.

One key aspect of architecture is its organization of component structure, interfaces, and operating concepts. One essential value of this organization is the idea of interchangeability. In 1793, Eli Whitney's mass production of muskets, based on the principle of interchangeable parts, announced the dawn of the industrial age. In the days before physical measurements were reliable, this was a daunting notion. Today in software, until abstractions can be reliably delimited, the notion of structural interchangeability is just as daunting, and just as significant. Commercial off-the-shelf components, subsystems, and compatible communications interfaces all depend on the idea of interchangeability.

There are still some significant unresolved issues, however, related to software development through composition. When the components that are candidates for importation and reuse are distinct subsystems that have been built with conflicting architectural assumptions, unanticipated complications may increase the effort required to integrate their functions. David Garlan has coined the term "architectural mismatch" to describe this situation [20]. Symptoms of architectural mismatch are the serious integration problems that occur when developers of independent subsystems have made architectural assumptions that differed from the assumptions of those who would employ these subsystems.

To resolve these differences, Garlan identifies the need to make explicit the architectural contexts for potentially reusable subsystems. Some design practices, such as information hiding, are particularly important for architectural consistency. Techniques and tools for developing wrappers[2] to bridge mismatches, and principles for composition of software are also needed. The most elemental need is for improved documentation practices, the inclusion of detailed pre-conditions for the use of interfaces, and conventions for describing typical architectural assumptions.

Architecture Permits the Functionality of a Component to be Separated from Its Component Interconnection Mechanisms

Traditional design approaches have been primarily concerned with the functionality of components. Architecture work seeks to elevate component relationships to the same level of concern. How components interact (coordinate, cooperate, communicate) becomes a first class design decision where the stated goal is to recognize the different fundamental qualities imparted to systems by these various interconnection strategies, and to encourage informed choices. The result is a separation of concerns, which introduces the possibility of building architectural infrastructure to automatically implement the architect's eventual choice of mechanism. The binding of this decision may be delayed and/or easily changed. Thus, prototyping and large-scale system evolution are both supported. Although proponents of this view speak of "first-class connectors" [37], they are actually making it possible for the question of connectors to be ignored in many cases. This contrasts to the programming paradigm, where connection mechanisms are chosen very early in the design cycle, are not given much thought, and are nearly impossible to change. Areas addressing this aspect include architecture description languages that embody connection *abstractions*, as opposed to mechanisms.

Less Is More: It Pays to Restrict the Vocabulary of Design Alternatives

Garlan and Shaw's work in identifying architectural styles [19] teaches us that although computer programs may be combined in more or less infinite ways, there is something to be gained by voluntarily restricting ourselves to a relatively small set of choices when it comes to program cooperation and interaction. Advantages include enhanced reuse, more capable analysis, shorter selection time, and greater interoperability.

Properties of software design follow from the choice of *architectural style*. Architectural styles are patterns or design idioms that guide the organization of modules and subsystems into complete systems. Those styles that are more desirable for a particular problem should improve implementation of the resulting design solution, perhaps by enabling easier arbitration of conflicting design constraints, by increasing insight into poorly understood design contexts, and/or by helping to surface inconsistencies in requirements specifications. Client-server[3] and pipe-filter[4] are example of architectural styles.

An Architecture Permits Template-Based Component Development

An architecture embodies design decisions about how components interact that, while reflected in each component at the code level, can be localized and written just once. Templates may be used to capture in one place the interaction mechanisms at the component level. For example, a template may encode the declarations for a component's public area where results will be left, or encode the protocols that the component uses to engage with the system executive. An example of a set of firm architectural decisions enabling template-based component development may be found in the Structural Modeling approach to software [1].

4. Architectural Views and Architecture Frameworks

4.1 The Need for Multiple Structures or Views

The contractor, the architect, the interior designer, the landscaper, and the electrician all have a different architectural view of a building. These views are pictured differently, but all are inherently related and together describe the building's architecture.

In Section 2 we said that software architecture is about software structure, but we also explained that defining "the overall structure" of a system was an inherently ambiguous concept. So, just as the "structure of a building" has many meanings depending upon one's motive and viewpoint, software exhibits many structures and we cannot communicate meaningfully about a piece of software unless it is clear which structure we are describing.

Moreover, when designing the software for a large, complex system, it will be necessary to consider more than one structural perspective as well as the relationships among them. Though one often thinks about structure in terms of system functionality, there are system properties in addition to functionality, such as physical distribution, process communication, and synchronization, that must be reasoned about at an architectural level. These other properties are addressed in multiple structures often referred to as architectural views. They are also sometimes referred to as architectural models, but again the terminology has not settled enough yet to be dependable.

Each different view reflects a specific set of concerns that are of interest to a given group of stakeholders in the system. Views are therefore abstractions, each with respect to different criteria. Each abstraction "boils away" details

---

2. A wrapper is a small piece of software that provides a more usable or appropriate interface for a software component. Users of the component invoke it through the wrapper, which translates the invocation into the form required by the component. The wrapper "hides" the (less desirable) interface of the component, so that only the wrapper software has to deal with it.

3. "Client-server" refers to two software components, usually implemented as separate processes, that serve as requestor and provider, respectively, of specific information or services.

---

4. A pipe is a mechanism for transporting data, unchanged, from one program to another. A filter is a program that applies a data transformation to a data set. This is a familiar style to programmers who use the Unix operating system; commands such as "cat data | grep 'keyword' | sort | fmt -80" are pipe-and-filter programs.

about the software that are independent of the concern addressed by the abstraction. Each view can be considered to be a software blueprint and each can use its own notation, can reflect its own choice of architectural style, and can define what is meant in its case by components, interrelationships, rationale, principles, and guidelines.

Views are not fully independent, however. Elements in one can relate to elements in another so while it is helpful to consider each separately, it is also necessary to reason rigorously about the interrelations of these views. Views may be categorized as follows:

- Whether or not the structures they represent are discernible at system runtime. For example, programs exist at runtime; one can determine the calls structure of a system by observing the execution of the system. Modules, however, disappear; modules are a purely static (pre-runtime) phenomenon.

- Whether the structures describe the product, the process of building the product, or the process of using the product to solve a problem. All the views discussed in this section are of the product. A model of the user interaction presents another view of the architecture of the system, and is typically represented via entity-relation diagrams. Still other views model the problem area or domain.

Some authors differentiate views by what kind of information they show. For instance, Budgen distinguishes between functional, behavioral, structural, and data-modeling viewpoints [10]. These all map, more or less, to the previous two categories.

Note that each view may be interpreted either as a description of the system that has been built, or a prescription that is engineered to achieve the relevant quality attributes.

4.2 Some Representative Views

There is not yet agreement on a standard set of views or terms to refer to views. In this section we list a typical and useful set. It should be noted that these views are given different names by various technologists. The perspective they represent is more important than the associated name.

Conceptual (Logical) View

The conceptual, or logical, architectural view includes the set of abstractions necessary to depict the functional requirements of a system at an abstract level. This view is tightly connected to the problem domain and is a useful communication vehicle when the architect interacts with the domain expert. The conceptual view is independent of implementation decisions and instead emphasizes interaction between entities in the problem space. This view is usually described by an informal block diagram, but in the case where object technology is utilized it may be expressed using class diagrams and class templates or in complex systems class categories.

Frameworks are similar to conceptual views but target not just systems but specific domains or problem classes. Frameworks are therefore close in nature to domain-specific architectures, to CORBA-based architecture models, and to domain-specific component repositories such as PRISM.

Module (Development) View

The module, or development, view is a frequently developed architectural structure. It focuses on the organization of actual software modules. Depending on how the modules are organized in the system, this view can take different forms. One form groups modules into identifiable subsystems, reflecting the software's organization into chunks of related code in the system, and often the basis for allocating development or maintenance work to project teams. For example, a module view might use the principle of information-hiding as the grouping criterion to facilitate maintainability [11]. A much different grouping would result by collecting modules together that interact with each other heavily at runtime to perform related tasks.

Another form groups the modules into a hierarchy of layers that reflect design decisions about which modules can communicate as well as predictions about the generality or application speciality of each module. In a layered system, modules within a given layer can communicate with each other. Modules in different layers can communicate with each other only if their respective layers are adjacent[5]. In this way each layer has a well defined and narrowly scoped interface to the software that makes use of it. In addition, traversing down the hierarchy shows modules of greater generality that are less likely to change in response to an application-specific requirements change. Layered systems are often comprised of four to six layers.

Figure 3 shows the five layers of an air traffic control system [23].

The module or layered organizations may or may not reflect the organization of the code as the compiler sees it in program libraries or compilation units. If not, then this compile-time structure is yet another view, which facilitates planning about the system build procedures.

Unlike the conceptual view, the module view is closely tied to the implementation. It is usually represented by module and subsystem diagrams that show interface imports and exports. As an architecture, this view has components that are either modules, subsystems, or layers, and the interrelationships are determined by import/export relations between modules, subsystems, or layers, respectively.

---

5. In some systems, the rule is that a module can only access modules in the same or lower layers. In other systems, the communication is limited to the same or immediately lower layer.

Layer 5	Human-computer interface External systems
Layer 4	ATC functional areas: flight management, sector management, and so on.
Layer 3	Aeronautical classes ATC classes
Layer 2	Support mechanisms: communication, time, storage, resource management, and so on
Layer 1	Bindings Common utilities Low-level services

Figure 3. Layers in an Air Traffic Control System [23]

Process (Coordination) View

While the conceptual and module views we've seen so far deal with static aspects of the system, the process, or coordination, view takes an orthogonal perspective; it focuses on the runtime behavior of the system. As such, the process view is not as much concerned with functionality as it is with how entities are created, with communications mechanisms such as concurrency and synchronization. Clearly the process view deals with the system's dynamic aspects.

The structural components in the process view are usually *processes*. A process is a sequence of instructions (statements) with its own thread of control. During system execution, a process can be started, shut down, recovered, reconfigured, etc., and can communicate and synchronize as necessary with other processes.

This view facilitates reasoning about a system's performance and runtime scheduling based on inter-process communication patterns.

The Physical View

The physical view shows the mapping of software onto hardware. Software that executes on a network of computers must be partitioned into processes that are *distributed* across these computers. That distribution scheme is a structure that affects (and allows reasoning about) system availability, reliability, performance, and scalability.

This mapping of the software on to the hardware needs to be flexible and have as little impact on the actual code as possible since physical configurations can actually vary depend-

ing upon whether or not the system is in test or deployment and depending on the exact deployment environment.

Relating the Views to Each Other

Each one of these views provides a different structure of a system, each valid and useful in its own right. The conceptual and module views show the static system structure while the process and physical views give us the dynamic or runtime system structure. The conceptual and module views, though very close, address very different concerns as described above. Some argue that the process and physical view should be combined [38]. Further, there is no requirement or implication that these structures bear any topological resemblance to each other.

While the views give different system structural perspectives they are not fully independent. Elements of one view will be "connected" to elements of other views, and one needs to reason about those connections. Scenarios, as described below, are useful for exercising a given view as well as these inter-view connections.

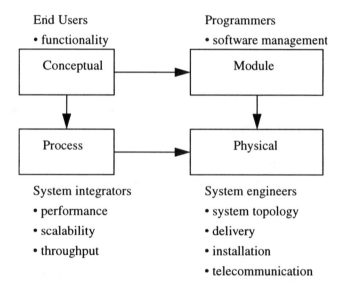

Figure 4. Architectural Views

All systems do not warrant multiple architectural views. Experience has shown that the larger the system, the more dramatic the difference between these views [23], but for very small systems the conceptual and module views may be so similar that they can be described together. If there is only one process or program there is clearly no need for the process view. If there is to be no distribution (that is, if there is just one processor) there is no need for the physical view. However, in the case of most systems of significant size and difficulty, if we were to attempt to combine these views into one structure we would limit evolvability, and reconfigurability, and add detailed complexity that would cripple the usefulness of the architecture as an artifact. This separation of concerns afforded by multiple views proves extremely beneficial in managing the complexity of large systems.

Figure 4 illustrates the views we have described, as well as their primary intended audiences and issues. It was adapted from a similar diagram shown in Kruchten [23]

Scenarios

Scenarios are scripts of individual pieces of a system's functionality. Scenarios are useful in analyzing a given view [12] or in showing that the elements of multiple views work together properly [23]. We can think about the scenarios as an abstraction of the most important system requirements. Scenarios are described in text using what is called a script and are sometimes described in pictures, for example object interaction diagrams. Scenarios are an important tool to relate different architectural views, because walking through a scenario can show how parts of different architectural views are related to each other.

4.3 Architecture Frameworks

While the conceptual view is often generalized for a problem domain into what was described as a framework, there has been some effort to actually make frameworks for architectures of systems from a given broad domain. The Technical Architecture Framework for Information Management (TAFIM) described below is one such effort.

Technical Architecture Framework for Information Management (TAFIM)

The context for the management, use, and evolution of an information system is today rarely a collection of manual activities as was the case forty years ago. Current information systems function as entities within larger systems of related automated processes; they support the operations of independent, but interoperating mission critical systems; they are intrinsic elements of embedded computer systems that control, assimilate, distribute, activate, and/or monitor the operations of complex hybrids of digital and electronic hardware. Partly as a result of this increasing integration with other mechanical, digital and electronic systems, it is increasingly important to recognize the common elements shared by all information systems. Whether an information system accumulates stand-alone data on financial trends, provides interactive feedback to process control systems developers on the performance of their designs, interprets and recognizes patterns as part of a distributed surveillance system, calculates navigation and guidance parameters as an embedded subsystem of a military weapons platform, or computes and distributes robotic machine control instructions at the heart of a factory automation system, it typically has three kinds of elements, each with its own typical life cycle of management and technology decisions. The three typical elements of any information system are (a) its data; (b) its mission-specific applications; and (c) its infrastructure of support applications, computing platforms and communications networks.

The TAFIM [16], being developed by the Department of Defense (DoD) advances a descriptive pattern for information systems architectures (ISA). This pattern recognizes the pervasiveness of the above three information systems elements. It thereby provides a means for tailoring common life cycle management and technology decisions appropriately for different kinds of information systems applications.

A technical architecture such as TAFIM is *not* a complete architecture in that it does not fully specify components and the connections between them. Rather it is a specification that constrains the architectural choices that can be made. Often it does this by specifying consensus-based standards to which the system and its architecture must adhere. Thus, the TAFIM expresses a pattern for describing an ISA, and recognizes that there are necessary and proper variations in the content of ISAs within different types of information systems applications, enterprises, mission areas, computing communities, etc. For instance, an ISA that is tailored for information systems supporting weather processing, where parallel processing computations are intrinsic and essential, will have unique content and features. However, its overall form will be intelligible to systems managers and executives via its consonance with the TAFIM pattern for describing ISAs. This pattern is the so-called technical architectural "framework."

5. Architecture-Based Development

5.1 Architecture-Based Activities for Software Development

What activities are involved in taking an architecture-based approach to software development? At the high level, they include the following that are in addition to the normal design-program-and-test activities in conventional small-scale development projects:

- understanding the domain requirements
- developing or selecting the architecture
- representing and communicating the architecture
- analyzing or evaluating the architecture
- implementing the system based on the architecture
- ensuring that the implementation conforms to the architecture

Each of these activities is briefly discussed below.

Understanding the Domain Requirements

Since a primary advantage of architectures is the insight they lend across whole families of systems, it is prudent to invest up front time in the life cycle to conduct an in depth study of requirements not just for the specific system but for the whole family of systems of which it is or will be a part. These families can be:

- a set of related systems, all fielded simultaneously, that differ incrementally by small changes
- a single system that exists in many versions over time, the versions differing from each other incrementally by small changes

In either case *domain analysis* is recommended. Domain analysis is an independent investigation of requirements during which changes, variations, and similarities for a given domain are anticipated, enumerated, and recorded for review by domain experts. An example of a domain is command and control. The result of domain analysis is a domain model which identifies the commonalities and variations among different instantiations of the system, whether fielded together or sequentially. Architectures based on domain models will yield the full advantage of architecture-based development because domain analysis can identify the potential migration paths that the architecture will have to support.

Developing (Selecting) the Architecture

While some advocate a phased approach to architectural design [39], experience has shown that architecture development is highly iterative and requires some prototyping, testing, measurement and analysis [23].

Ongoing work at the Software Engineering Institute posits that architects are influenced by factors in three areas [13]:

- requirements (including required quality attributes) of the system or systems under development
- requirements imposed (perhaps implicitly) by the organization performing the development. For example, there may be requirements, or encouragement, to utilize a component repository, object-oriented environment, or previous designs in which the organization has significantly invested.
- experience of the architect. The results of previous decisions, whether wildly successful, utterly disastrous, or somewhere in between, will affect whether the architect reuses those strategies.

Brooks argues forcefully and eloquently that conceptual integrity is the key to sound system design, and that conceptual integrity can only be had by a very small number of minds coming together to design the system's architecture [7].

Representing and Communicating the Architecture

In order for the architecture to be effective as the backbone of the project's design, it must be communicated clearly and unambiguously to all of the stakeholders. Developers must understand the work assignments it requires of them; testers must understand the task structure it imposes on them; management must understand the scheduling implications it suggests. The representation medium should therefore be informative and unambiguous, and should be readable by many people with varied backgrounds.

The architects themselves must make sure that the architecture will meet the behavioral, performance, and quality requirements of the system(s) to be built from the architecture. Therefore, there is an advantage if the representation medium can serve as input to formal analysis techniques such as model-building, simulation, verification, or even rapid prototyping. Towards this end, the representation medium should be formal and complete.

The field of architecture description languages (ADLs) is young but growing prolifically [14].

Analyzing or Evaluating the Architecture

The analysis capabilities that many ADLs bring to the table are valuable, but tend to concentrate on the runtime properties of the system—its performance, its behavior, its communication patterns, and the like. Less represented are analysis techniques to evaluate an architecture from the point of view of non-runtime quality attributes that it imparts to a system. Chief among these is maintainability, the ability to support change. Maintainability has many variations: portability, reusability, adaptability, extensibility; all are special perspectives of a system's ability to support change. There is emerging a consensus on the value of scenario-based evaluation to judge an architecture with respect to non-runtime quality attributes [22], [23].

Implementing Based on the Architecture and Assuring Conformance

This activity is concerned with ensuring that the developers adhere to the structures and interaction protocols dictated by the architecture. An architectural environment or infrastructure would be beneficial here. However, work in this area is still quite immature.

6. Current and Future Work in Software Architecture

As has been the sub-theme of this report, the study and practice of software architecture is still immature. Rigorous techniques need to be developed to describe software architecture so that they can be analyzed to predict and assume nonfunctional system properties. Moreover, architecture-based activities need to be more precisely defined and supported with processes and tools, and need to be smoothly incorporated into existing development processes.

There is an active research community working on technologies related to software architecture. This section examines ongoing technology work in software architecture and predicts areas of the most promising work that will bear fruit over the next five to ten years.

Problem areas in architecture and work that addresses them tend to be clustered around the following themes, arranged in terms of how and when the architecture is used during a system's life cycle:

- **Creation/selection:** How to choose, create, or select an architecture, based on a set of functional, performance, and quality requirements.

- **Representation:** How to communicate an architecture. This problem has manifested itself as one of representing architectures with linguistic facilities, but the problem also includes selecting the set of information to be communicated (i.e., represented with a language).

- **Analysis:** How to analyze an architecture to predict qualities about systems that manifest it, or how to evaluate an architecture for fitness. A similar problem is how to compare and choose between competing architectures.

- **Development:** How to build a system given a representation of its architecture.

- **Evolution:** How to evolve a legacy system when changes may affect its architecture; for systems lacking trustworthy architectural documentation, this will first involve "architectural archaeology" to extract its architecture.

See the Clements report[6] for a discussion of research opportunities in these areas.

Acknowledgments

This study and report were funded by the Office of the Assistant Secretary of Defense for Command, Control, Communications, and Intelligence. John Leary was a contributor to an earlier version of this document. Our thanks go to Nelson Weiderman, who provided excellent comments.

7. References

[1] Abowd, G.; Bass, L.; Howard, L.; & Northrop, L. *Structural Modeling: An Application Framework and Development Process for Flight Simulators.* (CMU/SEI-93-TR-14, ADA 271348) Pittsburgh, PA: Software Engineering Institute, Carnegie Mellon University, 1993.

[2] Abowd, G.; Bass, L.; Kazman, R.; & Webb, M. "SAAM: A Method for Analyzing the Properties of Software Architectures," 81-90. *Proceedings of the 16th International Conference on Software Engineering.* Sorrento, Italy, May 16-21, 1994. Los Alamitos, CA: IEEE Computer Society Press, 1994.

[3] Alexander, Christopher; Ishikawa, Sara; & Silverstein, Murray. *A Pattern Language.* New York City: Oxford University Press, 1977.

[4] Batory, D. & O'Malley, S. "The Design and Implementation of Hierarchical Software Systems with Reusable Components." *ACM Transactions on Software Engineering and Methodology 2,* 4 (1992): 355-398.

[5] Beck, K. & Johnson, R. "Patterns Generate Architectures," 139-49. *European Conference on Object-Oriented Programming.* Bologna, Italy, July 4-8, 1994. Berlin, Germany:

---

6. The pending SEI technical report authored by Paul Clements, *Coming Attractions in Software Architecture*, should be available by April 1996.

Springer-Verlag, 1994.

[6] Boehm, B. "Engineering Context (for Software Architecture)." Invited talk, First International Workshop on Architecture for Software Systems. Seattle, Washington, April 1995.

[7] Brooks, F. *The Mythical Man-Month—Essays on Software Engineering.* Reading, MA: Addison-Wesley, 1975.

[8] Brooks, F. *The Mythical Man-Month—Essays on Software Engineering(20th Anniversary Edition).* Reading, MA: Addison-Wesley, 1995.

[9] Brown, A.; Carney, D.; & Clements, P. "A Case Study in Assessing the Maintainability of Large, Software-Intensive Systems," 240-247. *Proceedings, International Symposium and Workshop on Systems Engineering of Computer Based Systems.* Tucson, AZ, March 6-9, 1995. Salem, MA: IEEE Computer Society Press, 1995.

[10] Budgen, David. *Software Design.* Reading, MA: Addison-Wesley, 1993.

[11] Clements, P.; Parnas, D.; & Weiss, D. "The Modular Structure of Complex Systems." *IEEE Transactions on Software Engineering SE-11,* 1 (1985): 259-266.

[12] Clements, P.; Bass, L.; Kazman, F; & Abowd, G. "Predicting Software Quality by Architecture-Level Evaluation," 485-498.*Proceedings, Fifth International Conference on Software Quality.* Austin, TX, Oct. 23-26, 1995. Austin, TX: American Society for Quality Control, Software Division, 1995.

[13] Clements, P. "Understanding Architectural Influences and Decisions in Large-System Projects." Invited talk, First International Workshop on Architectures for Software Systems. Seattle, WA, April 1995.

[14] Clements, P. "A Survey of Architectural Description Languages," *Proceedings of the Eighth International Workshop on Software Specification and Design.* Paderborn, Germany, March 1996.

[15] Dijkstra, E.W. "The Structure of the 'T.H.E.' Mulitprogramming System." *Communications of the ACM 18,* 8 (1968): 453-457.

[16] DoD Technical Architecture Framework for Information Management (TAFIM), Defense Information Systems Agency (DISA) Center for Information Management (CIM), Vol I (Concept) and Vol II (Guidance), V2.0. Reston, VA, October 1992.

[17] Gaycek, C.; Abd-Allah, A.; Clark, B.; & Boehm, B. "On the Definition of Software System Architecture." Invited talk, First International Workshop on Architectures for Software Systems. Seattle, WA, April 1995.

[18] Gamma, E.; Helm, R.; Johnson, R.; & Vlissides, J. *Design Patterns, Elements of Object-Oriented Software.* Reading, MA: Addison-Wesley, 1995.

[19] Garlan, D. & Shaw, M. "An Introduction to Software Architecture." *Advances in Software Engineering and Knowledge Engineering. Vol 1.* River Edge, NJ: World Scientific Publishing Company, 1993.

[20] Garlan, D. et al. "Architectural Mismatch (Why It's Hard to Build Systems Out of Existing Parts)," 170-185. *Proceedings, 17th International Conference on Software Engineering.* Seattle, WA, April 23-30, 1995. New York: Association for Computing Machinery, 1995.

[21] Hayes-Roth. *Architecture-Based Acquisition and Development of Software: Guidelines and Recommendations from the ARPA Domain-Specific Software Architecture (DSSA) Program* [online]. Available WWW <URL:http://www.sei.cmu.edu/arpa/dssa/dssa-adage/dssa.html>(1994).

[22] Kazman, F.; Basas, l.; Abowd, G.; & Clements, P. "An Architectural Analysis Case Study: Internet Information Systems." Invited talk, First International Workshop on Architectures for Software Systems. Seattle, WA, April 1995.

[23] Kruchten, Philippe B. "The 4+1 View Model of Architecture." *IEEE Software 12,* 6 (November 1995): 42-50.

[24] Martin, C.; Hefley, W. et al. "Team-Based Incremental Acquisition of Larger Scale Unprecedented Systems." *Policy Sciences.* Vol 25. The Netherlands: Kluwer Publishing, 1992.

[25] McMahon, P. "Pattern-Based Architecture: Bridging Software Reuse and Cost Management." *CROSSTALK 8,* 3 (March 1995): 10-16.

[26] Object Management Group. *Common Object Request Broker: Architecture and Specification.* Document 91.12.1. Framingham, MA, 1991.

[27] Parnas, D. "On the Criteria for Decomposing Systems into Modules." *Communications of the ACM 15,* 12 (December 1972): 1053-1058.

[28] Parnas, D. "On a 'Buzzword': Hierarchical Structure." 336-339. *Proceedings IFIP Congress 74.* North Holland Publishing Company, 1974.

[29] Parnas, D. "On the Design and Development of Program Families." *IEEE Transactions on Software Engineering SE-2,* 1 (1976): 1-9.

[30] Parnas, D. "Designing Software for Ease of Extension and Contraction." *IEEE Transactions on Software Engineering SE-5,* 2 (1979): 128-137.

[31] Perry, D.E. & Wolf, A.L. "Foundations for the Study of Software Architecture." *Software Engineering Notes, ACM SIGSOFT 17,* 4 (October 1992): 40-52.

[32] Saunders, T.F. et al. *A New Process for Acquiring Software Architecture.* MITRE Corporation Paper, M92B-126. Bedford, MA, November 1992.

[33] Schultz, Charles. "Rome Laboratory Experience with Standards Based Architecture (SBA) Process." Presentation at 7th Annual Software Technology Conference. Software Technology Systems Center (STSC), Hill AFB, UT, April 1995.

[34] Shaw, M. "Making Choices: A Comparison of Styles for Software Architecture." *IEEE Software 12,* 6 (November 1995):27-41.

[35] Shaw, M. "Conceptual Basis for Software Architecture." Invited talk, First International Workshop on Architecture for Software Systems. Seattle, WA, April 1995.

[36] Shaw, M. & Garlan, D. *Software Architectures.* Englewood Cliffs, NJ: Prentice-Hall, 1995.

[37] Shaw, M. *Procedure Calls Are the Assembly Language of Software Interconnection; Connectors Deserve First-class Status.* (CMU-CS-94-107) Pittsburgh, PA: Carnegie Mellon University, 1994.

[38] Soni, D.; Nord, R.; & Hofmeister, C. "Software Architecture in Industrial Applications." 196-210. *Proceedings, 17th International Conference on Software Engineering.* Seattle, WA, April 23-30, 1995. New York: Association for Computing Machinery, 1995.

[39] Witt, B.I.; Baker, F.T.; & Merritt, E.W. *Software Architecture and Design Principles, Models and Methods.* New York, New York: Van Nostrand Reinholt, 1994.

Toward a Distributed, Mediated Architecture for Workflow Management

Kurt Wallnau, Fred Long, Anthony Earl

Software Engineering Institute
Carnegie Mellon University
Pittsburgh, PA 15213

{kcw, fwl, ane}@sei.cmu.edu

Abstract

For workflow management technologies to be successfully adopted, they must address a range of challenging technical requirements imposed by a competitive and dynamic business and organizational environment. Specifically, workflow technologies must be interchangeable and integratable, must interoperate in a distributed and heterogeneous computing environment, and must support a wide-range of often divergent process management policies. Detailed functional and interface specifications for a comprehensive workflow management system will be difficult to adopt for a variety of reasons. However, a minimalistic specification focused only on the interaction of components within a workflow system may be more readily adopted by workflow technology vendors and customers. An outline for such an architecture is proposed, and our reasons for believing it is a viable approach based on early experimental results are discussed.

1. Introduction

If workflow technology is to become widely adopted by industry, it must evolve to meet new technical demands:

- Business models favoring the opportunistic integration of small, specialty-focused businesses into "virtual enterprises" are increasingly prevalent, especially in the manufacturing community. This presents challenges to support the integration of different kinds of workflow technologies that may be in use by the entities within a virtual enterprise.

- Diverse organizational theories are in operation today. Some theories favor small, independent teams, others a more constrained hierarchical model. This presents challenges to support flexible workflow policy definition and enforcement, and allow coexistence of different (and possibly conflicting) policies within a single executing process[1].

- Computing technology has continued its rapid evolution, most recently towards increasingly distributed applications running on a mix of hardware and operating systems. This presents a range of distributed-systems challenges—update consistency, resilience in the face of network failures, partitioning, and security, to name just a few.

To some extent, the Workflow Management Coalition (WFMC) is addressing these challenges[2][3]. Through its reference architecture the WFMC is helping to establish a common vocabulary of workflow management concepts and a functional partitioning of these concepts. However, our own experiences with integrated software engineering environments leaves us skeptical about the utility of moving from reference models to detailed interface specifications[4]. Our reasons include both socio-economic and technical factors.

On the socio-economic side, detailed specifications tend to take on a life of their own, and may easily become too complex and expensive to implement and adopt. Further, detailed interface specifications often run counter to the competetive needs of tool vendors to differentiate their products from competitor's products: a shared interface often implies a convergence of technical approaches that runs counter to this need. On the technical side, reference models are (necessarily) vague about implementation considerations and are therefore not a suitable foundation for deriving interfaces. While such derivation is possible, the resulting interfaces will lack the precision of interfaces derived from a software architecture. A software architecture is an intermediary abstraction between reference model and code that expresses structures that are tuned to a well-defined but narrow range of design and implementation issues[5].

In this paper we outline an architectural approach to workflow automation that addresses the technical demands described earlier while avoiding some of the pitfalls described above. The approach is architectural because it focuses on the large-scale structure and coordination of components[6] within a workflow system, not on detailed

Reprinted from *Proc. NSF Workshop on Workflow and Process Automation in Information Systems: State-of-the-Art and Future Directions,* 1996. Reprinted with permission.

functional interfaces. The approach also recognizes the role of both reference model and software architecture, and is thus complementary with WFMC objectives.

The paper is structured as follows. Section 2 discusses the specific technical challenges being addressed by the proposed architecture. Section 3 provides an overview of the proposed architecture. Finally, Section 4 discusses the current state of implementation experiments based on the architecture, and indicates directions for further work.

2. Requirements for Workflow Architecture

The specification of integration frameworks is fraught with peril: too little detail and the framework is meaningless, too much detail and it is too expensive to implement, too complex to understand and too restrictive for tool developers to adopt. Finding the right balance is a matter of being ruthless in defining a minimal set of key requirements. We believe the key requirements that must be satisfied by a workflow management architecture are those that address end-user adoption and marketplace economic issues, not low-level engineering issues.

Table 1 summarizes the requirements we address in our

Table 1. Key Adoption and Economic Requirements

Stakeholder	Requirement
End User.	Support multiple workflow policies.
	Support work in disconnected network.
Organization.	Support technology and vendor diversity.
	Support technology refreshment and evolution of organizational structures.
Tool Provider.	Low entry cost to use the infrastructure.
	Preserve existing technical approaches.

proposal and prototype, partitioned into three classes of stake holders: end-users of process technology; adopting organizations; and, workflow technology providers. The list of requirements and stakeholders is not exhaustive, and does not include important requirements in the area of security, administration, etc. However, we believe that a prioritized set of requirements would include very few "first-tier" requirements, perhaps fewer than ten. An alternative and promising formulation of requirements, referred to as *autonomies*, can be found in [7].

3. Overview of the Workflow Architecture

The workflow architecture must be independent of underlying implementation technologies (technology and vendor diversity also applies to a workflow infrastructure). Conversely, the use of specific technologies may provide opportunities for more sophisticated services than can be specified in a technology-neutral way. The solution to this dichotomy is to define the architecture in two forms:

- a reference architecture, which describes the major interfaces and coordination policies for components;
- a refined architecture, which is a technology-specific realization of the reference architecture.

Both forms are described in the following sections.

3.1 Reference Architecture

Figure 1 depicts a static view of the reference architecture. The static view describes the major functional components and interfaces, but does not describe any dynamic aspects of inter-component communication (referred to as "coordination model" in this paper). The architecture is

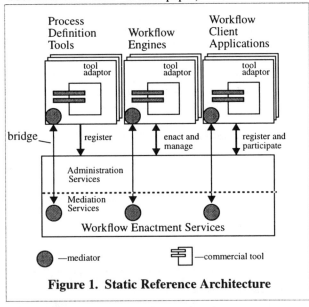

Figure 1. Static Reference Architecture

partitioned into two kinds of components:

- workflow enactment services, an infrastructure shared by a collection of interworking workflow technologies and applications; and,
- external workflow technologies and applications that are adapted to the infrastructure, i.e., native or "wrapped" components.

The architecture accommodates three kinds of adapted components: process definition, workflow engine and client application. In the interest of brevity a discussion of the role of these components is deferred to the discussion of the refined architecture. The infrastructure service is partitioned into two classes of services: administration and mediation. Administration services include only those services needed to support the coordination model (communication, registration, location, etc.).

Mediation services support interoperation of different workflow technologies with respect to a range of dimensions, both technical (e.g., process representation) and administrative (e.g., security). If two components differ with respect to some dimension, then a bridge must be constructed from one *interpretation* of that dimension to another. This is the role of mediator agents: bridges can be implemented in terms of agents, i.e., computational elements that map from one interpretation to another. If agents are registered with a mediation service, and are typed according to the kind of transformation (or bridge) they provide, then interoperation between two components could involve dynamic configuration of agents yielding an indirect transformation from one interpretation to another. Note that we can represent the WFMC workflow interchange format in terms of mediators that translate from proprietary representations to a common representation (this is referred to as a "half bridge" in [8]).

Readers familiar with the WFMC will see similarities between the WFMC reference model and the reference model depicted in Figure 1, particularly with respect to the kinds of components addressed (tools, engines, applications and enactment services). However, the reference model diverges from the WFMC model in a number of ways. Invoked tools are excluded from the architecture; these should be the responsibility of workflow applications and are outside the scope of the architecture. Also, administration services are subsumed by the infrastructure. Finally, the role of infrastructure is narrowed, and includes new (to the WFMC model) concepts of mediator (agents), bridges and adaptors.

Figure 2 depicts the dynamic reference architecture. For clarity of presentation communication services are depicted separately from mediation services. The key ideas expressed in the dynamic architecture are:

• executing workflow engines represent the instantiation of a process description (model), and a single model may be simultaneously instantiated by several workflow engines;

• a single executing workflow engine may involve arbitrarily many workflow client applications (i.e., per-user queues);

• a single workflow client application may participate in many executing processes (i.e., per-process queues); and,

• communication occurs via asynchronous messages.

These ideas reflect a minimal set of constraints on workflow technologies while also permitting a wide variety of interactions among clients, engines and process definition tools. The coordination model also provides a basis for defining administrative services for monitoring and controlling an executing system comprised of many active components. Lastly, the emphasis on asynchronous communication reflects the wide-area distributed nature of enterprise-wide workflow management.

Note that, as depicted, mediation services are used only to bridge technical implementations of static and executing process models. Mediation between workflow engines and client applications is also possible, and will most likely involve non-technical interpretations. However, for clarity this has been omitted from Figure 2.

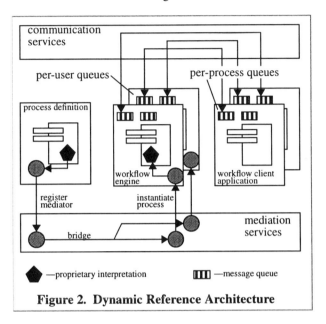

Figure 2. Dynamic Reference Architecture

3.2 CORBA Implementation

The reference architecture outlined the general principles and concepts, but it remained to demonstrate that these concepts can be implemented in a technology-neutral way. We selected CORBA[8] and TCL-DP[9] as implementation mechanisms. As most of our effort to date has been directed towards the use of CORBA we describe that implementation in this paper.

We first note that our prototype implementation addresses only portions of the reference architecture. In particular, we addressed the communication services and, to a much smaller extent, tool adaptors. We did not address mediation services in a significant way. Our rationale for focusing on the communications services (and the coordination model it supports) is that these aspects of the architecture will have the greatest impact on requirements for distributed workflow execution and was a logical and necessary "first step." Mediation services will be addressed as we integrate off-the-shelf workflow management components.

The static CORBA-based architecture is illustrated in Figure 3: it adds CORBA-specific details to the static reference architecture depicted in Figure 1. The static architecture is defined as a collection of object types (differentiated as object services and application objects for consistency with [10]). Although the interface definition language (IDL) specifications for these types are too detailed for this

71

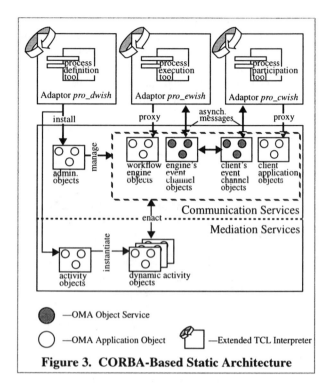

Figure 3. CORBA-Based Static Architecture

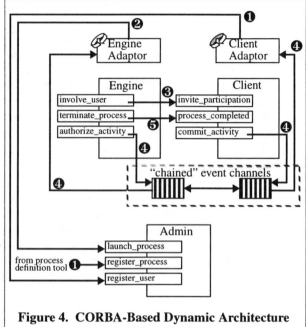

Figure 4. CORBA-Based Dynamic Architecture

paper, the role of objects of these types within the architecture are relatively simple:

- Administration objects provide services for registering users and processes and for managing collections of workflow sessions (i.e., a number of executing processes and participating users).

- Workflow engine and client application objects act as proxies for the workflow engine and end-user, respectively. Engines and users communicate via these proxies.

- Event channel objects buffer and forward messages between clients and engines. Buffering occurs on each end of the connection so that work can continue on each end even if a network partition occurs.

- Activity and dynamic activity objects represent process descriptions and active (executing) processes, respectively. In our initial prototype, activities were the native process formalism used by workflow tools, thus avoiding the need for mediation objects.

Tool adaptors were implemented as TCL interpreters extended with interfaces to the objects just described (thus, *pro_dwish* for "process developer window interactive shell"). The role of adaptors in the initial prototype is that of a placeholder: the tools they "adapt" are in fact encoded directly in TCL, and the activity object types are the native formalism of these tools. As we integrate commercial workflow tools, the role of adaptors (and mediators) will become more prominent.

The dynamic CORBA-based architecture is illustrated in Figure 4 and Table 2. The architecture focuses on the coordination between administration, workflow engine and client

application objects, and on the coordination of these objects with tool adaptors. The synchronous interfaces to objects are depicted as labeled entries on objects[1]; otherwise the iconography is as defined in Figures 1-3. Invocation of an operation is depicted via an arrow (e.g., *involve_user* invokes *invite_participation*). All operations depicted in the dynamic architecture are invoked: those without explicit incoming arrows are implicitly invoked by their associated adaptor (e.g., *involve_user* is invoked by the workflow engine adaptor).

The numbers annotating various invocations describe a rough sequencing of control, and are summarized in Table 2. The key points of this coordination model are:

- The use of synchronous services in some cases reflects a trade-off of abstractness and maintainability at the expense of increased synchrony; in general, synchronous interfaces are more easily reflected in "structure" (architecture) than message content.

- Units of workflow activity are distributed as objects via event channels. This requires object relocation to avoid wide-area synchronization; relocation is not yet supported by commercial CORBA implementations.

- Each component has a constrained role that is defined by the coordination model. Tools inserted into the "framework" need only concern themselves with the narrow range of invocations defined in Figure 4.

---

1. Activity objects are not depicted; however, they are interpreted by engines and clients, and exchanged via asynchronous message queues.

4. Key Observations and Future Work

We believe the reference architecture satisfies the requirements listed in Table 1. First, by restricting the role of the architecture to coordination of functionality rather than on specific functionality, a greater degree of technology autonomy is provided to meet the requirements of workflow technology providers. Second, mediation (though currently untested in the workflow context) reflects in the architecture the fact that interoperation is not a binary but rather a multidimensional phenomena; this addresses end-user requirements for policy flexibility and organizational requirements for technology refreshment. Lastly, distributed process execution is also supported to satisfy the remaining end-user requirement.

Table 2. Outline of Coordination Model.

	Component	Notes
❶	Process Definition	In the prototype, this created activity objects. More generally, this will look-up or register mediator agents.
	Client Application	This creates a surrogate application object for the user. This is done once per administrator; this object participates in all future processes.
❷	Workflow Engine	This creates one workflow engine surrogate. This object exists only so long as the process is executing.
❸	Workflow Engine	Users are "invited" into a process, establishing queues. Invitation can happen during process execution.
❹	Workflow Engine & Client Application	The workflow engine posts authorized activities to the appropriate user; the user completes work and commits the activity by returning it.
❺	Workflow Engine	The engine determines when the process is complete" and issues a termination message to all participants for finalization purposes.

The CORBA refinement shows to good effect the potential role of distributed object technology in supporting distributed workflow management. CORBA and the OMA object services in particular provided a good foundation for expressing and implementing architecture-level concepts, particularly those concerning distribution and concurrency. Further, while some aspects of the refined architecture clearly exhibit CORBA-specific properties (e.g., chained event channels are a particular OMA object service), other properties may prove to be technology independent, and may thus migrate into the reference architecture.

Clearly, many details about the refined architecture have yet to be worked out, especially with respect to mediation services. However, preliminary work suggests that the CORBA interface repository and dynamic invocation services will provide a good mechanism for run-time construction of mediation chains, and at worst will allow the construction of adaptors that are object-code independent of specific mediators (and thus independent of the technologies with which they interoperate).

While our prototype implementation is incomplete, we believe our results to date demonstrate the merit of the overall approach. Our next steps include integration of off-the-shelf workflow tools in order to flesh out the adaptors and mediators. We are also interested in exploring the use of alternative implementation mechanisms such as Java[11] in order to continue to refine the boundaries between reference model and refined architecture.

Acknowledgments

Thanks to Alan Christie, who's ideas about process technology and its adoption continue to shape this work.

Fred Long is a visiting scientist at the SEI from the University College of Wales, Aberystwyth, UK.

The SEI is sponsored by the U.S. Department of Defense.

5. References

[1] Ben-Shaul, I.Z., Kaiser, G.E., "A paradigm for decentralized process modeling and its implementation in the Oz environment," Proceedings of the 16th International Conference on Software Engineering, Sorrento Italy, 1994, pp. 179-88.

[2] Workflow Management Coalition Workflow Reference Model Specification, WFMC-TC-1003, January 1995, http://www/aiai.ed.ac.uk.wfmc.

[3] Workflow Management Coalition Interface 2 Application Programming Interface Specification, WFMC-TC-1009, November, 1995, http://www/aiai.ed.ac.uk.wfmc.

[4] Radar, J., Brown., A., Morris, E., "Operational use of CASE integration: An investigation of the state of the practice," Journal of Systems and Software, 1994.

[5] Garlan, D., Shaw, M., "An Introduction to Software Architecture," in Advances in Software Engineering and Knowledge Engineering, vol. I, World Scientific Publishing, 1993.

[6] Howard, L., Bass, L., "Structural Modeling for Flight Simulators," in proceedings of the Summer Computer Simulation Conference, Society of Computer Simulation, San Diego, CA, pp. 876-81.

[7]   Graw, G., Gruhn, V., "Distributed Modeling and Distributed Enaction of Business Processes," in proceedings of 5th European Conference on Software Engineering, Spain 1995, also Lecture notes in computer science, no. 989, Springer-Verlag.

[8]   The Common Object Request Broker: Architecture and Specification, Revision 2.0, July 1995, Object Management Group, Framingham, MA, 01701.

[9]   Ousterhout, J., TCL and the Tk Toolkit, Addison Wesley, ISBN 0-201-63337-X.

[10] Soley, R., Ed., Object Management Architecture Guide, 3rd ed., John Wiley and Sons, Inc., ISBN 0-471-14193-3.

[11] Shaio, A., Starbuck, S., van Hoff, O., Hooked on Java, Addison Wesley, ISBN 0-201-48837-X.

A Situated Evaluation of the
Object Management Group's (OMG)
Object Management Architecture (OMA)

Evan Wallace

National Institute of Standards and Technology
Manufacturing Engineering Laboratory
Gaithersburg, MD, 20899, USA
wallace@cme.nist.gov

Kurt C. Wallnau

Software Engineering Institute
Carnegie Mellon University
Pittsburgh, PA, 15213, USA
kcw@sei.cmu.edu

Abstract

It has been difficult to objectively assess the real value or maturity of the Object Management Group's Object Management Architecture (OMA). While experience reports have appeared in the literature, these have focused more on the functionality of the end-system than on (a) systematically exploring the strengths and weaknesses of the OMA, and (b) providing practical guidelines on the effective use of the OMA for specific software-engineering problems. In this paper we describe a case study in the use of the OMA to integrate legacy software components into a distributed object system. We assess the OMA in this problem context, and indicate strengths and weaknesses of the specification and current implementations. We extrapolate our experience to a broader class of component-based software systems, and recommend an architectural strategy for the effective use of the OMA to this class of systems.

1. Background

The Object Management Architecture (OMA) [1] continues to attract attention, with numerous implementations of the OMA common object request broker architecture (CORBA)[1] emerging in the commercial marketplace. How does an organization decide whether to embrace this technology? The stakes are high for this decision since the OMA can have a profound influence on the design and implementation of application software. A technology assessment strategy that can identify the value-added of a new technology, and simultaneously reveal how best to exploit this value added, is therefore of great potential value.

One such evaluation technique has been described and experimentally applied to the OMA [2]. The key idea of this evaluation technique is to situate a technology specimen (such as CORBA) in a model that describes peer technologies, identifies the way the technology specimen differs from its peers, and evaluates these differences in an application-specific context. For example, it can be asserted that remote procedure call (RPC) is a peer technology of CORBA[2]; however, while RPC and CORBA have many features in common, CORBA adds a substantial range of additional features. These additional features (called the *feature delta*) should form the focal point of a technology evaluation aimed at understanding the value-added of CORBA.

There are many ways of studying feature deltas. In some cases it is possible to isolate and benchmark elements of the feature delta, as illustrated by the comparative benchmarking of CORBA and RPC [3]. However, the lack of a specific problem context within which to evaluate the benchmarks can limit the effectiveness of this form of evaluation. To overcome this limitation, experimentally-focused case studies can be undertaken that apply the feature delta to representative problems of an application domain. Such case studies can be particularly fruitful. In addition to providing a problem context for evaluating a technology, case studies can also provide a wealth of practical experience in how to best apply a feature delta to these problems.

In this paper we describe one experimentally-motivated case study in the use of the OMA to an increasingly-important problem domain: the integration of component-based systems (systems comprised of stand-alone, independently-executing software packages). Section 2 provides background information on the engineering problems inherent to component-based systems. Section 3 provides further background on the manufacturing domain, and on the legacy collection of computer-aided design engineering (CADE) components that we modernized into a distributed, object-based system. Section 4 describes the impact of the OMA on the architecture of the modernized system, and Section 5 continues the discussion of the impact of OMA at a more detailed implementation level. Finally, Section 6 states our conclusions about the OMA based on this experiment.

---

1. We use CORBA to refer to only the message broker component of the OMA; we use OMA to refer to CORBA plus additional OMA services.

2. OMA and CORBA have other peers—see [2].

This paper appears courtesy of ACM, Inc. and will be presented at the *1996 Conference on Object-Oriented Programming, Systems, Languages, and Applications (OOPSLA),* Copyright © 1996 by the Association for Computing Machinery.

2. Background on Component-Based Systems

While all (real) systems are composed of components, in our usage *component-based* systems are comprised of multiple software components that:

- are ready "off-the-shelf," whether from a commercial source (COTS) or re-used from another system;
- have significant aggregate functionality and complexity;
- are self-contained and possibly execute independently;
- will be used "as is" rather than modified; and,
- must be integrated with other components to achieve required system functionality.

Examples of component-based systems can be drawn from many domains, including: computer-aided software engineering (CASE), design engineering (CADE) and manufacturing engineering (CAME); office automation; workflow management; command and control, and many others.

2.1 Architectural Mismatch: The Core Issue

In contrast to the development of other kinds of systems where system integration is often the tail-end of an implementation effort, in component-based systems determining how to integrate components is often the only latitude designers have. In our evaluation we were interested in whether the OMA suggested solutions to the core engineering problems in the integration of component-based systems: *architectural mismatch* [4].

The term "architectural mismatch" refers to the problem that components always embed assumptions about their intended operational context, and these assumptions often conflict with assumptions made by other components. For example, a component that uses a graphical human interface as the sole means of executing component functions has embedded an assumption that will render it unusable in a system that must run in batch mode—unless this mismatch can be removed by some form of component adaptation. Scores of other kinds of mismatches are commonplace involving, e.g., multi-users support, resource management, and security.

The term "architectural mismatch" implies more than just mismatched component assumptions: it also implies that mismatches can arise between components and a *software architecture* [5]. The general consensus is that software architecture deals with high-level design patterns[3] for structuring and expressing system designs. A sense of what is meant by "high level" is that these patterns are often expressed in terms of components, connectors and coordination. Components refer to units of functionality[4], connectors with the integration of components, and coordination as the manner in which components interact at run-time. Architec-

---

3. The terms "styles" and "idioms" are synonyms.
4. The component-based definition of this term is more restrictive than its use in software architecture literature.

tural mismatches can arise that inhibit component integrability and coordination.

Not all architectural styles are equally-well suited to a specific design problem. Many factors can influence the selection of a style—functional requirements, quality attributes (e.g., modifiability) and *a priori* design commitments (e.g., distributed system). Thus, a given set of software components may be assembled into a number of architectural styles, and may exhibit different kinds of architectural mismatches in each architectural setting. This suggests a reference model for describing the engineering practices involved in assembling component-based systems, as depicted in Figure 1..

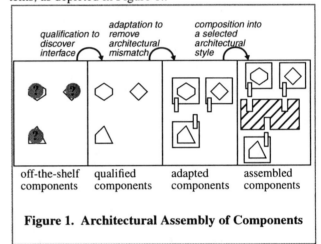

Figure 1. Architectural Assembly of Components

The vertical partitions depicted in Figure 1. describe the central artifact of component-based systems—the components—in various states:

- Off-the-shelf components have hidden interfaces (using a definition of interface that encompasses all potential interactions among components, not just an application programming interface[6]).
- Qualified components have discovered interfaces so that possible sources of architecture mismatch have been identified. This is (by the definition of interface) a partial discovery: only those interfaces that mismatch an architectural style or other components are identified.
- Adapted components have had their architectural mismatches removed. The figure implies a kind of component "wrapping," but other approaches are possible (e.g., the use of mediator agents).
- Assembled components have been integrated into an architectural infrastructure. This infrastructure will support component assembly and coordination, and differentiates architectural assembly from ad hoc "glue."

2.2 A Component-Based System Evaluation Context for the OMA

Although the reference model depicted in Figure 1. is simplistic, it is nonetheless sufficient to suggest the following questions for an evaluation of the OMA:

- Are certain architectural styles suggested by the OMA? If yes, does the OMA provide an adequate mechanism for implementing these styles? Are other mechanisms in addition to the OMA (as currently specified) required?

- Does the OMA introduce potential sources of architectural mismatch beyond those implied by architectural style? If yes, do these result from the OMA specification, or peculiarities of commercial implementations of the OMA?

- Are some kinds of components more readily adaptable to the OMA than others? If yes, what are the characteristics of components that make them more adaptable? What adaptation mechanisms work best with the OMA?

The case study described in detail, below, provided significant insight in answering these questions.

3. Background on CADE

While the nature of component-based systems provides a needed backdrop for focusing the OMA technology evaluation, the problem setting must be completed with requirements stemming from an application domain, and those stemming from the particular problem being addressed. We selected the manufacturing domain as a basis for this case study.

3.1 A Manufacturing Domain of the Future

The manufacturing processes required to move a product from concept to realization are many and varied, and often require the application of highly-specialized skills and computing resources. Job scheduling, shop layout, and manufacturability analysis are examples of such skills that are supported by software technology. In many cases these specialized skills are relatively independent of the underlying application domain—manufacturability analysis techniques for automotive parts and washing machine parts are quite similar. Some believe that a breakthrough in manufacturing efficiency can be achieved if these "horizontal" skills can be freed from their existing "vertical" market confinements, and allowed to develop in the free-market.

The challenge is how to re-assemble these horizontal specialties into *virtual enterprises*, i.e., otherwise independent manufacturing companies collaborating on a vertical manufacturing enterprises. Virtual enterprises are a means of supporting the flexible combination of the skills and tools from many highly-specialized companies; from this, faster market response time, reduced time-to-market, and increased manufacturing quality can be achieved. However, in addition to regulatory and business-model challenges of virtual enterprises, additional technology infrastructure is needed that will support:

- the integration of separately-developed, specialized, computer-aided manufacturing technologies;

- geographical distribution of computing resources, and support for heterogeneous computing environments;

- fee-for-service brokering of computer-based services to enable competition for specialized tools and skills.

In short, virtual enterprises in an increasingly specialized manufacturing world will rely more and more upon information technology such as supported by distributed object technology. However, the existing investment in computer-aided technology will need to be preserved, and adapted, to exploit distributed object technology.

3.2 A Legacy Manufacturing System

We needed a legacy manufacturing system for modernization to distributed object technology that would be simple enough to quickly prototype, yet sophisticated enough to constitute a reasonable test of the OMA. As a domain model of manufacturing activities suggests [7], there are many subdomains that might provide for fertile hunting. From this model we determined that the *design engineering* activity provided was suitably focused and automated.

Design engineering involves modeling and simulating part designs to test the performance of parts under certain expected real-world use conditions. This analysis can be used to determine the adequacy of a part design for performing a function, to optimize a part design, and to lower the cost and/or weight of a part while preserving confidence in its performance. A diverse range of software components have been developed that support design engineering, providing the basis for a OMA case study.

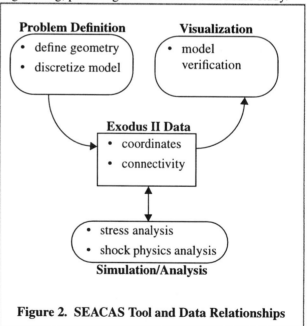

Figure 2. SEACAS Tool and Data Relationships

The Sandia National Laboratory Engineering Analysis Code Access System (SEACAS) provided us with a representative set of design engineering components. SEACAS supports functions such as problem definition, simulation, analysis, and visualization (see Figure 2.). Sandia has developed many components in each functional category, reflecting both the diversity of analysis problems being

77

addressed and the evolving sophistication of design engineering methods. For our case study, we selected a core set of SEACAS components that could represent a single thread through a design engineering scenario.

The general usage scenario for these tools is as shown in Figure 3., which uses a process description formalism similar to IDEF-0: the bubbles represent activities; data input appears on the left of activities, and data output appears on the right; mechanisms appear on the bottom of activities; and, control flow appears on the top of activities. The control flow "end-user" which would appear on each activity is omitted from Figure 3. for simplicity.

Following Figure 3., an analyst uses FASTQ to produce a *discretized*[5] model of the part to be analyzed. The visualizing tool BLOT then can be used to produce a graphical representation of the model for inspection by the analyst. Based on that inspection the analyst either re-runs FASTQ to correct the model or feeds the model to GEN3D to extrude the two-dimensional model into the third dimension. Another inspection/correction iteration may occur for the resulting three-dimensional model before the model is fed to the analysis tool. One or more analyses may be conducted, with results evaluated via the visualization tool or through inspection of other JAS3D output (not illustrated). As suggested by Figure 3., the process can be highly iterative, reflecting a process of convergence on a suitable design.

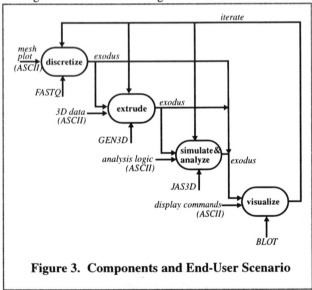

Figure 3. Components and End-User Scenario

As Figure 2. points out, many of these tools make use of a common data format (Exodus-II). This is an important property that greatly simplified the prototyping effort. However, there is more to component integration than data interchange. For example, in the scenario described above end-users are responsible for launching tools (often with personalized scripts), managing tool output (in private directories), and

---

5. A two- or three-dimensional mesh that models the contours of a solid.

preparing the output of one tool for use as input to another (sometimes with manual application of filters since not all SEACAS tools use the same version of the Exodus data format). In effect, the end-user is the system integrator, continually exposed to all of the low-level details and technology dependencies exhibited by the SEACAS components, and the environments in which they operate.

3.3 Objectives for OMA-Based Modernization

From the particular requirements of SEACAS, we determined that the case study should evaluate the use of the OMA to integrate a legacy collection of design engineering tools in order to:

- present a uniform virtual environment for end-users that would reflect the nature of the analysis activity and not the idiosyncrasies of specific SEACAS components;

- support wide-area distribution of SEACAS services while maintaining control over the software that provides these services (some of which contain classified algorithms);

- deliver reasonable, usable and predictable performance to end-users who are otherwise accustomed to using computer services in local area network settings.

These requirements extend and refine those of the underlying manufacturing application domain (Section 3.1).

4.   A Distributed Object Architecture for the SEACAS Components

The modernization objectives (cited above) can be thought of as *quality attributes*—externally-visible system properties that deal with issues other than functionality. The significance of quality attributes is that it has been demonstrated that the top-level design, or architecture, of a system is the key factor leading to the satisfaction (or lack) of these non-functional requirements [8]. Thus, for our evaluation of OMA we needed to determine how well it addressed architecture-level issues inherent to component-based systems (Section 2.2) as well as how it addresses component-based systems that exhibit these quality attributes.

In the following discussion it is useful to bear in mind that the purpose of the case study was an evaluation of the OMA feature delta. If the design problem is viewed strictly in terms of the four components integrated, then there were undoubtedly simpler design solutions to achieving the limited objectives outlined in Section 3.3. However, viewing the design problem as a representative one in a broader class of problems led us to design solutions that required a more elaborate use of the OMA, i.e., use of the OMA feature delta.

4.1 Architectural Overview

We quickly discovered that the OMA suggested an architectural approach that makes extensive use of the

OMA object model and the CORBA interface definition features; we were pleased to discover that this feature delta beyond the more primitive form of RPC interface definition had such significance. This central role for an object model in a component-based architecture is illustrated in Figure 4., which depicts a top-level view of the prototype architecture.

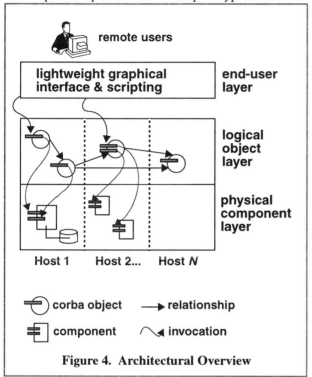

Figure 4. Architectural Overview

This architecture can be described in terms of how it supports integration—the core design activity in component-based systems (architectural mismatch is the inhibitor of integration). One useful way to think of integration is as a *relationship* between two integrated entities, where the relationship has four *aspects*: control, data, process and presentation [9][10]:

- Control integration describes how components make requests of (or invoke) each other's services.

- Data integration describes how components make data available to each other.

- Process integration describes what end-user process is supported by, or activates, the integration relationship.

- Presentation integration describes how end-users interact with the endpoints of an integration relationship.

The end-user layer addresses presentation and process integration through interactive, graphical client interface, and scripting logic that sequences and controls the execution of remote services. This layer will not be described in detail; we view it as an application layer supported by the architecture. However, we note that abstraction mismatches between the scripting language and the object model were introduced by our use of Tk/TCL; a mechanism such as Java would address this problem.

The physical component layer addresses the run-time aspects of the SEACAS components, and various platform dependencies. At this level a number of sometimes subtle interactions between components, operating system and CORBA implementation arose. These detailed implementation issues are discussed in Section 5.

The logical object layer addresses data and control integration. Interestingly, we discovered that the OMA suggested an architectural style to address these aspects that in effect blends two different styles: a *repository* style for data integration and a *structural* style for control integration. The remainder of this section will describe these styles and how they were realized with the OMA.

4.2 Object Layer as Data Repository

The repository-style architecture is characterized by a central data repository that is used as a principle means for components to coordinate their execution and share results. Numerous examples of repository-style architectures have been seen in the computer-aided software engineering (CASE) domain [11]; examples in the manufacturing domain are also emerging [12].

The repository-style architecture is motivated by two factors, both of which are relevant to SEACAS:

1. The data artifacts that are manipulated by software components are key assets that must be managed. Mechanisms for access control, versioning, backup and recovery, transactions, etc., are all important for the effective management of data assets.

2. The structure of data can be quite complex, with different kinds of data related in a complex network of aggregation and dependency relationships. Mechanisms for schema definition and evolution, query, and navigation are all needed to manage this complexity.

The two OMA services that we found to be most important for the SEACAS repository were *relationships* and *persistence*. Relationships were used to define links between various kinds of SEACAS artifacts while persistence allowed networks of object instances to persist beyond user sessions.

We used the object-oriented features of the CORBA interface definition language (IDL) to model SEACAS artifacts in a class hierarchy, and used relationships to express the derivation history from one class of artifact to another. A simplified object model is depicted in Figure 5., which shows the major object types and their relationships to each other and to the SEACAS components. For example, *exodus2d* (a two-dimensional mesh) inherits (and defines its own) operations and attributes from the *exodus* abstract superclass; *exodus2d* functionality is implemented by *FASTQ*; and, it participates in a 1:many relationship with *exodus3d* objects to indicate that a single two-dimensional mesh can be extruded into several three-dimensional meshes.

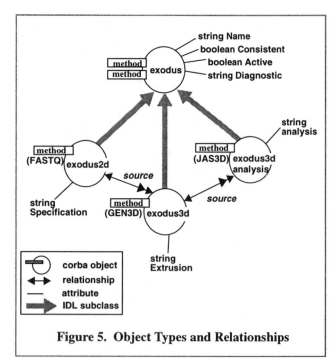

Figure 5. Object Types and Relationships

The net effect of populating the logical object model layer with instances of these object types and relationships is to create a distributed object repository of SEACAS objects. On a surface level, this would seem to indicate that the OMA provides a good foundation for repository-style architectures, and in the large this is true. Upon looking deeper, however, there are limitations to the OMA specification and commercial implementations of the OMA that may effect the scaleability and robustness of OMA-based data repositories.

With respect to commercial implementations, vendors are not required to implement any of the OMA services beyond CORBA. The object request broker we used did not support the relationship service, and it supported a non-standard persistence service. These missing services resulted in a substantial increase in programming complexity and a decrease in application functionality and robustness. For example, we implemented relationships as object-valued attributes; this required additional encoding of dependency management logic within *exodus* methods, and introduced subtle interactions with the persistence mechanism, which itself was quite complex. Also, the bi-directionality, arity and object type constraint checking, and compound object operations that would have been available with OMA relationship services were too expensive to implement.

Issues are also raised by the specification of the OMA services. For example, the underlying OMA assumption that object services can be separately specified and individually implemented is a cause for concern. There are, for example, specification and implementation dependencies between persistence and transactions, naming and security, and relationships and life cycle. While the OMA specification is sensitive to some of these dependencies, many more dependencies exist than can be conveniently specified or even anticipated.

The PCTE specification—a quasi-object based repository technology, is a broad indication of the level of complexity involved [13]. Other specification issues that will inhibit the development of robust OMA-based repositories include: the lack of various data management services (e.g., schema definition, administration, object ownership and sharing), and optimistic design assumptions about object granularity and network/interprocess communication performance.

However, while the OMA does have limitations regarding data management services, component-based systems might not, in general, require repositories that implement a full range of database management functionality. For our case study even simple OMA services—had they been available—would have sufficed. Thus, we concluded that

- Object services are both useful and essential for component-based systems integration; and,
- the OMA provides (barely) sufficient data management services, provided the designer is not over-exuberant.

4.3 Object Layer as Structural Architecture

The repository addresses issues of data and object management, but it does not address how the functionality of the SEACAS components is revealed through these objects, nor how these objects interact with the end-user level (the coordination model). There are two overall approaches to addressing these issues—a *functional* approach and a *structural* approach.

The functional approach is by far the predominant approach to component-based systems. This approach defines component interfaces in terms of their specific functionality. Occasionally, somewhat greater abstraction is obtained by generalizing component-specific interfaces into generic services, thus encapsulating some technology and vendor dependencies. Functional architectures are good for describing system functionality and for integrating specific functionality but are weak for addressing the run-time properties of a design. e.g., throughput, latency and reliability.

The structural approach has emerged as the study of software architecture has intensified. Rather than defining component interfaces in terms of functionality, structural styles define interfaces in terms of the role a component plays in a *coordination model*—a model that describes how the components interact. A simple illustration of a structural style is UNIX pipes and filters; more sophisticated illustrations include structural models for flight simulators [14], and the Simplex architecture for evolvable dependable real-time systems [15]. The structural approach has become more popular recently because it yields architectures that, by definition, support analysis of dynamic system properties.

CORBA IDL supports functional and structural styles equally well. However, we discovered that the structural approach is particularly well-suited to component-based systems; further, it is also suggested by the OMA. This conclusion can be demonstrated by a discussion of the simplified structural architecture depicted in Figure 6., which illustrates the key coordination interfaces of one type of SEACAS object[6]. The focus of attention for this discussion is on the structural model in Figure 6..

The essence of the SEACAS coordination model is that objects are data managers that are either in a consistent or an inconsistent state. A consistent object is one whose *input attribute* is consistent with the EXODUS data that has been derived from this attribute through the execution of a SEACAS component. The input attribute for the SEACAS object depicted in Figure 6. is *analysis*, which is a string containing simulation instructions for the finite element analyzer. Clients of an object can test whether an object is consistent using the *consistent?* probe, and can re-establish consistency by using the *update* method. The *update* method is non-blocking; clients can determine if an update is still in progress by using the *done?* probe. Clients can examine the results of an update in two ways: through a *view* method on the SEACAS object (not illustrated), or through an event queue. The *view* method can only be used on a consistent object, while the event queue can be used while an update is in progress (an object is not consistent until the update has successfully completed).

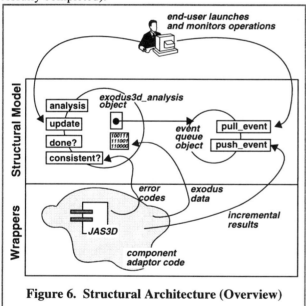

Figure 6. Structural Architecture (Overview)

Our conclusion that structural styles are particularly well-suited for component-based systems and for the OMA is based on these two observations:

1. Explicitly representing the coordination model via object interfaces addresses ambiguous and restrictive run-time semantics inherent in the OMA specification.

2. Coordination-focused object interfaces help identify areas of architectural mismatch, and suggest re-usable adaptation techniques for different kinds of mismatch. The first is discussed here, the second in Section 5.

The decision to make *update* a non-blocking method represents a departure from more straightforward use of CORBA features for client-side concurrency. Typically, pure[7] clients will use CORBA's dynamic invocation interface (DII)[8] if they not wish to block on a remote method; alternatively, multi-threaded clients could create a separate thread for each blocking method. Implementing a non-blocking *update* method appears to restrict the client's options—so why do it? There are two reasons.

The first reason is that finite element analysis may consume anywhere from a few seconds to several hours of wall clock time. Relying on a synchronous connection over a wide-area network for such durations will do violence to our reliability requirements—a momentary network failure would cause an update to fail. Making the *update* method a *oneway* call—another CORBA mechanism—is inadequate because this mechanism does not permit clients to be notified of the many exceptional circumstances that might indicate a problem with the update prior to the actual execution of SEACAS component services. Thus, had the update method been implemented using default CORBA synchronous logic, clients would have been forced to use the DII to achieve the desired level of system reliability. This is an unfair burden to place on clients; also, the architecture should ensure the reliability regardless of the form of client interface used.

The second reason concerns the way the CORBA basic object adaptor (BOA) addresses server-side concurrency, i.e., how to achieve concurrent execution of the methods of one or more objects within a server process. Clearly, servers that can exploit thread libraries will have a ready-made mechanism; however, the Object Management Group is loath to build implementation dependencies such as this into their specifications. Thus, the BOA specifies *activation policies* that (in increasing concurrency) associate a server process with:

- classes of objects ("shared" activation policy);
- individual objects ("un-shared" activation policy); or,
- individual methods ("per-method" activation policy).

By implementing *update* as non-blocking we subverted the BOA activation policy, since non-blocking semantics requires *de facto* concurrency of object implementations.

However, the un-shared and per-method policies require interprocess communication (IPC) for objects to invoke

---

6. The interfaces of other SEACAS objects are nearly identical.

7. Pure clients are applications; object implementations can also be clients, but are not "purely" clients.

8. The DII provides mechanisms for deferred synchronous communication.

each other's methods. Certainly this kind of coupling is to be expected where different object types are closely in a class hierarchy, as is the case with SEACAS objects (refer to Figure 5.). While it is possible to specify multiple sets of interfaces for objects—those for clients and "private" interfaces for friends, this can require substantial additional coding and in any event does not address the cost of the IPC or the creation of separate processes, especially in the case of per-method activation. Also, implementations of CORBA treat activation policy as a kind of configuration option for object implementations: different installations of the services may choose different policies. Again, such important system properties should be reflected in the architecture of the system, not in implicit coordination semantics and configuration options.

A final point on this topic is that these design and implementation decisions could have been taken even in a functional style, i.e., had the update method been a direct interface to a specific SEACAS function. However, the structural approach makes these coordination model decisions explicit in the object interface—there is no mistaking the assumptions concerning concurrency in the objects described in Figure 6.. Moreover, the structural approach addresses the coordination model the same way for each SEACAS component, as is evident in their common interfaces; this would be far less obvious in a functional style.

5. Component Adaptation Issues

As illustrated in Figure 6., there are several distinct relationships between the SEACAS components and the structural architecture. Each of the connections between component and structural model indicate an interaction between the architecture and a component, and hence an area of potential mismatch.

For example, from Figure 6., the *consistent?* probe should return "true" if and only if the SEACAS component executed properly. A failure could result from either a semantic fault or a system fault. SEACAS assumes that end-users will determine the success of an operation by reading diagnostic output; this does not match with the structural model, which assumes a more automated approach. System faults, such as a component crash, can also arise. SEACAS assumes such crashes will be evident since the end-user will have directly invoked the component; this also does not match with the structural model, which hides the component and its invocation.

Removal of these and other kinds of mismatches requires some form of component adaptation. In the above example, the diagnostic output needed to be parsed to determine if, and what kind, of semantic fault arose (if any, since the same output stream was used to report success and failure); also, the component process needed to be monitored for exceptional conditions and exit codes. Each of the other component-to-architecture connections depicted in Figure 6. exhibited such mismatches that needed to be resolved by component adaptation.

tion code (the "wrappers" in Figure 6.)—there were other areas of mismatch that were not depicted in the figure for reasons of clarity.

The term "wrapper" is very misleading—and its use in the figure is solely to make this point since the term is so widely, and imprecisely used. The term implies that component adaptation is accomplished through action taken on the component itself, i.e., encapsulating the component behind a veneer that presents an alternative, translated interface. However, this is just one approach to removing architectural mismatch. A better way of thinking of component adaptation is to observe that the mismatch occurs between two entities, in this case a component and an architecture, and that adaptation can occur at either or both ends of the relationship, or in the middle via an intermediary agent.

We do not know how to select among these options, nor do we have a model of adaptation techniques. However, the structural model did suggest a categorization of types of architectural mismatch that could arise, and our implementation provided at least one technique for addressing these mismatches. This confirms our earlier assertion that structural styles help focus attention on key areas of architectural mismatch. Also, since the structural model is quite general—there is little about Figure 6. that implies dependencies on the manufacturing domain—there is reason to hope for the development of architecture-specific adaptation techniques and mechanisms.

Unfortunately, while well motivated this last hope may be thwarted by the complexity of the adaptation, especially where the adaptation involves the architecture-side. We discovered that architecture-side adaptation is characterized by a thorny tangle of interactions between the coordination model, OMA semantics, vendor-specific features of the object request broker (ORB), operating system primitives, and characteristics of the components themselves. While a complete exposition of these issues would require 'a code walk-through, a high-level overview of one example may reveal the nature of this complexity. We take the accumulation of incremental output on an event queue, as illustrated in Figure 6., as our example.

Recall that the decision to make the update method non-blocking in effect mandated that the object server support concurrent execution of object services, and that we could not use the BOA per-object or per-method activation policy for reasons discussed earlier. To this we add that the ORB implementation we used for the case study did not support multi-threaded servers. As a consequence, we were forced to implement our own "homegrown" concurrency service. Those familiar with UNIX systems programming will not be surprised by our approach to this problem, and Figure 7. depicts the key elements of our solution.

The core of the solution makes use of UNIX asynchronous I/O and sockets. The idea is to have the main event

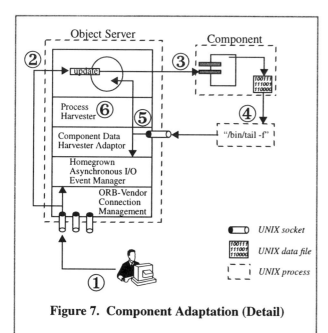

Figure 7. Component Adaptation (Detail)

loop in the object server "listen" (via the *select()* system call) for activity on any number of socket connections, and when activity is detected on a socket invoke a callback procedure that is appropriate to the kind of activity detected (e.g., data available). With this background in mind, the solution works as enumerated in the figure:

1. Client connections to an object service are implemented as sockets. These sockets are installed as they are created into the asynchronous event handler so that client requests for object services can be detected and dispatched. This installation depends upon ORB-vendor connection management services that allow the detection of new client connections, and the use of sockets.

2. A client request for an *update* is detected as activity on the client socket. The callback routine registered to handle this activity calls the ORB-vendor's implementation of the standard BOA object event handling method; thus, this part of the solution is fairly portable to different ORBs, provided the ORB allows server developers to access these routines (which is not true of one ORB we have used).

3. In response to the *update* request the SEACAS component is launched (via *fork()* and *exec()*). Different kinds of components may require different approaches to this step, for example the component could be a server that must be connected-to rather than launched. The process identifier of the launched tool is installed in the process harvester, and signal handlers are established to monitor the state changes of the process.

4. The component will begin writing its incremental output to a data file; component-side adaptation ensured that the file name was unique to each invocation. A monitor process is launched to detect state changes to the output file and report them to a socket established in step 3 for this

purpose; this requires delicate timing logic because the data file will appear an indeterminate time after the SEACAS component is launched.

5. Incremental output is detected on the data harvester socket. A callback procedure is invoked by the event manager to parse the data, since only portions of the data file that are being generated by the SEACAS component are of interest for the purposes of observing the progress of the finite element analysis. The parsed data is enqueued on an event channel.

6. The process harvester detects the termination of the SEACAS component, and determines whether the termination was normal or exceptional (needed to determine if the object is in a consistent state). Upon termination of the SEACAS component, the data monitoring process is terminated, sockets are closed, and I/O callbacks removed from the event handler.

This illustration, while gory in detail, serves to highlight a number of important points. First, adapting architectural mismatch may require low-level, intricate code. Techniques for making this process rational and repeatable will contribute greatly both to programmer productivity and system reliability: most of the problems our prototype experienced involved low-level adaptation code. Second, vendor-specific ORB features have an overwhelming influence on adaptation techniques. Another commercial ORB we have used requires completely different, but not less complex, adaptation approaches. Last, the possibility of developing architecture-specific adaptation techniques may be hampered by intricate ORB, tool, and operating system dependencies. However, this is only an issue if portable object implementations is desired—and the OMA does not support object implementation portability in any event.

6. Conclusions about the OMA

The technology evaluation we conducted on the OMA was robust because: it was based on a model that situated the OMA in the context of peer technologies, yielding a feature delta; and, the feature delta was applied to an important problem domain in a non-trivial application setting. As a result of this approach, we are able to reach substantiable conclusions about the use of the OMA to a specific class of engineering problems. Moreover, we are able to provide practical guidance on the use of the OMA to these problems based on actual experience rather than conjecture.

We conclude that the OMA is a good, if complex, vehicle for building component-based systems. The major elements of the OMA feature delta—object services and an object-oriented interface description—provided an excellent foundation for designing and implementing distributed component-based systems. In practice, developers will require the use of an even richer set of object services than currently defined; it remains to be seen whether vendors will as a rule provide implementations of these services. Developers will also find multi-thread support for object services to be increasingly useful, if not essential

We recommend an architectural approach to using OMA that combines elements of a repository-style with elements of a structural-style. While the OMA services are neither sufficiently rich nor sufficiently integrated to realistically implement an object-oriented database, the data management services should be sufficient for most component-based systems; an object-oriented database could in any event be one included as a component should those kinds of services be needed. The OMA object model and interface description capabilities are strongly suited to the development of application architectures; the structural style is well-suited to the OMA as a means of strengthening and applying OMA run-time features, and as a means for simplifying, and making rational, the identification and removal of architectural mismatches among components.

7. References

[1] *Object Management Architecture Guide, Revision 2.0*, Second Edition, OMG TC Document 92.11.1, Object Management Group, 492 Old Connecticut Path, Framingham, MA, 01701.

[2] Brown, A., Wallnau, K., "A framework for systematic evaluation of software technologies" to appear in the special issue of IEEE Software on assessment of software tools, September 1996.

[3] Wallnau, K., Rice, J., "ORBS In the Midst: Studying a New Species of Integration Mechanism", in Proceedings of International Conference on Computer-Aided Software Engineering (CASE-95), Toronto, CA, July 1995.

[4] Garlan, D., Allen, R., Ockerbloom, J., "Architecture Mismatch: Why Reuse is so Hard", IEEE Software V12, #6, pp17-26, November 1995.

[5] Garlan, D. and Shaw, M., "An Introduction to Software Architecture," in Advances in Software Engineering and Knowledge Engineering, vol. I, World Scientific Publishing Company, 1993

[6] Parnas, D., "Information distribution aspects of design methodology," in proceedings of IFIP conference, 1971, North Holland Publishing Co.

[7] Barkmeyer, E., SIIMA Reference Architecture Part I: Activity Models, NIST Technical Report (in publication).

[8] Abowd, G., Bass, L., Kazman, R., Webb, M., "SAAM: A Method for Analyzing the Properties of Software Architecture," in Proceedings of the 16th International Conference on Software Engineering, Sorrento Italy, May 1994, pp. 81-90

[9] Thomas, I., Nejmeh, B., "Definitions of tool integration for environments," IEEE Software 9(3), pp. 29-35, March 1992.

[10] Wasserman, A., "Tool integration in software engineering environments," in F. Long, ed., *Software Engineering Environments, Lecture Notes in Computer Science 467*, pp. 138-150, Springer-Verlag, Berlin, Germany, 1990.

[11] Brown, A., et. al., *Principles of CASE Tool Integration*, Oxford University Press, 1994, ISBN 0-19-509478-6.

[12] Brown, A., Judd, R., Riddick, F., "Architectural issues in the design and implementation of an integrated toolkit for manufacturing engineering" submitted to the International Journal of Computer Integrated Manufacturing.

[13] Wakeman, L. and Jowett, J., "PCTE: The Standards for Open Repositories", Prentice-Hall, 1993.

[14] Abowd, G., Bass, L., Howard, L., Northrup, L., *Structural Modeling: An Application Framework and Development Process for Flight Simulators*, SEI Technical Report, CMU/SEI-93-TR-14, 1993, Software Engineering Institute, Carnegie-Mellon University, Pittsburgh, PA.

[15] Sha, L., Rajkumar, R., Gagliardi, M., A Software Architecture for Dependable and Evolvable Industrial Computing Systems, SEI Technical Report, CMU/SEI-95-TR-005, 1995, Software Engineering Institute, Carnegie-Mellon University, Pittsburgh, PA.

The Gadfly:
An Approach to Architectural-Level System Comprehension

Paul Clements, Robert Krut, Ed Morris, Kurt Wallnau

Software Engineering Institute
Carnegie Mellon University
Pittsburgh, PA 15213-3890

{clements, rk, ejm, kcw}@sei.cmu.edu

Abstract

Technology to support system comprehension tends to reflect either a "bottom-up" or "top-down" approach. Bottom-up approaches attempt to derive system models from source code, while top-down approaches attempt to map abstract "domain" concepts to concrete system artifacts. While both approaches have merit in theory, in practice the top-down approach has not yielded scalable, cost-effective technology. One problem with the top-down approach is that it is very expensive to develop domain models, and it is difficult to develop models that are sufficiently general to be applied to multiple systems (and hence amortize the development cost). This paper describes the Gadfly, an approach for developing narrowly-focused, reusable domain models that can be integrated and (re)used to aid in the process of top-down system comprehension.

1. Introduction

A primary purpose of program understanding technology is, ultimately, to assist maintainers to develop a system-level understanding of an application so that changes to the application can be introduced in a rational, consistent way. Unfortunately, although source code is often the most reliable arbiter of what a system does, it does not reflect all of the attributes of an application necessary to develop a true system-level understanding: there is more to understanding a system than understanding what function it computes. System characteristics such as performance, robustness, security, etc., must also be understood. We refer to such characteristics as quality attributes, and quality attributes are related more to the architecture of a system than to its code [16].

This paper describes a knowledge-based software assistant called the Gadfly. The Gadfly is intended to help designers *create* applications that attain a selected set of quality attributes[1], as well as to help maintainers *understand* how an existing application has achieved those properties. The construction and understanding guidance of the Gadfly is at the *architectural* level, which deals with allocation of functionality to components and inter-component interaction, rather than the internal workings of individual components. To motivate the architectural approach to system comprehension based on quality attributes, the paper makes the following points:

- Software architecture provides a level of understanding at which a system's quality attributes can be best managed and understood, because they most often depend on inter-component relationships and cannot be discovered from source code alone.

- Quality attributes represent coherent domains of specialized design knowledge that can be separately modeled and combined in different ways to support both forward engineering and system comprehension.

- Quality attribute knowledge is similar to the knowledge represented by specialized design schemas and similar concepts found in program comprehension literature, and is amenable to knowledge representation modeling.

- Software architecture can be used both as a framework for integrating sets of quality attribute domain models, and as a juncture between top-down and bottom-up strategies for program comprehension.

The rest of the paper is structured as follows: Section 2 provides an overview of current approaches to program and system comprehension, and describes the program understanding context for the Gadfly. Section 3 surveys the key concepts of software architecture, and outlines the potential role software architecture can play in both forward-engineering and system comprehension activities. Section 4 describes the Gadfly, and illustrates its use through an operational scenario. Section 5 summarizes the key contributions of the Gadfly to program comprehension, and outlines potential next steps.

---

1. The Gadfly prototype addresses only the information security attribute.

Copyright © 1996 by The Institute of Electrical and Electronics Engineers, Inc. All rights reserved.

2. Program comprehension technology

2.1 Top-down and bottom-up approaches for system comprehension

Current program understanding models identify a number of different types of knowledge that a maintainer uses to comprehend software, including knowledge of programming, knowledge of the real-world situation represented in the software, and knowledge of the application domain. All of these types of knowledge are important to the maintainer, since they embody different abstractions and impart different kinds of understanding of software systems. These kinds of knowledge are used in a top-down or bottom-up manner, or some opportunistic combination of these approaches.

The bottom-up model of program comprehension suggests that a model of the application is built starting with program knowledge and works to produce higher abstractions, using strategies like "chunking". Program knowledge[1] reflects the maintainers' understanding of programming idioms, program structure, algorithms, and flow of control and data (the programming domain), and is typically related to a bottom-up approach.

Alternately, a top-down model of program comprehension suggests that comprehension proceeds from higher level abstractions down to lower level program idioms, algorithms, etc. Pennington [1] suggests that, in addition to program knowledge, expert maintainers also rely on an understanding of the real-world problem addressed by the software in order comprehend a particular software system. This world knowledge is referred to as a situation model, which describes the problem domain from a higher level of abstraction than program models. According to Pennington, program comprehension involves employing both bottom-up and top-down strategies to relate and coordinate information from the program model with that of the situation model[2].

Brooks suggests that, in order to comprehend a programming problem, experts employ a top-down, hypothesis driven problem solving approach[3]. In applying this approach, Soloway and Ehrlich found that expert programmers employ high-level schemas (plans) that strongly influence expectations about what a program should look like[5]. Koenemann and Robertson demonstrated that for experienced programmers, program comprehension occurred primarily in a top-down manner using such schemas; however, programmers resort to bottom-up strategies when they lacked hypotheses, when hypotheses failed, or for close scrutiny of relevant code[4]. Subjects determined what program segments were relevant based on their knowledge of the task domain, general programming knowledge, and their current understanding of the program. Letovsky suggests that program comprehension can best be viewed as an opportunistic application of bottom-up and top-down strategies[7].

Guindon, Curtis, and Krasner also addressed the question of opportunistic system comprehension, but from the standpoint of the design of highly complex systems[6]. In experiments requiring the design of logic to control the functioning of lifts (elevators), the authors found that the primary determinant of performance was the presence (or lack) of computational techniques, called specialized design schemas, that correspond to characteristics of the application domain. These specialized design schemas encode a solution template and the situations under which the solution is appropriate. Examples of specialized design schemas employed by the experiment subjects included scheduling and routing, message communication, and concurrency. Guindon, etl al., found that subjects applied these schemas in a highly opportunistic manner, building partial solutions at various levels of abstractions.

Clearly, program comprehension relies on the application of a set of domain models (variously called specialized design schemas, situation models, program models, etc.). We expect that program comprehension relies on processing analogous to those suggested by Guindon for design.

2.2 Approaches to building domain models

Current tool support for the application of domain knowledge to aid in program comprehension suffers from several limitations. While a number of approaches to codifying domain knowledge have been developed (e.g., [9][10]), to date they have demonstrated only limited success. Nor are tools based on source code parsing sophisticated enough to produce domain models or recognize architectural designs within systems.

The existing approaches to supporting the maintainer by supplementing their domain knowledge can be classified into two broad categories:

- approaches that attempt to automatically extract the high-level domain knowledge from source code and other system artifacts; and,

- approaches that attempt to codify and organize the knowledge of experts about specific systems.

The former approach (automatic extraction of high-level abstractions from source code) has proven difficult. For example, automatic recognition of algorithms is complex due to the wide variance in the manner in which a specific algorithm can be encoded, and the huge volume of code in which the algorithm may be embedded. In addition, this approach still requires an expert maintainer to relate any algorithms found to domain concepts.

The latter approach (building knowledge bases from expert input) has led to a number of interesting tools that provide some support for software maintainers. However, the effort necessary to create the knowledge base is extremely high, relying on time-consuming interviews involving system experts and often "knowledge engineers" who specialize in the organization of knowledge into appropriate rules.

In addition to being expensive to develop, the completed knowledge bases are inflexible and hard to maintain [11]. They mix information that spans multiple views or abstractions in a system (e.g., algorithms, architecture, requirements), domain knowledge that crosses multiple software domains (e.g., security, fault-tolerance, distribution, performance), knowledge unique to the application domain (e.g., banking, health informatics, command and control), and knowledge specific to a single system (e.g., a specific air-traffic control system). It is hard to see how information within the resulting knowledge bases can be generalized to other systems within (or outside of) the application domain. Thus, their heavy development cost cannot be amortized across other applications.

2.3 A new approach for knowledge-based system comprehension

In this paper, we suggest a new approach to developing domain knowledge to support system understanding, and describe a prototype implementation of this approach, called the Gadfly. The Gadfly is based on these premises:

- There is a strong symmetry, largely unexploited to date, between developing a system and comprehending it after the fact. Comprehension seeks to understand the artifacts produced during construction. Hence, the knowledge structures that served to guide the construction tend to be the same ones that provide the framework against which the legacy artifacts can be understood.

- Systems are comprehended, at least in part, from the vantage of codifiable domains of knowledge. The Gadfly recognizes that more than one kind of domain applies to a system. For example, to build a secure command-and-control system requires knowledge about command-and-control systems as well as methods for achieving security in computer systems. These domains may be orthogonal in many ways; in any case, knowledge about them can be separately modeled and combined in different ways to reveal different aspects of a system under investigation.

- Just as domain knowledge can be partitioned into different kinds of expertise (e.g., security, fault-tolerance, command-and-control), so, too, it can be partitioned and mapped to systems in terms of different views or kinds of understanding (e.g., code, architecture and problem statement views). Thus, system comprehension involves understanding a system, through various abstractions, in terms of different kinds of domain knowledge.

- The architecture of system is an abstraction that is particularly fruitful as a basis for system comprehension, and the concepts of software architecture can provide a foundation for structuring the investigation of a system, and for integrating supportive domain knowledge.

The Gadfly is a system that guides its user through an analysis of a system, based on separate knowledge bases dealing with the application domain and relevant system quality attributes. The prototype Gadfly was built to render analytical assistance with secure command-and-control systems; hence, it was armed with one knowledge base about kinds of command-and-control systems, and a second knowledge base about computer security.

3. Software architecture and comprehension

Software architecture refers to a view of a system that focuses on the nature and interactions of the major components. While not a new concept— the fundamental notion dates back at least to 1968 when Dijkstra pointed out that carefully structuring a system imparts useful properties and should be considered in addition to just computing the right answer [13]—software architecture as a topic of study is enjoying a flurry of interest. See, for example, [14].

A software architecture represents the integration of application domain concepts with system design expertise to ensure that the application will meet (or, in the case of program understanding, how it has met) its requirements. System design expertise is used to make (or understand) design trade-offs, e.g., performance vs. modifiability or security vs. ease of use. These and other quality attributes are manifested at the architectural level of systems, and cannot be discerned or analyzed from individual system components.

More generally, an architecture represents a body of knowledge with multiple uses for both the designer and maintainer:

- Architecture enables communication and can be used to convey the decisions of designers to maintainers.

- Architecture represents a transferable abstraction of a system that can be applied to other systems exhibiting similar requirements. *Domain-specific software architectures* describe the features of a family of systems [15].

- Architecture suggests a recipe book for designers and maintainers to assist them in selecting and identifying the design idioms that guide the organization of modules and subsystems into complete systems.

- Architecture simplifies system construction and guides program understanding by acting as a framework that constrains the manner in which components interact with their environment, receive and relinquish control, manage data, communicate, and share resources.

- Architecture enables a system to satisfy its quality attributes. For example, modifiability depends extensively on the system's modularization, which reflects the encapsulation strategies; performance depends largely upon the volume and complexity of inter-component communication and coordination, etc.

- Architectural constructs are institutionalized in the development and maintenance organization's team structure, work assignments, management units, etc.

Therefore, crucial information about the social context of a system, vital for understanding, is embodied in its architecture.

Most research in software architecture has tended to focus on forward engineering. Architecture description languages (ADLs) continue to be an active area of research [12]. The key challenge for ADLs is to express the unchanging characteristics of a system in addition to describing allowable variation. Closely related to work on ADLs is research on automated composition of systems from architectural models [17][18]. Architecture-level composers tend to view system building as an exercise in constraining the variability of an underlying design until no variation remains and the result is an executable system.

In contrast, relatively little research has been undertaken to understand how software architecture can be used to aid in system comprehension. The software architecture analysis method (SAAM) [16] is an architecture comprehension technique that designers can use to validate that design decisions support selected quality attributes. SAAM is essentially a guide to architecture-level comprehension if quality attributes. However, SAAM is focused mostly on the methodology for comprehension; there is less emphasis on codifying design heuristics associated with any particular quality attribute.

The Gadfly draws upon advances in both areas of software architecture research (forward engineering and comprehension) by recognizing that the kinds of knowledge needed to compose a system are, by and large, the same kinds of knowledge needed to comprehend an existing system. The kinds of analysis a designer subjects a hypothetical design are similar to the analysis of operational (fielded) designs, whether the intention is to perform a design trade-off for a particular quality attribute (forward engineering), or to discover the presence of a quality attribute (system comprehension).

4. The Gadfly

The Gadfly prototype is a knowledge-based software assistant (KBSA)[2] that supports the development and comprehension of command, control and communications (C3) systems. These functions are supported in this way:

- Development: portions of command centers[3] can be semi-automatically composed from components and a generic command center architecture.

- Comprehension: specific command center designs can be evaluated from an information security perspective.

- Integrated composition and comprehension: comprehension services may be invoked from

---

2. In general, a KBSA is an application that uses deductive reasoning to provide expert assistance to humans engaged in knowledge-intensive activities.

3. A specific (headquarter) function within a C3 system.

composition services to provide guidance in the composition process.

We first describe the knowledge and computational models used by the composition function of Gadfly, since these models are used (though extended) by the comprehension function. We then describe the overall Gadfly architecture and how the composition and comprehension functions interact. Finally, we annotate a sample session using the Gadfly for system comprehension purposes.

4.1 The Gadfly computational model

The composition function of the Gadfly is built upon a domain model—a model which describes, in this case, the structure and operational context of command centers. The command center domain model is represented in RLF [20], which employs a structured-inheritance network (similar to Brachman's KL-ONE [21]) and a specialized forward-chaining rule-based inferencing system. The domain model includes descriptions of command center tasks (e.g., situation monitoring and threat assessment), links between these tasks and architectural components in a command center (e.g., geographic information system) and links from architecture components to specific technologies (e.g., DeLorme mapping system).

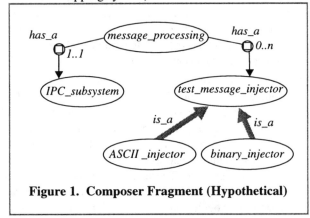

Figure 1. Composer Fragment (Hypothetical)

The composer allows command center designers to interactively develop portions of command centers through a refinement process: navigating among, and converging decision points in a domain model. These decision points represent various alternatives in the design and implementation of a family of command centers described by this domain model. The composition process is strongly analogous to various hardware composition systems developed in the 1980's [19].

To illustrate the knowledge and computational models of the composer, consider the simplified fragment of the command center domain model illustrated in Figure 1. This fragment represents a small portion of the generic architecture encoded within the domain model. It asserts that the message processing component of the architecture has exactly one inter-process communication (IPC) system and zero or more components for injecting test messages into the IPC subsystem. Further, there are exactly two kinds of injectors: one injects ASCII-encoded messages, one injects binary-encoded messages.

The composer works by navigating through such network models, asking questions pertinent to the current "focus" (the semantic network concept it is examining) of the composer, and acting upon these answers. At the point when the focus of the composer is at the message processing system, for example, the designer might be asked whether a test message injector is desired, and, if so, how many and of what kind.[4] Similar questions might be asked about the IPC subsystem, for example if the model described specific products that could provide this functionality. As the designer answers questions, the composer emits an instantiation of the generic model (a refinement) to record the decisions made by the designer and any consequences of these decisions; in some cases it can also emit build scripts for automatically constructing prototype systems.

We refer to the semantic network (as illustrated in Figure 1) as encoding structural knowledge. Extra-structural knowledge is also encoded in the model as different types of rules that are linked to the structural model. Rules are used to capture domain knowledge not easily encoded in a semantic network, and are used to propagate design decisions through the network. For example, the decision to select a binary injector might be made automatically if an earlier design decision determined that the class of messages processed by the command center included binary messages; this, in turn, could have been deduced (and propagated) from a still-earlier decision regarding the mission of the command center (also modeled in the domain model).

We developed a proof-of-concept composer based upon the model just described. However, we discovered that application domain knowledge alone was an insufficient foundation for the composer. While the domain model described alternative components and compositions, it provided little engineering guidance on how to select among these alternatives. Frequently, such decisions could be made on the basis of desired quality attributes. To help designers make such decisions, knowledge about these quality attributes and how they can be achieved by different design decisions must also be consulted. The Gadfly prototype is an extension of the original composer that augments the application-specific domain model (C3) with quality attribute domain knowledge.

4.2 The Gadfly architecture

The initial customer for the Gadfly was concerned with evaluating systems (proposed and existing) from an information security perspective. They had already developed a domain model of information security principles to aid in

4. The following questions can be deduced from the structure of the model. Other questions, derived from extra-structural knowledge, might also be asked.

analysis and evaluation efforts, but found the model difficult to employ because it lacked an application-specific context. This problem was the complement to limitations of the composer prototype, which had an application context but lacked quality attribute models.

The purpose of the Gadfly prototype was to demonstrate the re-use of security expertise for designing new systems, and for evaluating existing systems, from a security perspective. The Gadfly architecture reflects the integration of application-domain knowledge with different kinds of highly-specialized design knowledge; it also reflects our contention that there is a symmetry between system design and system comprehension, and that a single technology can accommodate both kinds of activities.

Similarly to the C3 domain model, the information security domain model was encoded in a structural model augmented with extra-structural rules. The structural model encodes information such as:

- a threat model, which describes a range of potential security threats that confront systems, e.g., disruption, deception and disclosure; each threat is the root of its own taxonomy (e.g, there are many kinds of disruption);

- a security service model, which describes basic classes of countermeasures for meeting various threats, e.g., hardware redundancy, cryptographic checksum, password protection; and,

- a security mechanism model, which describes and links various "approved" mechanisms that may be useful for implementing all or part of one or more security services.

Extra-structural rules encode procedural knowledge, referred to as strategies in [8], for applying this knowledge in specific contexts. These strategies include the kinds of information that security analysts will seek regarding the operational and maintenance context of a system, as well as concrete analysis processes, such as mathematical models for deriving the seriousness of a threat (for example, balancing factors such as the potential gain for the intruder, the damage incurred by the system, the risk of detection to the intruder, and the cost of detecting the intruder).

The Gadfly architecture is illustrated in Figure 2. The elicitor (the top-most box in Figure 2) is the function that manages the dialogue between the Gadfly and the designer. To conduct this dialogue the elicitor needs to modulate between C3 domain knowledge and information security domain knowledge. The elicitor "walks" the structural models, asking questions depending upon rules and facts associated with various concepts in the structural model, emitting instantiations of concepts where appropriate, and shifting focus to new nodes in the structural model. Links between concepts instantiated from the C3 domain model and information security domain model represent the assignment of security concepts to the application architecture[5]. The process continues in cyclic fashion (fire the rules, ask questions, shift focus in the network) until the session is complete (no more nodes to visit or questions to ask)..

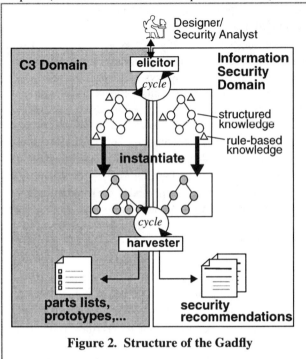

Figure 2. Structure of the Gadfly

The Gadfly can be used for system composition, in which case security knowledge can be consulted as a means of determining, for example, which components to select for a given system. Alternatively, Gadfly can be used when for constructing a cognitive model of security concepts within an existing system. Moreover, it is not even strictly necessary that the system description be encoded in a domain model to use the Gadfly in this way. If an architectural model did not exist for a system, the execution of the Gadfly would result not in an assignment of security concepts to an architectural description, but rather in a framework for investigating the system from a security perspective. That is, the questions asked by the elicitor and the instantiated security model generated from the dialogue would provide a basis for further investigation of the system using whatever system artifacts are available (code, design notes, or the developers themselves). In effect, then, the Gadfly helps maintainers by allowing them to re-use highly specialized system comprehension strategies [8].

---

5. The prototype did not go so far as to create these links, since the operational concept of the composer was that instantiated networks were transient, and existed only so long as needed by the harvester. The links exist conceptually, and are illustrated in the annotated report generated by Gadfly (Section 4.3 of this paper). The generalization noted here is easily achieved, however.

4.3 Annotated output from a Gadfly session

The ten-page report that forms the basis of the following annotations was generated from a session in which an analyst was using the Gadfly to investigate the security properties of the message processing component of the command center architecture.[6] There are six sections of the Gadfly-generated report (not counting a prologue which provides context information on the report itself), each illustrated in turn in Figures 3a through 3f.[7]

The message processing component is itself an aggregate concept comprised of several kinds of components, including: message translators and validators, interprocess communication components, message generation components, human-machine interface components, etc. In the following scenario, specific off-the-shelf components that implement these functions had already been selected. Thus, the scenario reflects a comprehension task: the analyst is attempting to infer security properties of a design where several key decisions have already been made.

```
You specified the following sets of
threat consequences as being the most
important to counter:

* disruption via incapacitation
* disruption via corruption
* disruption via falsification
* disclosure via intrusion
* disclosure via interception
* disclosure via exposure
```

Figure 3. Threat Context and Prioritization

Figure 3 reflects a security prioritization scheme for the particular system under investigation. This information represents requirements and design assumptions for the command center: comprehension of more detailed security properties (and the relationship of these properties to other aspects of the command center design) is not possible without this kind of information.

This is an important feature of the Gadfly: it addresses information that is best specified (or found) in architectural-level specifications, i.e., issues of system and component context and inter-component relationships. Since this information is not likely to be found in code, this aspect of Gadfly reflects the reuse of a system comprehension strategy: the application of the strategy produces a framework for investigating security properties of the command center in question.

---

6. The report corresponds to "security recommendations" depicted in Figure 2.

7. The content of the report has been edited slightly for formatting purposes.

Figure 4 summarizes the specific threats to which this

```
Specific threats most concerned about:

*disclosure: intrusion penetration
*disclosure: interception scavenging
*deception: falsification insertion
*deception: falsification substitution
*disruption: corruption tamper malicious
*disclosure: intrusion cryptoanalysis
(etc.)
```

Figure 4. Known Threats

command center must respond. As was stated about the threat context and prioritization information depicted in Figure 3a, this information reflects design context; however (as will be illustrated) this information provides a basis for concept assignment of specific security threats to specific components in the command center architecture.

Figure 5 summarizes aspects of a command center that might be associated with system-level documentation, but seldom with software-level documentation: the physical environment in which the software will execute. This information, too, is crucial for comprehending the security aspects of the software.

```
You specified the component would operate
in the following environment/context:

The factor: has the attribute(s):

component_info:
    source code available to: nobody
    outside net connection: satellite
physical site:
    network components in: unsecure area
    component housed in: secure area
    spot checks by guards: not performed
(etc.).
```

Figure 5. Physical System Context

Armed with this context information (Figures 3-5), the Gadfly can proceed with the task of assigning security concepts to elements of the command center. Further, the Gadfly can *infer* new threats not explicitly specified by the analyst. Figure 6 is an excerpt of the security concepts directly assigned to command center components.[8] Figure 3e is an excerpt of the threats inferred from the system context. These inferences result from sometimes subtle interactions between environmental context, threat priority and component attributes. These inferred threats are then assigned to the appropriate components.

---

8. DEC_Message_Q, PRISM_MTV, etc., are the names of specific off-the-shelf components used to implement this instantiation of the command center architecture.

```
Threats for component: DEC_Message_Q:
    deception->falsification->substitution
    disruption->corruption->
        malicious_logic_corruption
    disclosure->interception->wire_tapping
(etc.)
Threats for component PRISM_MTV:
    deception->falsification->substitution
    disclosure->interception->penetration
(etc.)
Threats for component ASCII_PRISM_MSG_GEN:
    deception->falsification->insertion
(etc.)
```

Figure 6. Threat (Concept) Assignment

Finally, the Gadfly is able to derive a set of security services that should be present in a system if it is to meet the assigned threats. As in Figures 6 and 7, the Gadfly is able to make a direct assignment of security concepts (services, in this case) to components: it is also able to infer the need for additional services. For brevity, only the former is illustrated in Figure 8.

```
Since:
    component_info:
        component on network machine:
        outside of building
    and you are worried about disclosure
infer new threat:
    disclosure->exposure->logic_tapping

Since:
    component_info:
        component on network machine:
        outside of building
    and you are worried about disclosure
infer new threat:
    disclosure->intrusion->
        reverse_engineer
(etc.)
```

Figure 7. Inferred Threats

As noted earlier, the information security domain model underlying the Gadfly also maps security services (Figure 8) to approved security mechanisms (e.g., software components). As a result, the kinds of mechanisms needed in the architecture to achieve a specific set of quality attribute objectives (security in this case) have been identified; the identify of these mechanisms can be used as a basis for a more fine-grained pattern matching within the code (e.g., search for cryptographic or password services in code).

5. Conclusions

5.1 Gadfly Contributions

The Gadfly is a knowledge-based assistant for helping designers create command centers, and for helping security analysts comprehend the security properties of existing (and perhaps evolving) command center systems. The Gadfly makes three separate but related contributions to program understanding: a focus on architecture-level specifications, a partitioning of domain models into separately-modeled and individually-selectable knowledge bases, and a demonstration of the symmetry between system design and system comprehension.

```
A primary service for disclosure->
    corruption->tamper_malicious
for DEC_Message_Q component
    is data_redundancy

A primary service for deception->
    falsification->substitution
for DEC_Message_Q component
    is password
(etc.)
A primary service for disclosure->
    intrusion->reverse_engineering
for ASCII_PRISM_MSG_GEN
    is access_control
(etc.)
```

Figure 8. Service Assignment and Inference

Architecture is the appropriate locus for specifying and comprehending system-wide properties. Continuing with security as an example, a component that is susceptible to logic tampering may represent a vulnerability in one system, but if it is enclosed within a more secure component (in inter-component relationship) or within a secure operating environment (a system boundary relationship), then it will not be a vulnerability. Thus, the property of vulnerability needs to be assigned to a specification of the system at a level that spans individual components: namely, the architecture level.

The second contribution of Gadfly—separable domain models—is as much an economic contribution as it is a technical one. The idea of developing separable, reusable domain models is not new—it is a founding principle of the Knowledge Sharing Initiative, which is developing techniques for creating "shareable ontologies" [22]. The economic and technical justifications for shareable ontologies are strong: cost amortization, community standards, evolutionary refinement of shared models, etc.

While we are not suggesting that the information security model is a shareable ontology—it lacks some of the characteristics specified by [22] that would make it one—we do claim it plays the role of shareable ontology within the Gadfly system. That is, constraining Gadfly domain models (currently, information security and C3) in various ways makes it possible to develop domain models that are focused on, for example, comprehension strategies and concept assignment to architectural components (as opposed to lines of code).

Thus, it is not hard to envision generalizations of the Gadfly that would allow designers to consult construction or comprehension strategies focused on fault-tolerance, distribution, real-time performance, or other quality attributes of systems. The development of specialized domain (comprehension strategy) models is more economically feasible than developing one-of-a-kind, system-specific mixed-content domain models that do not easily transfer to new applications.

Finally, the Gadfly demonstrates that the same kinds of human expertise needed to design systems are also needed to comprehend systems. Although design requires a synthesis of many kinds of expertise, system comprehension can be (and in practice often is) narrowly focused to the search for specific kinds of properties. The Gadfly demonstrated how one technology framework could re-use knowledge for both constructive (forward-engineering) and deconstructive (reverse-engineering) activities.

5.2 Future Direction

Although the Gadfly architecture admits the possibility of integrating arbitrarily many domain models to support construction and comprehension of systems, the current system requires that the elicitor have knowledge of the specific knowledge-bases being employed. Ideally, the elicitor would be able to independent of domain models. However, while it might be simple to implement this feature, it is equally important not to subject designers to "information overload." Some way of pruning or focusing the dialogue will be important, and this will be more difficult to accomplish. Similarly, modeling and managing the interaction between domain models (e.g., distribution and fault tolerance) will also be difficult, as these interactions imply trade-off reasoning that may be difficult to formalize.

A more practical extension of the Gadfly would be the development of domain models covering other kinds of quality attributes. While some work has been done to formalize static quality attributes such as modifiability, it would be interesting to see if this work could be formalized in such a way that it could be used by the Gadfly. Similarly, design heuristics for narrow ranges of issues such as real-time and fault tolerance could also be developed.

Acknowledgments

Special credit to: Mark Simos (Organnon Motives), who originated the Gadfly concept in the mid 1980's; Paula Matuszek (Loral), whose expertise in reasoning systems made the latest Gadfly possible; and Brian Koehler (US. Government) for his security expertise. The SEI is sponsored by the US Department of Defense.

6. References

[1] Pennington, N. Comprehension strategies in programming. In G. M. Olson, S. Sheppard, and E. Soloway (editors.) Empirical Studies of Programmers: Second Workshop. Norwood N.J. Ablex Publishing Co. 1987. pp 100-112.

[2] Pennington, N., Grabowski, B., The Tasks of Programming. In Psychology of Programming, J.M. Hoc, Green, T., Samurcay, R., and Gilmore, D., editors, Academic Press 1990, ISBN 0-12-350772-3.

[3] Brooks, R., Towards a Theory of the Comprehension of Computer Programs, in International Journal of Man-Machine Studies, vol. 18, pp. 543-554.

[4] Koenemann, J., Robertson, S., "Expert Problem Solving Strategies for Program Comprehension," in Proceedings of Computer Human Interaction (CHI'91), New Orleans, LA, April 1991, pp. 125-130.

[5] Soloway, E. & Ehrlich, K. "Empirical studies of programming knowledge" IEEE Transactions on Software Engineering, SE-10(5), September, 1984.

[6] Guindon, R., Curtis, B., Krasner, H., A Model of Cognitive Processes in Software Design: An Analysis of Breakdowns in Early Design Activities by Individuals, Microelectronics and Computer Technology Corporation (MCC) technical report STP-283-87, August 1987.

[7] Letovsky, S., Cognitive Processes in Program Comprehension, in Empirical Studies of Programmers, Soloway, E., Iyengar, S. eds., pp. 58-79, 1986, Ablex publishers, Norwood, NJ.

[8] von Mayrhauser, A. & Vans, A.M. "Comprehension processes during large-scale maintenance" in Proceedings of the 16th International Conference on Software Engineering. Sorrento, Italy, May 16-21, 1994. IEEE Computer Society Press. Los Alamitos, CA. 1994. pp. 39-48.

[9] Lutz, E. "The Knowledge Base Maintenance Assistant" in Proceedings of the Eight Knowledge-Based Software Engineering Conference, Chicago, Illinois, September 20-23, 1993. IEEE Computer Society Press, Los Alamitos, CA., 1993. pp. 86-95.

[10] Layzell, P., Freeman, M., and Benedusi, P. "Improving reverse-engineering through the use of multiple knowledge sources." Software Maintenance: Research and Practice. Vol. 7, 1995. pp. 279-299.

[11] Yen, J. and Hsiao-Lei, J. "An approach to enhancing the maintainability of expert systems." in Proceedings of the Conference on Software Maintenance 1990. IEEE Computer Society Press. Los Alamitos, CA. 1990. pp. 150-160

[12] Clements, Paul, "A Survey of Architecture Description Languages," to appear in Proceedings of the 8th International Workshop on Software Specification and Design, Paderborn, DE, 1996.

[13] Dijkstra, E., W., "The structure of the 'T.H.E.' multiprogramming system," CACM, vol. 11, no. 5; pp. 453-457, 1968.

[14] IEEE Transactions on Software Engineering, special issue on software architecture, April, 1995.

[15] Hayes-Roth, R., "Architecture-Based Acquisition and Development of Software: Guidelines and Recommendations from the ARPA Domain-Specific Software Architecture (DSSA) program," http://www.sei.cmu.edu/arpa/dssa/DSSAexp.html, 14 January, 1994.

[16] Abowd, G., Bass, L., Kazman, R., Webb, M., "SAAM: A Method for Analyzing the Properties of Software Architecture," in proceedings of the 16th International Conference on Software Engineering, Sorrento, Italy, pp. 81-90, May 1994.

[17] Parnas, D., "On the design and development of program families," IEEE Transactions on Software Engineering, vol. SE-2, no. 1, pp. 1-9, 1976.

[18] Moriconi, M., Qian, X., Riemenschneider, R., "Correct Architecture Refinement," IEEE Transactions on Software Engineering, vol 21, no. 4, April 1995.

[19] Searls, D., Norton, L., "Logic-Based Configuration with a Semantic Network," in The Journal of Logic Programming, Vol. 8, 1990, pp. 53-73.

[20] Wallnau, K., Solderitsch, J., Simos, M., "Construction of knowledge-based components and applications in Ada," in proceedings of AIDA-88, Fourth Annual Conference on Artificial Intelligence and Ada, pp. 3/1-21.

[21] Brachman, R., Schmolze, J., "An overview of the KL-ONE knowledge representation system," Cognitive Science, Vol. 9, No. 2, pp. 171-216.

[22] Neches, R., Fikes, R., Finin, T., Patil, R., Senator, T., Swartout, W., "Enabling Technology for Knowledge Sharing," AAAI, Fall 1991.

Part IV. Software Understanding and Evolution

Reengineering: An Engineering Problem

Peter H. Feiler

Software Engineering Institute
Carnegie Mellon University
Pittsburgh, PA, 15213, USA
phf@sei.cmu.edu

Abstract

This paper discusses a conceptual framework for reengineering that is based on a view of reengineering as an engineering problem. Under this view the objective of reengineering is to facilitate the disciplined evolution of a software-intensive system from its current state to a desired state. Applied to legacy systems this view offers a strategic approach to migrating legacy systems into systems that are maintained by incremental evolution. This view of reengineering, which takes the whole software engineering process into account, fosters a growth path by leveraging promising emerging software engineering technologies.

1. Introduction

In the last few years, the world has realized that the number of large systems being built from scratch is rapidly diminishing while the number of legacy systems in use is very high. New system capabilities are created by combining existing systems. At the same time, the context in which these systems have been built has changed. Changes range from changes in the application environment in which these systems operate (e.g., new sensors) to changes in hardware and software technologies (e.g., dramatic increases in processor speed and memory, high-level languages, improved methods). Some of the technologies used when these systems were built can hinder the system's ability to evolve to meet ever-changing demands in a cost-effective way.

As a result of these problems, a number of technology solutions have sprung up under a variety of labels, including reengineering, reuse, recycling, modernization, renovation, reconstitution, reverse engineering, design recovery, redocumentation, respecification, redesign, restructuring, and retargeting. Their focus is primarily on deriving information from code of legacy systems (reverse engineering), on restructuring and retargeting code, and on mapping derived design information into a new implementation. In particular, a number of tools exist to migrate information systems implemented in COBOL to new platforms and to upgrade their data representation into a relational form. Summaries

of reverse and reengineering markets and technologies are found in reports such as [14]. Categorizations of reengineering tools can be found in [7] and [8], as well as [12]. For a summary of software reengineering technology, the reader is referred to [1].

While reengineering tools will help in certain aspects of reengineering, reengineering is no more about tools than engineering is about tools. Just as engineering implies a disciplined process supported by engineering methods and automated tools, reengineering practice requires a disciplined process supported by methods and tools. In short, reengineering should be viewed as an engineering problem that requires an analysis of the problem, consideration of engineering trade-offs in its solution, and a disciplined practice of implementation. This captures the spirit of the American Heritage Dictionary (2nd edition) definition of *engineering* as "the application of scientific and mathematical principles to a practical end".

1.1 Definition

In this paper we are building on Chikofsky's work on a taxonomy [4], the results of the First Software Reengineering Workshop of the Joint Logistics Commanders Joint Policy Coordinating Group on Computer Resources Management [15], as well as insights from ARPA sponsored work including STARS, DSSA and from European efforts sponsored under the auspices of ESPRIT, Eureka (Eureka Software Factory), and the Institute for Systems and Software Technology of the Frauenhofer Gesellschaft [9].

Definitions for reengineering found in the literature include:

- the examination and alteration of an existing system to reconstitute it into a new form and the subsequent implementation of the new form;
- the process of adapting an existing system to changes in its environment or technology without changing its overall functionality;
- modification and possible further development of an existing system;

0-8186-7718-X/96 $5.00 © 1996 IEEE

• improvement of a system through reverse engineering (and restructuring) followed by forward engineering.

Figure 1 illustrates a taxonomy of terms related to reengineering by Chikofsky. In this commonly-accepted taxonomy, software system abstractions are represented in terms of life-cycle phases. Shown are requirements, design, and implementation. The traditional process of developing a system by creating these abstractions is referred to as *forward engineering*. *Reverse engineering* is the process of analyzing an existing system; identifying system components, abstractions, and interrelationships; and creating the respective representations. Redocumentation and design recovery are two forms of reverse engineering. Redocumentation refers to the creation and revision of representations at the same level of abstraction, while design recovery refers to the utilization of external information including domain knowledge in addition to observations of the existing system to identify meaningful higher levels of abstraction. The third process component of reengineering is restructuring. *Restructuring* is the transformation of representations at the same level of abstraction while preserving the system's external behavior. *Reengineering* is an engineering process to reconstitute an existing system into a new form through a combination of reverse engineering, restructuring, and forward engineering.

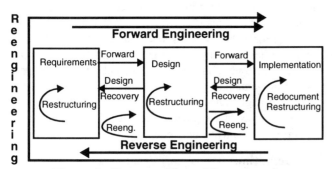

Figure 1. Common View of Reengineering

Reengineering relates closely to *maintenance*, which is generally viewed as consisting of corrective, perfective, preventive, and adaptive maintenance. According to ANSI/IEEE Std 729-1983, software maintenance is the "modification of a software product after delivery to correct faults, to improve performance or other attributes, or to adapt the product to a changed environment." In this paper we use the term *system evolution* to include software maintenance.

For the purposes of this paper, we take an encompassing view of *reengineering* as *addressing the engineering problem of (improving) cost-effective evolution of large software intensive systems, both existing and future, through appropriate application of effective best-practice engineering methods and tools*. Evolution of many existing systems is considered as not being cost-effective and cannot keep pace with changes in the application (domain) environment and changes in the computing environment and software engi-

neering technology. The term *legacy system* has been attached to systems with such characteristics. Changes in the application environment (the external environment the application system operates in) as well as in the implementation environment (the hardware/software platform) have to be assumed as a given and have to be accommodated (*engineering for change*). This need for engineering for change applies to both existing systems and new (or future) systems.

1.2 Context

The focus of this paper is on technical aspects of reengineering. However, economic, management, and acquisition aspects play as important a role in the successful improvement of the capability to reengineer legacy systems.

The cost of incremental change to a legacy system needs to be reduced. Criteria for deciding on the need for reengineering range from heuristics such as age of code and excessive maintenance personnel training cost (as found in a 1983 NIST document) to parameterized cost models (see [9, 16]). Improvement in this cost is anticipated by investing more than the minimal amount into reflecting the requested change. The additional investment would go into improving the way the system has been engineered with the result of smaller incremental cost in the future. If several legacy systems have to be reengineered, their similarities can be captured in a common reusable architecture, treating them as a family of systems rather than isolated point solutions. The cost models for reengineering, together with better understanding of the effectiveness of different engineering techniques, will allow software engineers to make reasonable engineering trade-offs as they choose a particular evolutionary reengineering strategy for a legacy system.

Engineering effectiveness is influenced by how well an organization is able to manage its engineering process and improve its engineering capability. SEI has provided leadership for government and industry to improve these organizational software process capabilities through work on the Capability Maturity Model (CMM)[sm] and its use as an assessment and improvement tool [6]. In the context of this paper we assume that the reader understands the relevance of such capabilities for an organization's ability to systematically, efficiently, and effectively reengineer legacy systems.

Successful improvement of legacy systems through reengineering also requires attention to improvements in the acquisition process and to legal concerns. The Joint Logistics Commanders Joint Policy Coordinating Group on Computer Resources Management has held a workshop series to address acquisition issues at the policy level [15]. One result is a Software Reengineering Assessment Handbook [16] which addresses a number of the economic and decision making issues. For further discussion of these and other inhibitors to successful transition of improved software engineering practice see the work done on transition models by SEI and others [13, 11].

2. A Reengineering Framework

In this paper we have cast reengineering as an engineering problem. As illustrated in Figure 2, problem solving involves an understanding of the problem, i.e., a clear understanding of the root causes in terms of its existing state, an understanding of the desired state, and a path (plan) to evolve from the current state to the desired state. The salient difference between engineering and reengineering as problem solving activities is that, with reengineering, a solution in form of the legacy system already exists. It imposes certain restrictions on the problem solving activity and the solution space.

The current state reflects properties of the existing system and the process by which the system is engineered (developed and maintained). A subset of those properties is undesirable, reflecting the problem to be solved. System understanding reflects the process of creating and maintaining an understanding of a system (through analysis, elicitation, and capture). System evolution represents the engineering activity of migrating the existing system to the desired state. Based on an understanding of the current and desired system state and available (re)engineering technology, an analysis making engineering trade-offs by considering technical, management, and economic risks and constraints results in a (re)engineering plan. During the execution of this plan (i.e., the actual evolution of the system through engineering activity), the plans may be reassessed taking into consideration changes in the context (e.g., technical changes such as promising new technologies or economic changes such as budget reductions or increases).

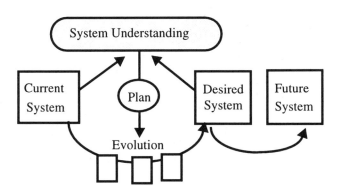

Figure 2. Reengineering Problem Solving

2.1 The Current System State

The root causes for the lack of cost-effective evolution fall into two categories: management of the engineering process and the engineering process itself. Management of the engineering process is addressed by process improvement technologies such as the Capability Maturity Model (CMM)[sm],

and will not be elaborated here. The second category represents technology root causes, i.e., the engineering process, methods, and tools. It will be the focus of further discussion.

Reengineering is considered when existing legacy systems enjoy properties worth preserving. Legacy systems also have a number of properties that are worth preserving. Examples include:

- Legacy systems are deployed and have undergone the scrutiny of real users with respect to their functionality meeting their real needs.

- Nonfunctional properties such as performance and accuracy have been fine-tuned.

- Corrective maintenance has resulted in "hardened" code and a wealth of test and validation capabilities.

- System history exists in the form of original designers, current and past maintainers, as well as bug report and change order records.

However, the same history of maintenance that stress-hardened the system causes a problem: the system becomes ``brittle" and increasingly resistant to change. The technology root causes to this brittleness can manifest themselves in a number of ways. Some examples are:

- Data structures not cleanly implemented. Communication concepts may not have been understood and shared memory (e.g., Fortran COMMON) is used as the communication mechanism.

- System representations such as architectural and design descriptions reflecting the application domain and the implementation approach may never have been created or documented; the documentation (and sometimes even the source code) is out of date.

- Assumptions about the application environment have been hardcoded in the implementation. Examples include assuming a point solution including fixed number and types of real-world objects.

- The computing environment evolved through several generations. For example, early hardware platforms were memory-limited, resulting in a number of sometimes (in today's view) convoluted implementation "tricks," such as overlay, instruction reuse, and cryptic user interaction. No operating system support was assumed. Today's computing environments typically consist of COTS standard operating systems, DBMS, window systems, and networking support, and are geared toward a high degree of interactiveness and "user-friendliness."

- The implementation technology has evolved from machine code with absolute addressing; to symbolic assembler, high-level algorithmic languages (COBOL, FORTRAN, ALGOL); to languages supporting data abstraction, modularity, information hiding, concurrency support, data modeling capabilities, etc. Design and implementation methods have been coming and going, each leaving its trademark in the code of legacy systems. This code may or may not accommodate the changes demanded from systems today.

Some of the root causes and their implications may be understood by some experts, but are not documented and available to the majority of software engineers. Information about legacy systems is often quite sparse, usually limited to the source code and/or executable, perhaps operations manual, and people maintaining the system. System representations such as architectural and design descriptions reflecting the application domain and the implementation approach may never have been created or documented; the documentation (and sometimes even the source code) is out of date. This lack of up-to-date documentation causes problems when migrating the current system to its new desired state.

2.2 The Desired System State

The desired system state is a combination of properties of the existing system to be maintained, properties expected of a system as part of state-of-the-art software engineering practice and implementation technology, and properties that have their roots in changing environments and are reflected in the system history, but may not have been explicitly expressed by the system user. Examples of maintained properties are functionality, performance, and accuracy. Examples of properties resulting from best practice software engineering and implementation technology include portability, modularity, structure, readability, testability, data independence, documented system understanding, openness (open system), interoperability, and seamless integration. Properties that address continuous change and provide flexibility include localization of information regarding certain different types of change in both the application domain and the implementation, introduction of virtual machine abstractions, and parameterization (dynamic as well as generation technology), COTS, and reuse of components. Properties that encourage reuse of existing engineering know-how include the existence of domain models, domain-independent software architectural principles, domain-specific architectures, and adaptable components.

The desired system state may be known to system users, system maintainers, original system builders, and best software engineering practice experts. The customer (user) may not necessarily be aware of all the potentially desired properties and may only be willing and able to invest in some. Some desired properties can be provided with proven technology, while others depend on emerging technology whose maturity for practical application has not been demonstrated.

2.3 System Understanding

The current state of an existing system and its desired state represent an understanding of the system. This understanding is based on artifacts of the existing system; knowledge and experience with the system as it may exist in users', maintain-

ers', and original builders' heads; and documented system history in the form of bug reports and change records.

Figure 3 illustrates the potential sources of information for system understanding. The artifacts are source code, manuals, and the executing system. The knowledge and experience with the system include understanding of engineering decisions, rationale, and possible or considered alternatives, as well as undocumented history and (typically nonfunctional) properties such as performance, robustness, work-arounds, etc. History provides insight into robustness of system components, types, and frequency of changes in the environment (and implementation).

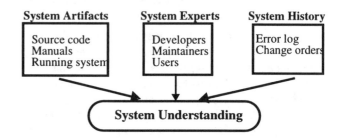

Figure 3. Creating System Understanding

Capture, representation, currency, and accessibility of this system understanding is a big challenge. As illustrated in Figure 4, a central component of system understanding is the system design record that document system representations at different levels of abstraction. This is complemented with rationale for design decisions, the software engineering process and methods used, and the evolution history.

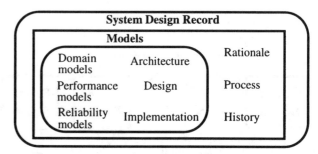

Figure 4. Representing System Understanding

These representations are *models* of the system. Models reflect views of the system focusing on certain aspects with different degrees of detail. The purpose of a model is to present a view that is understandable, i.e., not too complex. This is accomplished by the model capturing those abstractions that are relevant from a particular perspective. Some models focus on architectural issues while other models focus on data representation, behavioral, reliability and performance aspects of a system. Examples of models are domain models, domain-specific architectures, real-time scheduling models such as found with rate monotonic analysis (RMA) [10], performance models based on queuing theory, etc.

Models have different degrees of formality and may have the ability to be executed. The models may reflect designs (i.e., the notation they are expressed in needs to be transformed into executable implementations), or they may be executable and capture all the desired user functionality and can act as prototype implementations, which can be made more robust or efficient through reimplementation (i.e., transformation into a modeling notation that more appropriately satisfies the need).

As more than one system is considered, models can show their similarities and differences. Systems can be grouped into families. Some models focus on information about the application domain (domain models) while others focus on the implementation architecture. Domain models and domain-independent architectural modeling principles are combined to create domain-specific architectures. Those architectures are populated with components and adapted to the particular application needs. The result is a technology base of models that can be (re)used for a number of systems, leveraging existing engineering know-how. Domain analysis and architectural analysis contribute to the population of this technology base, while application engineering can get adapted utilizing these models (see Figure 5). Furthermore, the technology base can be expanded by the emergence of new modeling concepts, e.g., safety modeling.

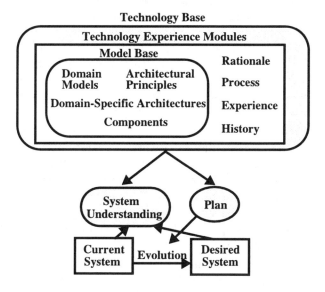

Figure 5. Engineering Technology Base

While some models represent the executing system itself, other models reflect constraints the system must satisfy. Those are models used to validate desired system behavior. Examples of such models are assertions validated in design reviews or verification, or translated into test suites and test data validating the behavior of the running system. When reengineering a legacy system, such test and validation models exist and have stood the test of time. They can be leveraged for verification and validation of the desired system. Depending on the particular migration path to the desired system, alternatives to full regression testing may be considered. One example is validation of functional equivalence at a certain level of abstraction through comparison of event traces [3].

Engineering decisions, rationale, and alternatives complement these models. They may be captured through elicitation process. The models together with the engineering knowledge are known in other engineering disciplines as *experience modules.*

In this idealized view, the amount of engineering information available to the engineer grows tremendously, resulting in information overload. In order to cope with this situation an intelligent intermediary (intelligent engineering assistant or engineering associate) will become essential to the successful utilization of the system understanding. Technologies that are potential contributors to this notion of intelligent assistant include case-based reasoning and intelligent tutoring.

2.4 Evolutionary Migration Path

The understanding of the system, both the current and the desired system state, is the technical basis for determining the particular reengineering strategy to be chosen. It requires analysis, considering alternatives, and making engineering trade-offs. Such a technical engineering analysis consists of two major components: choosing the degree of legacy leverage, i.e., what can be taken over and what has to be newly created; and choosing the approach for migrating over to the desired system, i.e., how to introduce the changes into the system. The reengineering case study by Britcher [3] nicely illustrates that no single approach is appropriate, but engineering trade-offs need to be considered.

The ability to utilize (recycle) as much as possible of the existing system in the process of evolving to the desired system may be termed *legacy leverage.* Both the existing and the desired system can be described in terms of a collection of models. For the legacy system, code exists. Other models may have to be derived from the code or other information sources. Certain abstraction may not exist in the legacy system or may reflect undesirable properties. The goal is to eliminate undesirable properties while at the same time introduce desirable properties. Choices have to be made as to which legacy system models to ignore, which ones to transform, and which ones to leave intact. This is illustrated in Figure 6.

The choices are driven by our understanding of the legacy and desired system properties as well as their reflection in the different models. In concrete terms this means that in some cases, undesirable properties of legacy systems can

101

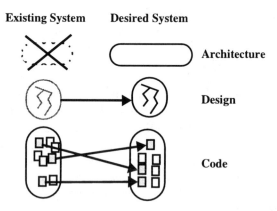

Figure 6. System Evolution

be eliminated by massaging the code or transforming the data representation, while in other cases a new architecture or data model has to be developed and only a few system components can be translated into the new implementation language.

The reengineered system can be introduced into the operational environment in a number of ways. The following are three classic approaches:

- **Complete rebuild** The desired system may be built separately from the legacy system, although parts of the legacy system may have been recycled. Once completed the new system is put into operation while the old system is shut down.

- **Incremental This approach incrementally phases out pieces of the legacy system.** The architecture of the desired system may be created and a skeleton implementation developed. A mapping between the data representation of the legacy and the desired system, implemented as a two-way transformation filter allows the skeleton desired system to run as a shadow of the "live" legacy system, while parts of the desired system implementation are completed and incrementally added to the skeleton.

- **Evolutionary** This approach evolves the current system towards the desired system by phasing in new features over time. The legacy system code may be restructured to introduce modularity and partitioning. Desired system properties are incrementally introduced into the existing system resulting in an incremental evolution of both the architecture and the system components.

Hybrid approaches are possible. Operational systems may be upgraded by both improving parts of the legacy system code (for continued use in the desired system), and by introducing a new architecture and a layer of wrappers as mediators between the legacy code and the desired system skeleton. One of the more innovative ways of evolving operational systems incrementally and on-line is discussed in [17].

Validation of the desired system can utilize existing testing capabilities. Validation can be decomposed into validating that the desired system still provides equivalent functionality

and into detection of bugs introduced in the reimplementation.

Risk analysis plays an important role in determining the evolutionary migration path from the current to the desired system. The choice of the particular reengineering strategy is affected by the risks inherent in alternative approaches and the ability to mitigate these risks. Some of the risks to consider include:

- cost, time, and effort of reengineering
- ability to eliminate or reduce undesirable system properties
- the maturity of new technology inserted into the system
- ability for system maintainers to adopt the new technology
- impact of deployment of the reengineered system
- impact of system changes on performance and robustness.

In summary, reengineering is an engineering activity that involves system understanding and evolution through application of appropriate engineering practices. The framework outlined here does not promote particular techniques but accommodates emerging technologies as they mature.

3. Conclusion

Reengineering has been presented from the perspective of an engineering problem. This framework takes a holistic view of reengineering that perceives reengineering as a problem solving approach to evolving legacy systems. Key elements are understanding of both the current and desired system and choice of a migration path, possibly in multiple steps, from the current to the desired system. The framework accommodates a range of strategies for reengineering and advances in software technology, such as domain modeling and software architecture-based solutions.

The reengineering framework presented above can be viewed as a framework for engineering of software-intensive systems that has been tailored for reengineering. A full discussion of this generalized framework is beyond the scope of this paper. However, the following characterization serves to quickly illustrate the validity of this claim (the reader may want to review Figure 5).

Gaining understanding of the desired system is in essence a requirements elicitation process. In this particular case, there is the added constraint that the desired system has to be evolvable from the current system. Similarly, gaining understanding of the current system is an activity that is not specific to reengineering. Techniques ranging from code analysis to domain and architectural analysis contribute to building up insight into a system. New system development is characterized by the fact that an existing software-intensive system may be non-existent or totally replaced without utilizing any parts. In this case understanding the existing state involves understanding the current operational environment into which the desired system is to be inserted. The new system may be developed and released in multiple iterations, and the migration plan may take on the characteristics of a spiral model of development [2]. As models of the current and desired system are established they may take on a number of characteristics. The models may emphasize commonality and explicitly represent variability among several instances of a system. As such they capture product line thinking. The models may focus on an open systems approach, i.e., having clearly defined interfaces between components of a system, allowing the components to evolve and be interchange while complying to the interface specification. Developers may look beyond the desired system, trying to anticipate future evolution of the system and evolve an architecture that accommodates such evolution.

3.1 Acknowledgments

This paper is a revised and shortened version of [5]. The thoughts expressed in this paper have been evolving within the SEI as well as in the software engineering community. The author attempted to condense them into these pages. I am particularly thankful for Floyd Hollister's inspiration to view reengineering from a problem-solving perspective. The content of this paper was shaped by discussions with and input from Bernd Bruegge, Maribeth Carpenter, Sholom Cohen, Larry Druffel, John Goodenough, Floyd Hollister, John Salasin, Dennis Smith, Scott Tilley, Doug Waugh, Jim Withey.

4. References

[1] Arnold, R.S., *Software Reengineering*, IEEE Computer Society Press, Los Alamitos, CA, 1993.

[2] Boehm, B.W., "A Spiral Model of Software Development and Enhancement." IEEE Computer, May 1988.

[3] Britcher, R.N., "Re-engineering software: A case study," *IBM Systems Journal*, Vol. 29, No. 4, 1990., pp. 551-567.

[4] Chikofsky, E.J. & Cross II, J.H., "Reverse Engineering and Design Recovery: A Taxonomy," *IEEE Software*, January 1990, pp. 13-17.

[5] Feiler, P.H., "Reengineering: An Engineering Problem." Technical Report CMU/SEI-93-SR-5, Software Engineering Institute, Carnegie Mellon University, July 1993.

[6] Humphrey, W.S., "Characterizing the Software Process: A Maturity Framework." IEEE Software, March 1988.

[7] *IEEE Software*, Editor-in-Chief: Ted Lewis, Published by the IEEE Computer Society, Elsevier Science Publishing Co. Inc., New York, NY, May 1990.

[8] Software Engineering Technical Committee Newsletter, IEEE Computer Society/TCSE, Editor: Samuel T. Redwine, Jr., Vol. 11, No. 3, January 1993.

[9] Witschurke, R., "Wiederverwendung in der Informationsverarbeitung: Re-use, Re-engineering, Reverse Engineering," ISSN 0943-1624, Institut fur Software und Systemtechnik, Universitat Dortmund, Germany, December 1992.

[10] Klein, M.H., Ralya, T., Pollak, B., Obenza, R., Harbour, M.G., "A Practitioner's Handbook for Real-Time Analysis: Guide to Rate Monotonic Analysis for Real-Time Systems", Kluwer Academic Publishers, 1993.

[11] Leonard-Barton, Dorothy, "Implementation as Mutual Adaptation of Technology and Organization." *Research Policy*, 17 (5), pp. 251-267, October 1988.

[12] Olsem, M.R., Sittenauer, C., Reengineering Technology Report. Technical Report, Air Force Software Technology Support Center, August 1993.

[13] Przybylinski, S.R., Fowler, P.J., and Maher Jr., J.H., "Software Technology Transition," a tutorial presented at the 13th International Conference on Software Engineering, Austin, TX, May 12, 1991.

[14] Rock-Evans, R.; Hales, K.: *Reverse Engineering: Markets, Methods and Tools*. London: Ovum LTD. 1990.

[15] Proceedings of the First Software Reengineering Workshop, JLC-JPCG-CRM, Joint Logistics Commanders, Santa Barbara, CA, November 1992.

[16] Software Reengineering Assessment Handbook. JLC-HDBK-SRAH, Air Force Software Technology Support Center, March 1995.

[17] Sha, L., et al., "Evolving Dependable Real Time Systems", Proceedings of the IEEE Aerospace Applications Conference, February 1996.

Coming Attractions in Program Understanding

Scott Tilley & Dennis Smith

Software Engineering Institute
Carnegie Mellon University
Pittsburgh, PA, 15213, USA
{stilley, dbs}@sei.cmu.edu

Abstract

This paper identifies a set of emerging technologies in the field of program understanding. Technical capabilities currently under development that may be of significant benefit to practitioners within five years are presented. Three areas of work are explored: investigating cognitive aspects, developing support mechanisms, and maturing the practice.

1. Introduction

This paper identifies a set of emerging technologies in the area of program understanding that are expected to lead to advances that will be available to advanced practitioners over the next five years.[1] Most of these technologies are based upon current research focus areas; a few are based on the judgment of the authors. Promising areas are those that hold potential for most positively affecting software engineers in the next five years, either by providing revolutionary new technologies that enable them to perform tasks in a (semi)automatic manner that previously were completely manual, or by enhancing their current capabilities through evolutionary improvements in existing program understanding tools and techniques.

Program understanding is the (ill-defined) deductive process of acquiring knowledge about a piece of software through analysis, abstraction, and generalization. Increased knowledge facilitates common activities as performing corrective maintenance, reengineering, and redocumentation. While much current research is focused on ways to automate program understanding, such significant amounts of domain knowledge, practical experience, and analytical power are required that today it is largely a manual task.

The issue of program understanding is critical in our ability to both maintain and reengineer legacy systems. Many organizations are faced with the problem of maintaining aging software systems constructed to run on a variety of hardware, programmed in obsolete languages, and suffering from the detritus that accumulates from prolonged maintenance. As the software ages, the task of maintaining it becomes both more complex and more expensive. Software engineers must spend an inordinate amount of time attempting to create an abstract representation of the system's high-level architecture by exploring its low-level source code.

A legacy program may be inherently difficult to understand for several reasons. The complexity of the problem domain can make the realization of the solution (i.e., the program) itself complex. Poor design, unstructured programming methods, and crisis-driven maintenance practices can contribute to poor code quality, which in turn affects understanding. Programming language-based structuring mechanisms create a problem of compatibility between the structure of the program and the structure of the mental model the individual may have of the program. In many cases the only up-to-date, complete, and trustworthy information about a system is the source code; all other information must be gleaned from this.

Problem areas in program understanding can be clustered around the following three broad themes:

- **Investigating cognitive aspects**: How humans apply problem-solving techniques when attempting to understand a program. Issues include comprehension strategies, computer-supported cooperative understanding (CSCU), and maintenance handbooks.

- **Developing support mechanisms**: How tools can be used to aid comprehension. Issues include alternate data gathering techniques, advanced knowledge organization schemes, and hypertext-based information exploration.

- **Maturing the practice**: How emerging technology can be matured such that it becomes part of the state-of-the-practice. Issues include making technology sufficiently robust that it is applicable to real-world problems, performing empirical studies to test the effectiveness of

---

1. Since this paper attempts to summarize a changing field, it is intended to be dynamic in nature; it will be updated at regular intervals. Comments are invited and suggestions for inclusion are welcome.

This paper will also appear in *Proc. CASCON '96*. Reprinted with permission.

105

support mechanisms, and defining a universally accepted lexicon of terms.

Each of the three central themes are discussed in turn below. Cross-cutting issues that affect each of these themes, such as scaleability, extensibility, and applicability, are discussed in Section . These issues do not represent specific areas of program understanding work *per se*, but are extremely important nonetheless.

2. Investigating cognitive aspects

Investigation into the *cognitive aspects* of program understanding focuses on studying the problem-solving behavior of programmers engaged in understanding tasks. Because there are wide differences in the productivity of maintenance programmers, it can be fruitful to analyze the strategies used by those who are successful. This will lead to tools and techniques that better support program understanding activities.

2.1 Comprehension strategies

Software engineers employ *comprehension strategies* when they are attempting to understand a program. Investigating comprehension strategies involves identifying what information programmers use and modeling how they use it to understand a piece of source code. It is a fundamental area of research that crosses many disciplines, including software engineering, education, and cognitive science. Better understanding of these strategies will enable the development of tools and techniques that provide much greater support for program understanding than is currently possible.

Numerous theories have been formulated to explain the problem-solving behavior of maintainers and programmers engaged in program understanding. An excellent survey of this area compared six cognitive models of program understanding [1] . The different cognitive models are usually variations on the theme of top-down understanding, bottom-up understanding, iterative hypotheses refinement, or some opportunistic combination of the three. The bottom-up approach reconstructs the high-level design of a system, starting with source code, through a series of "chunking" (mentally clustering logically related code fragments together) and concept assignment steps. The top-down approach begins with a pre-existing notion of the functionality of the system and proceeds to earmark individual components of the system responsible for specific tasks. The iterative refinement method involves creation, verification, and modification of hypotheses until the entire system can be explained using a consistent set of hypotheses. The opportunistic model describes the maintainer as someone exploiting both top-down and bottom-up cues as they become available.

Studies show that maintainers regularly switch between these different models depending on the problem-solving task at hand. Consequently, no single model explains all program understanding behavior, even though some models subsume other models. By investigating new comprehension strategies that better reflect actual understanding approaches used by expert programmers, the circumstances under which specific comprehension strategies are more appropriate will become clearer.

2.2 Computer-supported cooperative understanding

The cooperative use of tools by multiple people working together to solve a problem is known as computer-supported cooperative work (CSCW). Applying CSCW techniques to program understanding can be called *computer-supported cooperative understanding* (CSCU). While still in its infancy, CSCU shows promise in program understanding tasks requiring the effort of more than a single software engineer.

As software systems grow, both in size and in complexity, it will become increasingly common for teams of programmers to perform maintenance tasks together. This means the traditional approach to program understanding, which has focused primarily on a single person working in isolation, will have to evolve to support cooperative understanding. CSCU will enable software engineers with diverse areas of expertise to contribute their knowledge to analyzing and modifying legacy systems.

2.3 Maintenance handbooks

As more knowledge is gained about how people actually understand programs, through the development of cognitive models and their validation in comprehension experiments, it would be beneficial to codify this knowledge. This could take the form of *maintenance handbooks* that capture expertise and strategies proven effective for both general and specific maintenance scenarios. Such handbooks would provide practitioners with prescriptive solutions to common problems.

Programmer experience seems to be a significant factor in the success of an understanding task. Experienced programmers tend to have superior programming knowledge, make better use of tools, and employ systematic comprehension strategies to make the task more tractable. They also tend to have invaluable domain expertise that can be used when confronted with a new task that resembles a previous one. Instead of concentrating on how the program works (as a less experienced person might), a more experienced software engineer tends to form representations of "what the program does." They attempt to reuse knowledge and expertise from previous tasks by first looking for a link between what they perceive and an existing model structure before conceiving a new model.

A maintenance handbook that captures such expert strategies would be advantageous to others who lacked the same experience. Other engineering disciplines make extensive use of similar handbooks. For example, electronics technicians have reference handbooks to guide them while repairing complex circuitry.

3. Developing support mechanisms

One way of helping software engineers with program understanding tasks is through computer-aided *support mechanisms*. Such tools and techniques can significantly help manage the complexities of program understanding by facilitating the extraction of high-level information from low-level code. The support mechanisms attempt to free the software engineers from various tedious, manual, and error-prone tasks such as extensive code reading, searching, and pattern matching by inspection.

Reverse engineering is a particularly important type of program understanding support mechanism. It is seen as an activity which does not change the subject system; it is a process of examination, not a process of alteration. It can aid program understanding through the identification of artifacts, the discovery of their relationships, and the generation of abstractions. The discussion below categorizes the support mechanisms according to three canonical reverse engineering activities identified in [2]: (1) data gathering; (2) knowledge organization; and (3) information exploration (includes navigation, analysis, and presentation).

So far, reverse engineering has been relatively successful in aiding program understanding. It is more robust and scaleable than pure artificial intelligence-based automated program understanding tools, more tractable than formal methods based on theorem-proving, and more attractive than non-computer-aided techniques such as code reading. Promising work on support mechanisms can be classified as extending the capabilities of one (or more) of the three canonical activity areas.

3.1 Data gathering

In order to identify a system's artifacts and relationships and use them for later construction and exploration of higher-level abstractions, the gathering of raw data is required. Hence, *data gathering* is an essential reverse engineering activity. New developments in data gathering techniques will benefit practitioners by providing them with more accurate and extensive capabilities with which they can extract artifacts of interest from their programs.

3.2 Leveraging mature technology

The predominant technique used for data gathering is parsing the subject system's source code to extract abstract syntax trees with a large number of fine-grained syntactic artifacts and dependencies. To accomplish this, many researchers have spent an inordinate amount of time building parsers for various programming languages and dialects. However, mature technology already exists in the compiler arena to parse source code, perform syntactical analysis, and produce cross-reference and other information usable by other tools, such as debuggers; it is not necessary, in most cases, to recreate these tools.

By leveraging proven compiler-based technology for data gathering, users of reverse engineering tools will be assured of predictable results. This is not currently the case: there are several extraction tools in use that, when applied to the same source code, produce widely different results [3]. Practitioners and researchers alike will benefit greatly once the data already available from traditional tools are properly used in newer program understanding tools.

3.3 Alternate sources of data

In addition to using data gathered from traditional sources such as compiler-based static analysis, there is work on integrating *alternate sources of data* into reverse engineering toolsets. Examples include dynamic analysis (e.g., profiling), natural-language content analysis (e.g., from comments and/or other documentation), and informal data extraction (e.g., interviewing). These non-traditional techniques can provide a basis for more balanced and complete understanding of a program by emphasizing different attributes of its artifacts and relationships. This can be especially beneficial to software engineers working with programs that are difficult to understand based solely on data gathered through static source code analysis. For example, dynamic analysis can provide data that aids understanding of distributed, real-time, client-server programs (applications that are becoming increasingly predominant).

In-line comments are a potentially rich source of data about the program, and are often used by human experts when attempting to understand a piece of code. However, automatic analysis of such commentary, and other written documents such as program logic manuals, is more difficult. Techniques such as natural language analysis are needed to parse the commentary. In addition, some judgment must be used to link comments to the code it (purports to) describe. The comments may be isolated in the code, or (even worse) they may no longer reflect reality and in fact may provide conflicting information if they were not updated in tandem with the code they are associated with. Nevertheless, comments represent such a potentially rich data source that work continues to focus on their analysis.

A third source of data about the program is not the subject system itself, but is rather derived from its human maintainers. Interviewing techniques can used to capture the expertise such people have. This type of "corporate knowledge" is a potentially invaluable asset if it can be applied to program understanding.

3.4 Data filtering

No matter what the source, the amount of data gathered for understanding very large systems can be enormous. Large quantities of data can easily overwhelm our ability to assimilate it. Therefore, the use of intelligent *data filtering* techniques will play an important role in aiding program understanding. Simply presenting the user with reams of data is insufficient; understanding is gained only through the assimilation of the data. In a sense, a key to program understanding is deciding what is material and what is immaterial: knowing what to look for---and what to ignore [4].

Data filters can be used to extract selected artifacts and/or relationships from a rich data source. For example, a profiling tool may be used to gather complete run-time call information from a program, but the software engineer may only be interested in a subset of these calls. Such filters can also be used to interface between common data representations shared among tools and information specific to selected tools.

3.5 Knowledge organization

For program understanding, gathered data must be put into a representation that facilitates efficient storage and retrieval, permits analysis of the artifacts and relationships, and yet reflects the users' perspective of the subject system's characteristics. This representation is usually based on a data model. A data model enables us to understand the essential properties and relationships between artifacts in a system. Without some form of model, raw data is almost impossible to understand. Humans rely on *knowledge organization* techniques to create, represent, and reason about data models.

Advanced modeling techniques

Classical physical data models, such as the hierarchical, network, and relational models, capture data and their relationships in the form most suited to computer manipulation. In contrast, *advanced modeling techniques* capture data and their relationships in a form more suited to human understanding. They provide abstraction mechanisms that aid the software engineer in organizing knowledge about the subject system.

One such technique is conceptual modeling, which is that it is closer to the human understanding of a problem domain than to a computer representation of the problem domain [5]. The emphasis is on knowledge organization (modeling entities and their semantic relationships) rather than on data organization. The descriptions that arise from conceptual modeling activities are intended to be used by humans---not machines. This is one of the reasons that conceptual modeling is eminently suited to aiding program understanding: the focus on the end user is paramount.

Iterative domain modeling

Domain modeling is the process of identifying, organizing, and representing the structure and composition of elements in a problem area. It can be used as an aid in organizing knowledge about a subject system. The construction of the domain model can precede reverse engineering (in which case it is used to guide the understanding process by supplying expected constructs), or it can be constructed during reverse engineering (if no previous knowledge about the domain was

available). These two uses, as a guide to and as a product of reverse engineering, can also be combined into *iterative domain modeling* to support exploratory understanding. The benefit to the software engineer is to provide a new method of tool-assisted program understanding: standard components can be automatically recognized by tools and used to populate the domain model, while non-standard components can be semi-automatically or manually classified and used to extend the domain model.

Scaleable knowledge bases

As stated above, the volume of data produced during the reverse engineering of a large-scale software system is considerable. Such size and complexity necessitate *scaleable knowledge bases* using fundamentally different approaches to repository technology than is used in other domains. For example, not all software artifacts need to be stored in the repository; it may be perfectly acceptable to ignore certain details for program understanding tasks. Coarser-grained artifacts can be extracted, partial systems can be incrementally investigated, and irrelevant parts can be ignored to obtain manageable repositories. Once available, scaleable knowledge bases will enable improved understanding of large software systems.

3.6 Information exploration

Because the majority of program understanding takes place during *information exploration*, it is perhaps the most important of the three canonical reverse engineering activities. While data gathering is required to begin the reverse engineering process, and knowledge organization is needed to structure the data into a conceptual model of the application domain, the key to increased comprehension is exploration: it facilitates iterative hypothesis refinement. Exploration includes navigating through the hyperspace that represents the information related to the subject system, analyzing and filtering this information with respect to domain-specific criteria, and using various presentation mechanisms to clarify the resultant information.

Navigation

Large software systems, like other complex systems, are non-linear and may be viewed as consisting of an interwoven and multi-dimensional web of information artifacts. The web's links establish relationships between the artifacts. These relationships can be component hierarchies, inheritances, data and control flow, and others generated as part of the reverse engineering process. *Navigation* allows programmers to traverse the information web as part of their exploratory understanding activities.

Reducing disorientation: As the size of this web grows, the well known "lost in hyperspace" syndrome limits navigational efficiency. Several solutions are being investigated to solve this classical problem of *reducing disorientation* within a large information space. These include maps, multiple windows, history lists, and tour/path mechanisms

[6] . Unfortunately, many of these methods do not scale up well.

A more promising approach is the use of composite nodes; they reduce web complexity and simplify its structure by clustering nodes together to form more abstract, aggregate objects [7] . Composite nodes deal with sets of nodes as unique entities, separate from their components. Navigation tools that support such clustering will be very useful in program understanding.

WWW-based interfaces: Notwithstanding the disorientation problem discussed above, hypertext-based navigation can empower the software engineer to choose and deploy navigation strategies that are most suitable to the task at hand. There are several current reverse engineering systems that employ a hypertext user interface. However, such interfaces usually remain proprietary and require users to learn new interaction methods and tools to use them effectively. Work is underway on evolving these hypertext-based systems to use more generally available graphical user interfaces, most notably browsers for the World-Wide Web (WWW). The explosive growth of both the Internet and the WWW will make it possible for program understanding technology to be delivered to practitioners in a manner that is consistent with their current environment, using *WWW-based interfaces*, and which integrates reverse engineering support mechanisms independent of their actual installation location.

Advanced pattern matching: Pattern matching is an essential part of program understanding. Much effort is spent locating relevant code fragments that implement the concepts in the application domain. Reverse engineering involves the identification, manipulation, and exploration of artifacts in a particular representation of the subject system via pattern recognition: either mentally by the programmer, or mechanically by the support mechanism. Artifacts are segmented into features, which are then pattern-matched against stored collections of expected structural motifs. The success of this process depends critically on the recollection of existing structural knowledge and on the ability of the person (or tool) to recognize its presence in a noisy map.

An emerging trend is the development of *advanced pattern matching* techniques that concentrate more on the meaning of the code rather than on its form. They will enable the software engineer to reduce the amount of time and effort spent switching between domains (e.g., from the application domain to the implementation domain) during program understanding. If the patterns searched for can be represented in terms more closely related to the application domain---in whose terminology most change requests are couched---then the programmer can make more changes to the source code more easily and will less unforeseen circumstances.

Analysis

The critical step in which abstractions are derived from the raw data is *analysis*. The resultant information is used to develop further insights for understanding the system. There

are many new analysis techniques currently under investigation that may have significant impact on practitioners in a few years. One example is slicing [8] , where the program code fragments that may affect the value of selected variables are identified. By isolating only those statements that can change the value of a variable (or variables), the cognitive overhead of understanding a large piece of code is reduced significantly.

End-user programmability: Rather than limiting software engineers to only designer-defined analyses that are invoked using canned methods, it is better to provide mechanisms through which programmers can define their own analyses. Various leading-edge reverse engineering systems that aid program understanding provide full-fledged programming languages in which analysis methods can be encoded. The use of *end-user programmability* in reverse engineering support mechanisms will enable analysis techniques to be developed on an as-needed and task-specific basis, thereby increasing the likelihood of their applicability to software systems with unique characteristics.

Automation level: It is important to develop a tradeoff between the functions that are handled automatically by a reverse engineering tool and the capability of the tools to accept human input and guidance. Work is currently focused on how to best balance between automatic, semi-automatic, and manual approaches, where each is more applicable, and how the support mechanism can "know" when to ask for expert guidance. Using the correct *automation level* can affect both the time taken to complete a program understanding task, and the level of comprehension achieved.

Higher-order impact analysis: Estimating the effect of changes before they are irrevocable has always been an important part of program understanding. Engineers try to avoid causing massive changes to a system due to maintenance, in part due to practical issues such as recompilation delays, but more importantly because they are unwilling to create "change waves" that ripple throughout large parts of the system; the potential for induced errors is too great. Current tools perform impact analysis primarily at the syntactic level. Newer research focuses on *higher-order impact analysis* tools that allow "what if" scenarios to be performed and the result of proposed changes known beforehand. This will enable the programmer to interact with the impact analysis tool more at the application-domain level than the implementation-domain level. For example, estimating the impact of a change to a module on the system's architecture.

Presentation

Because humans make considerable use of visual metaphors for communicating and understanding information, it is important to have flexible *presentation* mechanisms. Currently, most reverse engineering systems provide the user with fixed presentation options, such as cross-reference graphs or module-structure charts. While this set might be considered adequate by the system's producers, there will always be users who want something else. It should be possible to create multiple, perhaps orthogonal, structures and view them using a variety of mechanisms, such as using different graph layouts provided by external toolkits.

Advanced visualization techniques: Exploiting research in graph layout theory has already proven effective in aiding program understanding; witness the proliferation of graphical representations of source code in current reverse engineering systems. Refinements to this traditional area also show promise, for example using so-called "fish-eye" views to provide emphasis on selected focal points while still retaining relative location information [9] . Exploratory work is underway on more *advanced visualization techniques* using three-dimensional data imaging, virtual reality "code walk-through," and user-defined views. It is hoped that one more of these techniques will provide new insights into program understanding.

Tailorable user interfaces: Presentation integration can occur at different levels (e.g., the window system, the window manager, the toolkit used to build applications), and the toolkit's "*look and feel*" [10] . The standardization provided by presentation integration lessens the "cognitive surprise" experienced by users when switching between tools. However, what is really needed is a *tailorable user interface* that permits the user to impose their own personal *taste* on the common look and feel. This refinement of presentation integration moves the onus---and the opportunity---for reducing cognitive overhead induced by the user interface from the tool builder to the tool user.

Multimedia: Presentation of analysis results has traditionally taken the form of charts, tables, or graphs. The recent proliferation of *multimedia*-enhanced computers opens a door to new ways of presenting this same information. Work into the use of audio and video annotations as a way of commenting source code, capturing programmer rationale, and presenting information to the user in more familiar and readily accessible ways shows promise.

4. Maturing the practice

Until recently, much work in program understanding focused on "toy" programs that bore little resemblance to real-world legacy systems. Fortunately, this has begun to change. As the state-of-the-art *matures* and becomes the state-of-the-*practice*, promising work is focusing on facilitating the insertion of program understanding technology, on performing empirical studies, and on creating an agreed-upon lexicon of related terms. The benefit to practitioners will be to make program understanding tools and techniques easier to use, more applicable to everyday tasks, and more widely perceived as a legitimate technology capable of solving real-world maintenance problems.

4.1 Technology insertion

For program understanding technology to make more of an impact and gain wide-spread use, it must address several transition issues, including scaleability, extensibility, and applicability. Only then can *technology insertion* take place on a larger scale. The benefit of inserting program understanding technology into the current development and maintenance processes will be to make the new capabilities available to more users in a more uniform manner, so that using new techniques such as slicing becomes as commonplace as established techniques such as browsing cross-reference charts.

Real-world legacy software systems can contain millions of lines of source code. Support mechanisms need to be sufficiently robust to function effectively at this scale. Increasing the extensibility of the support mechanisms through end-user programmability, such as scripting or macro languages, will make the integration of program understanding tools and existing tools in the practitioners toolkit easier. Such extensibility will also increase the applicability of the overall toolkit, so that current reverse engineering techniques (which are sometimes narrowly focused) become more generally applicable.

It has been repeatedly shown in other fields (e.g., CASE) that for a new technology to be successful it must coexist with existing tools and processes; forcing programmers to adopt radically new ways of working rarely works. It is only through pragmatic technology insertion that program understanding will become less of a novelty and more of an accepted practice.

4.2 Empirical studies

Experimentation should play an important role in both the theory (investigating cognitive aspects) and the practice (developing support mechanisms) of program understanding. Without *empirical studies*, there is no systematic way to validate (or refute) hypotheses or claims of functionality. With empirical studies, practitioners will be able to make better and more informed decisions as to the applicability of certain program understanding technologies to their specific problems.

Most engineering disciplines conduct empirical studies, either as initial investigation or as theory validation. The level of sophistication of the empirical studies carried out is a good yard-stick by which one can measure the maturity of a field. While there have been efforts in performing program understanding experiments, much more work is needed. Towards this end, there is a clear need for a common test suite: a subject system (or systems) that can be used to perform metrics measurement on. It is extremely important for the continued maturation of the field that scientific, verifiable, and repeatable empirical studies be performed. Such studies will benefit software engineers by providing them with independent and indisputable proof of the gains possible using program understanding technology, rather than relying on unsubstantiated claims.

Practitioners also stand to gain through participating in early-adoption trials and case studies. Such experiments can be win-win situations. Researchers and tool developers gain by validating, strengthening, or refocusing their work on practical problems. Users gain by hands-on experience with the technology before others. They also have the opportunity to guide its development so that it will be more beneficial to their daily work.

4.3 Common terminology

Established fields of study usually have a common vocabulary with agreed-upon meanings for key phrases. As the program understanding community matures, it too will develop *common terminology* that will aid researchers and practitioners alike. By facilitating clear and unambiguous exchanges of information, one of the hallmarks of a developing field will be addressed: confusion over the meanings of new "buzz words."

A seminal paper in reverse engineering by Chikofsky and Cross appeared in the January 1990 issue of IEEE Software [11]. It represents the first attempt at creating a taxonomy of common terminology related to program understanding, providing often-cited definitions of "reverse engineering" and many related terms. Unfortunately, different interpretations of this and other related phrases remain. For example, there are several near-synonyms for "reengineering," illustrating the relative immaturity of the field's nomenclature. Work is continuing on refining and expanding this early lexicon.

Practitioners will benefit from common terminology by forcing vendors to use the same words to represent the same functionality. For example, if a tool claims to extract "business rules" from source code, there must be a clear definition of what a business rule is in this context and how it is represented. The move towards common terminology represents a coming attraction in program understanding that is long overdue.

5. Summary

This paper presented coming attractions in program understanding: improved technical capabilities under development that could be ready for evaluation and demonstration in the next five years. Three promising lines of research were discussed: investigating cognitive aspects, developing support mechanisms, and maturing the practice. These new capabilities have the potential to make a significant positive impact on forward-looking practicing software engineers.

5.1 Acknowledgments

Thanks to John Salasin, Paul Clements, and Alan Brown for providing comments on early drafts of this paper. This work was supported in part by the U.S. Department of Defense.

6. References

[1] A. von Mayrhauser and A.M. Vans. "Program Comprehension During Software Maintenance and Evolution." IEEE Computer, pp. 44-55, ugust 1995.

[2] Scott R. Tilley and Dennis B. Smith. "Towards a Framework for Program Understanding." Proceedings of the 4th Workshop on Program Comprehension (WPC '96: March 29-31, 1996; Berlin, Germany), pp. 19-28, IEEE Computer Society Press, 1996.

[3] Gail C. Murphy, David Notkin, and Erica S.-C. Lan. "An Empirical Study of Static Call Graph Extractors" Proceedings of the 18th International Conference on Software Engineering (ICSE-18: March 25-29, 1996; Berlin, Germany) , pp. 90-99, IEEE Computer Society Press, 1996.

[4] Mary Shaw. "Larger Scale Systems Require Higher-Level Abstractions." ACM SIGSOFT Software Engineering Notes, 14(3):143-146, May 1989.

[5] Bent B. Kristensen and Kasper Osterbye. "Conceptual Modeling and Programming Languages." ACM SIGPLAN Notices, 29(9), September 1994.

[6] Jacob Nielsen. Hypertext and Hypermedia. Academic Press, 1990.

[7] Marco A. Casanova, Luiz Tucherman, Maria J.D. Lima, Jose L.R. Netto, Noemi Rodriguez, and Lui F.G. Soares. "The Nested Context Model for Hyperdocuments." Proceedings of Hypertext 91 (San Antonio, TX; December 15-18, 1991), pp. 193-201.

[8] Mark Weiser. "Program Slicing." IEEE Transactions on Software Engineering, SE-10(4):352-357, July 1984.

[9] Margret A.-D. Storey and Hausi A. Muller. "Graph Layout Adjustment Strategies." Proceedings of Graph Drawing 95, September 1995.

[10] Anthony I. Wasserman. "Tool Integration in Software Engineering Environments." Proceedings of the International Workshop on Environments (Chinon, France; September 18-20, 1989), pp. 137-149, Springer-Verlag (G. Goos and J. Hartmanis, eds.), 1989.

[11] Elliot J. Chikofsky and James H. Cross II. "Reverse Engineering and Design Recovery: A Taxonomy." IEEE Software, 7(1):13-17, January 1990.

Discovering a System Modernization Decision Framework:
A Case Study in Migrating to Distributed Object Technology

Evan Wallace

National Institute of Standards and Technology
Manufacturing Engineering Laboratory
Gaithersburg, MD, 20899, USA
wallace@cme.nist.gov

Paul C. Clements, Kurt C. Wallnau

Software Engineering Institute
Carnegie Mellon University
Pittsburgh, PA, 15213, USA
{clements, kcw}@sei.cmu.edu

Abstract

Many organizations face a serious challenge introducing new technologies into existing systems. Effective modernization requires knowing and articulating specific goals for the reengineering effort, conscious selection of technologies and technical approaches that can achieve those goals in the context of the class of system being upgraded, a staged migration plan, and an integration strategy to make in-hand components work under the newly adopted architecture. Although the study of reengineering is moving towards an engineering discipline, there are as yet no proven decision frameworks that allow an organization to rationally choose a modernization strategy. This paper provides an in-depth look at the engineering trade-offs made in modernizing a manufacturing engineering design system to use distributed object technology. From this case study the outlines of a more general re-engineering decision framework can be seen, and are discussed.

1. Issues in System Modernization

System modernization is a specialized application of system reengineering, which is the disciplined evolution of a system from its current state to a new one [12]. Modernization involves substantial technical and business risk, because by its very nature it is the result of a prediction about the desirability of that future state. Substantial capital investment may be committed (such as adopting new support environments, or investing in intensive reprogramming), and the system often must continue operation free of disruption in the meantime.

Faced with the question of modernization, management must answer many questions, many of which may not ever be explicitly articulated and thus not given sufficient consideration. What is to be gained through modernization? What aspects of the system and its supporting infrastructure will be modernized? What are the technology options that can be brought to bear? Are they of sufficient maturity and acceptable risk? Is the current system well-enough understood at the architectural level to judge the feasibility and risk in

migrating to the chosen new technology? How will the stages of migration be managed? What will the effects be on the organization's business and customer base? These and other questions must be considered carefully; the alternative is a baseless migration towards a technology with glossy brochures, that may not be in the organization's best interests at all.

On the other hand, prudent modernization and technology refreshment can increase an organization's capabilities in many tangible and intangible ways. The system may take on new functionality, better performance, higher modifiability, tighter security, or become able to interoperate with a new or important class of partner systems. Derivative systems may be spun off quickly and reliably in a product line approach. Personnel may become fluent in state-of-the-art tools and techniques, thus increasing their value. Productivity and morale may be lifted. Market share may be increased.

The decision-making process is a complex one, with dozens of variables, many of which depend on each other. A decision framework that enumerates the decision points, articulates the questions that must be answered at each decision point, and suggests strategies based on those answers would, we believe, be of enormous practical importance. The purpose of this paper is to propose the foundations for such a decision framework. A complete framework is far beyond the scope of the reported work, but it is hoped that by identifying the decision points, the contributing factors to each, and the decision algorithms for at least some, that we will lay a foundational skeleton that the community as a whole might work together to fill.

This paper reports on our experience from a case study in system modernization. The system was a toolset for analyzing manufacturing designs; the reengineering effort involved migrating to an integrated, distributed, object-based paradigm. The case study highlighted important lessons about this class of technology migration, out of which emerges the basis of an embryonic decision framework for modernization.

This paper will also appear in *Proc. Int'l Conf. Software Maintenance*, 1996.
Copyright © 1996 by The Institute of Electrical and Electronics Engineers, Inc. All rights reserved.

113

The remainder of the paper is organized as follows: Section 2 provides necessary background on the constraints and influences which governed the technical decision-making processes within the case study. Section 3 describes the case study in detail, and assesses the final result. Section 4 generalizes from this assessment of a specific modernization effort to an outline of a re-engineering decision framework, and populates this framework with illustrations from the case study. Finally, Section 5 states the key conclusions of this paper and indicates possible avenues for further work.

2. Influences on Case Study

A modernization effort involves a delicate balancing of many kinds of constraints and influences. The most important classes of such influences are described in the following sections.

2.1 Organizational Influences

NIST and the SIMA Project

The U.S. National Institute of Standards and Technology (NIST) has a long-standing role in investigating technologies for the integration of manufacturing systems. NIST's role in aiding U.S. industries' competitiveness is through facilitating the development of non-proprietary standards and advocating their use. The Common Object Request Broker Architecture (CORBA) being developed by the Object Management Group (OMG) consortium is viewed as one such potential standard that could provide a means for improved integration for the manufacturing industry [13]. OMG has over five hundred members and is still growing, and vendors are supporting CORBA on the platforms that are commonly used for manufacturing (product realization) activities.

The NIST Systems Integration for Manufacturing Applications (SIMA) program has a goal to increase the flexibility and integration of computer based activities that comprise the whole product realization process from beginning part design through part production [31]. To this end, SIMA sponsored a project to test and demonstrate the viability of CORBA technology, and to determine whether the standard is suitable for agile manufacturing and virtual enterprises.

Sandia and the TIE-In Project

Sandia National Laboratories is a federally-funded research and development laboratory that supports the U.S. Department of Energy (DOE). Among its many activities, Sandia investigates the manufacture of high-quality, dependable systems. This has resulted in the development of numerous software components to support manufacturing engineering design, some of which formed the basis for the case study.

Sandia is interested—as are other U.S. government agencies—in exploring the transfer of internally-developed technologies to commercial application. The DOE Technical Exchange of Information to Industry (TIE-In) project is tasked with making DOE-developed technology available

outside of DOE. Among other things, TIE-In is interested in knowing whether CORBA can help make this technology available to U.S. industry while also addressing obvious security issues.

SEI and the Component Integration Project

The Software Engineering Institute (SEI) is a federally-funded research and development institute whose mission is to improve the state of software.

Within the SEI, a component integration project addresses issues relating to the integration of complex systems from pre-existing software parts. The project focuses on systems that are comprised of commercial off-the-shelf (COTS) components. One objective of the project is to define software architectures, integration techniques, and technologies to support component integration in distributed, heterogeneous computing environments. The current technology focus of the project is on the use of distributed object technology, and CORBA in particular, for component integration.

2.2 Application Domain Influences

Manufacturing processes for product realization are many and varied and require specialty skills. For example, job scheduling, shop layout, and manufacturability analysis are all specialized skills, often requiring specialized support technology. The notion of virtual enterprise is seen as a means of supporting the flexible combination of these specialty skills and tools from many highly-specialized companies, and as a means of improving U.S. manufacturing competitiveness through faster market response and higher manufacturing quality. Technology for virtual enterprises must support:

- the integration of separately-developed, specialized computer-based technologies covering a range of manufacturing processes;
- geographical distribution of computing resources and heterogeneous computing environments;
- fee-for-service brokering of computer-based services to enable free-market competition.

SIMA has developed a model that identifies the constituent activities of manufacturing and the data needs and data outputs of these activities [32]. We searched through this activity model for a candidate activity around which to build a prototype integrated system using CORBA. Such a candidate needed to be simple enough to quickly prototype, yet sophisticated enough to constitute a reasonable test of the integrating technology. We found such characteristics in the engineering design analysis activity.

Engineering analysis is a computer simulation performed on part designs to test a part's performance under certain real-world use conditions. This analysis can be used not only to determine a design's adequacy at performing its function but also be used in the optimizing a design, and lowering a part's cost and/or weight while preserving confidence in its performance. Due to the specialized nature of design software and the expertise needed to perform the design function, it is a good candidate for computer network-based fee-for-service applications. Also, the kinds of software needed to support engineering analysis often require specialized computing resources (supercomputers, graphics display, etc.), thus serving our desire to address distributed, heterogeneous systems.

2.3 Current Sandia System and Desired Outcome

Sandia provided components from the Sandia National Laboratory Engineering Analysis Code Access System (SEACAS) for the modernization case study. SEACAS is a collection of components that perform the computer based processing tasks needed to support the analysis activity: they provide functions such as defining test conditions (problem description), analysis simulation, and visualization (see Figure 1.). These tools share a common data format called EXO-

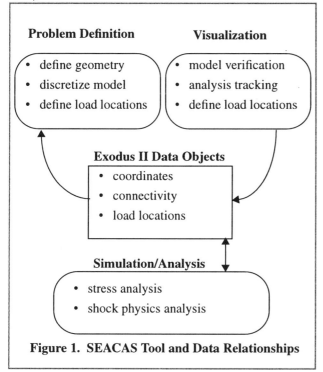

Figure 1. SEACAS Tool and Data Relationships

DUS II [33]; thus these tools already have a form of data integration. The analysis function is done using a Finite Element (FE) approximation technique[30]. The problem definitions describe how to break up the part being analyzed into elements, how to connect the elements together as well as the conditions to be modeled and simulated, such as material characteristics and forces to apply in the simulation

The SEACAS toolset has many components in each functional category both as a result of the history of its development and the wide variety of approximations appropriate to each actual analysis. We met with experts from Sandia and developed a scenario incorporating a subset of the tools in the

SEACAS toolset. This included two problem definition tools FASTQ and GEN3D, an analysis simulator JAS3D and a visualizer BLOT. The general usage scenario is as shown in Figure 2..

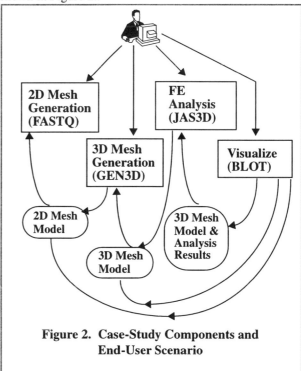

Figure 2. Case-Study Components and End-User Scenario

An analyst uses FASTQ to produce a *discretized*[1] model of the part to be analyzed. This model is stored in a file in the EXODUS shared data format. The visualizing tool BLOT then can be run against the model producing a graphical representation for inspection by the analyst. Based on that inspection the analyst either reruns FASTQ to correct the model or he feeds the model to GEN3D to extrude it into a three dimensional model. Another inspection/correction iteration may occur for the resulting three dimensional model before the model is fed to the analysis tool. One or more analyses may be conducted, with results evaluated via the visualization tool or through inspection of other JAS3D output. Iteration among the various steps is also possible, for example the analysis results might suggest changes to the underlying 2D or 3D mesh.

In the scenario described above end-users are responsible for launching individual tools (often with personalized scripts), managing tool output (in private directories), and preparing the output of one tool for use as input to another (sometimes with manual application of filters since not all SEACAS tools use the same version of the Exodus data format—both format and tools have evolved over time). In effect, the end-user is the system integrator, continually

---

1. A two- or three-dimensional mesh that models the solid as a set of many smaller linked solids.

exposed to all of the low-level details and technology dependencies exhibited by the SEACAS components.

TIE-In (the NIST and SEI projects as well) wanted to demonstrate a modernization of SEACAS that would:

- present a uniform virtual environment for end-users that would reflect the nature of the analysis activity and not the idiosyncracies of specific SEACAS components;

- support wide-area distribution of SEACAS services while maintaining control over the software that provides these services (some of which contain classified algorithms);

- provide a measure of security not just against theft of software but also reliability and prevention of malicious or inadvertent denial of service; and,

- deliver reasonable, usable and predictable performance to end-users who are otherwise accustomed to using computer services in local area network settings.

It seemed to us that distributed object technology, and CORBA in particular, might provide a means of achieving these objectives—or at least the SEACAS modernization would reveal limitations of CORBA in meeting these objectives—either of which would meet our organizational and project objectives.

2.4 Technology Influences

Many organizations will have made some technology commitments in advance of a thorough requirements analysis and design trade-off analysis. It is important to understand the consequences of these commitments on both the target system and software development strategies. Our decision to use CORBA as a foundation for the modernization effort represents an important technical constraint:

- CORBA is new technology, and although there are numerous commercially-available object request brokers (ORBs), the underlying CORBA specifications are changing. The instability of implementations and specifications is an important design factor.

- CORBA is intended to be only a communication infrastructure within a larger distributed object technology—the object management architecture (OMA) [14]. ORB vendors are not required to implement OMA services. Thus, the decision to rely upon a vendor's implementation of OMA services presents risks, as does the decision to implement interim services in anticipation of OMA services not yet available.

- There are no well-established architectural *styles* [17] for distributed object technology that have been demonstrated to be effective with the OMA. It is possible to analogize from established architectural styles; however, there may be subtle mismatches between these and the OMA. For example, a repository-style integration architecture [19] can in theory be supported by the OMA. However, the OMA lacks support for critical database features, and

assumptions concerning object granularity, security, etc., could cause severe performance problems.

- The OMA specifications describe services from an object consumer's perspective, not from the perspective of an object supplier. Thus commercial ORBS exhibit a wide range of non-standard implementation features. Such vendor dependencies represent potential risks to the survivability of a re-engineering solution given the volatility of the OMA specifications and marketplace. Unfortunately, it is not always easy to identify such dependencies, nor to avoid them if identified.

2.5 Systems influences

Different kinds of system properties will strongly influence modernization strategies. System properties may either be intrinsic to the system, or they may be extrinsic properties that the system must exhibit. Examples of intrinsic properties include: distributed processing, client-server orientation and multi-processing. Examples of extrinsic properties (or *quality attributes* [15]) include fault tolerance, multi-level security and performance[2].

Different systems exhibit different patterns of intrinsic and extrinsic properties; some of these patterns arise with sufficient frequency to warrant classification as a kind of system. We refer to the kind of system that was the subject of the case study as a *component-based* system. While all (real) systems are composed of components, in our usage the term component-based refers to systems that are comprised of multiple software components that:

- are ready "off-the-shelf" whether from a commercial source (COTS) or re-used from another system;

- have significant aggregate functionality and complexity, i.e., play the role of subsystems in the final system;

- may be self-contained and execute independently;

- will be used "as is" rather than modified; and,

- are treated as black- (or very opaque-) boxes in that their implementations are independent of each other.

Examples of component-based systems can be drawn from many domains, including: computer-aided software engineering (CASE), design engineering (CADE) and manufacturing engineering (CAME); office automation; workflow management; and command and control.

The stipulation that multiple components must be involved is important since this intrinsic system property defines a range of problems that must be addressed and dictates the kinds of engineering techniques and technologies needed to address these problems. One key problem intro-

---

2. One way to differentiate these classes of properties is to consider intrinsic properties as representing bound design and implementation decisions, while quality attributes are externally-visible system properties that deal with issues other than functionality.

duced by component-based systems can be summed up with the phrase *architectural mismatch* [16]: components embed assumptions about the architectural and operational context in which they operate, and these assumptions often conflict with the architecture of the target system and with assumptions manifested by other components.

The engineering techniques that are needed to address architectural mismatch are centered on the notion of systems integration as a design activity. In contrast to the development of other kinds of systems where system integration is often the tail-end of an implementation effort, in component-based systems determining how to integrate components is often the only latitude designers have. Quality attributes such as usability, availability, and maintainability are influenced by and help shape integration decisions such as: which components need to be integrated to which; how component execution is coordinated; which architectural mismatches must be resolved, and which mechanisms are used to adapt components to remove these mismatches.

To understand where such mismatches might arise when integrating two or more components, it is useful to have some idea of what it means to integrate components—and this turns out to be surprisingly elusive. One useful way to think of integration is as a *relationship* between two integrated entities, where the relationship has four dimensions, or *aspects*: control, data, process, and presentation [20][21]:

- Control integration describes how components make requests of (or invoke) each other's services.

- Data integration describes how components make data available to each other.

- Process integration describes what end-user or business process is supported by the integration relationship.

- Presentation integration describes how end-users interact with the integration relationship, i.e., how to achieve a uniform model of human interaction.

All four aspects will be reflected to different degrees in each integration relationship. Although these aspects are entirely qualitative and descriptive, and there are no causal connections between these and quality attributes, they provide a useful if limited framework for discussion, and will be referred to in the following discussion.

2.6 Architectural Influences

Frameworks vs. Opportunistic Integration
We refer to technology infrastructures that present a coherent and common view of integration within a class of systems as *integration frameworks*. A number of integration frameworks have been developed to support component integration in the CASE domain, each with its own particular emphasis on one or more aspects of integration [26]. For example, PCTE [27] provides a range of integration services that emphasize data integration, while ToolTalk [28] provides services that emphasize control integration. Within the manufac-

turing domain the SEMATECH CIM[3] application framework is both an integration framework and an instance of an architectural style referred to by the object-oriented community as an *application framework*[4]; it emphasizes control and process integration.

The cost of developing or using application or integration frameworks can be great, and includes both the cost of developing or licensing the framework and the cost of introducing changes in engineering practices. In some situations a more opportunistic approach to integration may be desirable. That is, rather than use a framework that imposes a common approach to all integration problems, each integration problem is viewed as a unique problem. While opportunistic integration may result in extra effort and inconsistent solutions, it is flexible and can address application-specific design problems and can accommodate new integration technologies. Opportunistic integration does not imply hacked, ad hoc solutions; indeed, there are several architectural styles that may be applicable to component-based systems that do not depend upon integration frameworks (e.g., the "communicating objects" style [17]).

Functional vs. Structural Architectures
A major design issue is whether to adopt an architectural style that emphasizes the functionality of the system and its components, or a style that emphasizes the structure of a system based on how the components interact rather than on what functions they provide. We refer to the former class of styles as functional styles, and the latter class as structural styles.

Functional styles are far and away the predominant approach to component-based systems; this approach defines components in terms of their functionality, e.g., database. The interfaces between components are often expressed as function-specific application programming interfaces (API) or as standard mechanisms (e.g., SQL for databases). Numerous examples of functional architectures can be found in [19]; a good example for the CAME domain is found in [22]. Functional architectures are good for describing what kinds of technologies are needed to implement a desired system functionality, the overall role each technology will play and which technologies are likely to interact. They are weak when it comes to describing non-functional properties of a design (throughput, reliability, etc.), and generally result in an ad hoc integration

---

3. SEMATECH is an industry consortium; the Computer Integrated Manufacturing (CIM) Application Framework is one product of the consortium.

4. The term "framework" in application framework and integration framework describes different concepts: the former describes a partial application that is completed by the developer or integrator, while the latter describes infrastructure that is independent of application functionality.

where each particular inter-component relationship is implemented as component-specific "glue."

Structural styles are of more recent vintage but have been emerging as the study of software architecture has intensified. Rather than defining component interfaces in terms of specific functionality, structural styles define interfaces in terms of the role a component plays in the architecture—often describing a *coordination model* (i.e., control and data flow). A commonplace illustration of a structural style is UNIX pipes and filters; more sophisticated illustrations include structural models for flight simulators [23], the Simplex architecture for evolvable real-time systems [24], and UNAS for distributed, concurrent systems [25]. Since the structural form of the architecture is often directly related to the architecture's intrinsic coordination model, a range of quality attributes can be understood from any particular design expressed using the structural form; further, the structure defines a uniform strategy for inter-component integration. However, it may be difficult to determine just what function is being computed by a system from a structural architecture.

3. Modernization Case Study

With these technical and non-technical influences in mind, it is possible to describe the architecture and implementation of the prototype, and to describe in some detail how a particular trade-off analysis of the influences and technical approaches described above are reflected in the solution.

3.1 Architectural Issues and Trade-offs

Figure 3. depicts a top-level view of the prototype architecture. The three layers reflect the different kinds of integration issues being addressed:

- The (top-most) presentation and process layer addresses presentation and process integration. Both aspects are addressed in the prototype by Tk/TCL [29]. It is depicted as a separable entity from the lower layers, principally because it can be designed and implemented in a way that is independent of object location or how the objects are implemented, thus providing some support for the desired end-user "virtual environment."

- The (middle) logical object layer addresses control and data integration. Control integration is achieved using a structural rather than functional interface (this is discussed in more detail later); data integration is achieved by object persistence and relationships. It is at this layer that most of the detailed architectural issues related to quality attributes are addressed.

- The (bottom-most) physical component layer addresses the management of physical resources (files, operating system processes, etc.) and issues of architectural mismatch between the components and the architectural forms reflected by the logical object model (discussed more fully in Section 3.2).

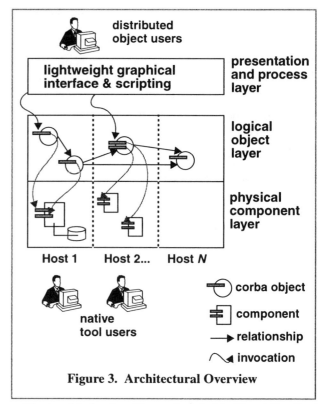

Figure 3. Architectural Overview

The two kinds of end-users depicted in Figure 3. reflect a non-intrusive modernization strategy. It was important to preserve the existing methods and mechanisms for accessing tool services since (a) we were dealing with a technology that had many unknowns (CORBA), and (b) we were only migrating a portion of the SEACAS system to distributed object technology. Supporting both classes of users involved additional coding effort, for example to provide complementary tool data management services to those provided in the native environment, so that object-based users did not interfere with native tool users (and visa versa). But the extra effort was deemed less important than supporting a non-intrusive modernization.

Figure 4. depicts the logical object layer in more detail. The objects that implement the structural architecture are referred to as structural objects in Figure 4.. Two kinds of structural objects are depicted in Figure 4.: application objects and framework objects. Application objects implement system functionality and most of the coordination model, while framework objects provide needed integration infrastructure services (which were needed despite our desire to pursue an opportunistic integration approach). Framework objects are discussed in detail in Section 3.2.

The coordination model is implemented by application objects that behave as state machines that are either consistent or inconsistent with respect to some specification. Specifications represent human input (e.g., mesh models, analysis instructions), and consistency represents whether component-generated data was derived from the specification. Components are invoked as a result of update opera-

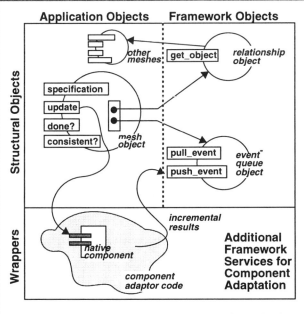

Figure 4. Structural Architecture (Overview)

tions; they return diagnostic data directly to the invoking object (not shown); they may also return other data, such as incremental results from long-running analysis sessions, via event channels.

This structural approach simplified the task of understanding and analyzing how the object model would behave in a wide-area distributed setting. For example, we were able to tune the coordination model to various kinds of network failure modes (partition, node crashes, etc.), and to express these tunings directly in the structure of the architecture. The structural approach also helped to focus the component adaptation/wrapping to those aspects of the design that were sensitive to coordination issues, for example whether simultaneous invocations of the component were supported, how to address network disconnections.

We considered adopting a functional approach, essentially just wrapping the SEACAS components "as is" using a remote procedure call (RPC) metaphor[5]. We rejected this because the approach would not address data integration requirements: this would have required us to develop additional data management services, or else to parameterize the RPC interfaces to allow data interchange of lengthy data streams—neither of which was desirable. Beyond these problems, an RPC approach would have exposed tool technology to the programming interface; this would make the modernized SEACAS system less adaptive to new components and component upgrades, as the revealed technology dependencies are invariably reflected in end-user systems and interfaces such as we developed.

---

5. Using the earlier concepts, we can describe the RPC approach as opportunistic integration (minimal or no use of framework services) in a functional architecture.

3.2 Detailed Design Trade-Offs

A number of modernization trade-off decisions arose at more detailed levels of the design and implementation of the modernized system. For discussion purposes these have been categorized according to the aspects of integration which they addressed (process, presentation, control and data integration).

Process, Presentation Integration in Distributed Systems

The detailed design of our prototype was driven largely by the end user process it supports. There were many similarities in steps between the user process activities for two dimensional mesh generation, three dimensional mesh generation and mesh analysis. These similarities led naturally to the model shown in Figure 5., which depicts the major

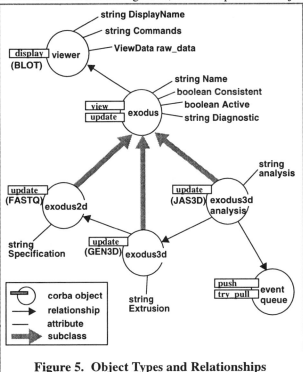

Figure 5. Object Types and Relationships

object types found in the logical object model layer of the architecture (Figure 3.). The structure of these objects reflects the end-user process: an analyst using the SEACAS tools is primarily concerned with data elements, (e.g. input commands, output diagnostics, and mesh binaries), and relationships among them. These relationships are expressed in the object model as object relationships, and are modified by the value of attributes such as Consistent. Relationships and their modifying attributes capture the evolution of a mesh instance through the user process from 2D to 3D and finally to a full analysis.

The decision to express end-user processes in the form of a logical object model represents a major design trade-off between the desire to achieve a tight coupling between an object model and end-user processes versus the potential need to evolve end-user processes over time: all data schemas embed process assumptions, and tighter coupling between process and data model implies a less evolvable data model [34]. For this case study we decided that the process of describing and analyzing solid models was sufficiently mature that drastic changes to the process model were not likely. The point to note, however, is that this modernization decision was informed both by quality attributes (evolvability) and domain-specific influences (the stability of end-user processes in this case).

In an interactive system issues of performance are closely related to end-user process. Because of the compute-intensive character of analysis simulation, we anticipated that this could be run on a supercomputer, while we expected an analyst to be sitting in front of a workstation (PC or supermicro), and operating in a remote (to the simulation service) location. Thus, another set of trade-off decisions involved where on a network topology objects live, and how much visibility end-users have on object location and on the performance characteristics of the underlying hosts (for example, to estimate the time required to complete an analysis session).

For this design, we opted to make object location and host details as transparent as possible to end users. This involved a trade-off between end-user flexibility and complexity. Our decision to opt for object location transparency was informed by an objective assessment of the state of CORBA and CADE technology and the current state of manufacturing engineering: there simply was no technical or business basis upon which to develop or anticipate the use of advanced service brokering services that might require greater visibility into object and network topologies. This decision also represented a desire to introduce the minimum number of new concepts to the existing system that are necessary to support our modernization objectives. Nevertheless, despite this simplification, details of object location were reflected on the structural model in the way visualization and the event queue objects are defined.

Control, Data Integration: Needed Framework Services

Since the OMA is not yet a sufficiently mature integration framework, and since the ORB implementation we were using did not implement OMA services beyond the minimal CORBA specification, we were predisposed to try to use the OMA to support opportunistic integration. However, we discovered that even an opportunistic approach to integrating component-based systems requires an extensive range of integration framework services (as this term is defined in Section 3.1). Two categories of integration framework services were needed: one to deal with integration in the logical object model layer, and one to deal with tool adaptation at the physical component layer.

At the logical object layer both control and data integration services were required. While both forms of integration are

supported OMA services, our ORB implementation did not support them. This necessitated a trade-off among:

- the degree to which we wanted our logical object model to mirror the end-user process model;
- the amount of code we were willing to write to implement OMA-compliant services; and,
- the degree to which we were willing to have the design reflect a non-standard approach by implementing subsets or alternative forms of OMA services.

In the final analysis, we opted to introduce non-standard forms of OMA services. We determined that the initial technical objective—providing a virtual environment to the end-user—was important enough to justify integration at the logical object layer, but we knew that this would require use of OMA services such as object persistence and relationships. At the same time, resource constraints on the effort made the implementation of standard OMA services problematic. Therefore, we implemented the needed OMA services, but only partially and in ways not consistent with the OMA specifications. This resulted in a design that was functional but that does not reveal the capabilities of the OMA; this represents a compromise to NIST and SEI objectives.

At the physical component level integration services are required that support what are referred to as "wrappers" in Figure 3.. These services include: operating system process and file management; management of process families; detection of component failures and crashes; and system diagnostics. From this list it is obvious that these services are highly dependent upon the host platform and properties of the components being adapted. What is less obvious is that there are additional services needed that are dependent upon the target system's software architecture. While this is not surprising when one considers that the purpose of tool wrapping is to resolve *architectural mismatch*, and must therefore address both architecture and component aspects of adaptation, it is not generally realized that architectural design must also accommodate the cost and complexity of developing architecture-specific component adaptation services.

To illustrate architecture-specific integration consider, from Figure 4., the connection of component output to an event channel. This clearly requires adaptation services to support an interface from the tool wrapper to an OMA object. However, depending on the nature of the components and host platform, a range of other wrapper-level services may also be necessary to support this connection. For example, in our implementation, sending incremental results to the event channel required the assistance of a "helper process" that monitored component output files for changes in status; new data on these files was filtered and passed to the event channel. The use of helper processes required additional services to support parsing and filtering of tool data, and also services for managing the life cycle of process families (e.g., termination of the component should terminate helper processes).

4. Outlines for a Re-engineering Decision Framework

The case study has illuminated several of the goals, approaches, and influences at work in a non-trivial modernization (technology incorporation) effort. As suggested in the introduction, we believe that these aspects form the embryonic basis for a decision framework for this kind of reengineering. Specifically, we see evidence for a framework whose structure is greatly simplified in Figure 6. We will discuss each of the named outputs in turn.

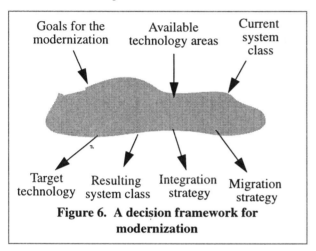

Figure 6. A decision framework for modernization

Technology Target

What technology will be imported into the enterprise and its products as a result of the modernization effort? The first task for deciding this is to explicitly articulate the motivations and goals for the effort. Technical goals often include enhancing the qualities or utility of the subject system. These typically include better performance or resource utilization, new or enhanced functionality, or the addition of qualities such as security, availability, or support for multiple users in a distributed environment.

The last was an explicit goal of the modernization effort described in the case study and drove us to adopt distributed object technology. Further motivation included adoption of a technology (CORBA) whose use was widespread and growing, in order to be able to provide systems that were compatible with it. Although this effort had a decided research or investigative theme, the desire to support a popular technology often occurs in production organizations as well. A tool vendor adopts a widely-used technology to make his products compatible and hence more marketable. A consumer is motivated by the high level of support and flexibility offered by popular technologies. Market forces often transcend issues of technical superiority.

Organizational goals may include the ability to rapidly turn out new versions of the system, or to deploy the system in multiple versions as a product line. Sometimes, as was the case for us, the organization's goal is to become adept at handling a particular technology.

Two themes may be seen. The first theme is that the new technology has been chosen *a priori*, for market or organizational reasons. The second is that other qualities are being sought, and the choice of technology to achieve those qualities is still unresolved. In between lies the case where a technology area has been chosen (such as distributed object technology), but the precise instantiation of it (such as CORBA) has not. The model in Figure 7 is suggested.

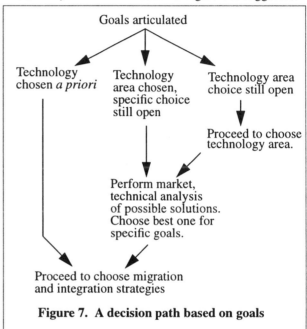

Figure 7. A decision path based on goals

But more generally, we see that choice of technology—if articulating the goals fails to identify it directly—is a function of the motivating goals for the effort, as well as properties of available technology areas such as maturity, available, breadth of user community, expense, in-house expertise, suitability of purpose in achieving the goals, and the ability of the current software architecture to accommodate the technology. One such decision-making process is described in [18].

Resulting System Class

Our case study illustrated modernizing a component-based system. This is in contrast to organic systems whose parts are built or modified in-house, and also in contrast to tightly confederated systems where the components work together via tightly interactive protocols (such as complex application programmer interfaces). In the latter case, the components are less able to do useful work in isolation. These two classes suggest quite different strategies for integrating the parts, and maintaining the integrity of the integrated whole.

Other classes of systems that have equally broad implications for system-building, but which were not explicitly addressed in our case study, were real-time systems. As is the custom, we distinguish between hard-real-time systems (which must meet concrete process deadlines), soft-real-time systems (whose correctness criteria are often phrased in terms of non-unit probabilities or process priorities), and non-real-time systems (which have implicit timing requirements). Likewise, the decision about whether the system will work in a distributed or parallel computing environment has broad ramifications for its migration to new technology.

The choice of system class is influenced most heavily by the choice of imported—for example, CORBA strongly supports non-real-time component-based distributed systems— but also a function of the system class before modernization begins. Organizations will find it harder, and hence less likely, to shift the class of system.

Migration Strategy

At least four factors play a role in determining if modernization should be all at once, or staged incrementally.

The first factor is the difference between the current system and the desired state of the new system. For example, adding hard-real-time constraints to a non-real-time system represents a major migration effort that is much different than upgrades to achieve a new system in the same class.

The second factor is whether or not the goals for modernization include any that would be met by intermediate products developed by an incremental update strategy.

The third factor is a function of the organization. How much expertise, over and above what is available in the organization, will be required for importing and deploying the chosen technology?

The fourth factor is a function of the chosen technology area. A mature technology, with an active user community and plentiful support tools can be fielded with less risk than a new technology with little community experience.

Figure 8 shows how goals, system class, organizational factors, and technology suggest a migration strategy.

Figure 8. Choosing a migration strategy

Integration Strategy

Integration strategy has to do with how to make the components in a component-based system interact with each other in a correct, usable, and efficient manner. Integration strategy may have a different meaning for a system in another class; this is an area of the framework that we have not explored. However, for component-based systems, the issues (each discussed previously) are as follows.

One is the issue of frameworks versus opportunistic integration, which was discussed in Section 2.6. Resolving this choice will be a function of the technology chosen (for example, choosing CORBA as provided by the OMA framework resolves this choice), the components at hand, and the organization's expertise. Another, also discussed in Section 2.6, is the issue of functional versus structural architectures. A third is concerns aspects of integration (control, data, process, or presentation), discussed in Section 2.5. The last is strongly influenced by the first; a framework-based approach will emphasize a particular range of integration aspects.

5. Conclusions and Potential Next Steps

We have described a case study in reengineering via technology modernization. The case study was a high-fidelity exercise in that its motivations were authentically motivated by real-world concerns such as supporting a distributed client base and making separately-developed tools work seamlessly to perform industrially useful work.

In addition to providing specific lessons and trade-offs about the introduction of distributed object technology in a component-based system, we have shown how the modernization exercise was influenced by several factors such as the goals nature of the participating organizations, the class of system being updated, and the choice of technology. We believe that a decision framework for modernization exists, and that our case study represents a single path through that framework. The case study has illuminated the path we travelled, suggested nearby paths, and hinted at the existence of the framework as a whole.

We have presented the work in terms of the decision framework, because we believe that now is an opportune time to challenge the reengineering community to work collaboratively towards building and instantiating as much of this framework as possible. Real-world reengineering case studies will become more common and available as the field matures. We hope and expect that an industrially robust decision framework for reengineering, based on sound experience, may soon be within our collective grasp.

Acknowledgments

The SEI is sponsored by the U.S. Department of Defense. Neil Christopher of NIST Manufacturing Engineering Laboratory deserves a large measure of credit for making this work possible and for setting out the broad objectives for the work.

6. References

[12] SEI Reengineering Project Description, http://www.sei.cmu.edu/~reengineering

[13] *The Common Object Request Broker: Architecture and Specification, Revision 1.1*, OMG TC Document 91.12.1, Object Management Group, 492 Old Connecticut Path, Framingham, MA, 01701

[14] *Object Management Architecture Guide, Revision 2.0*, Second Edition, OMG TC Document 92.11.1, Object Management Group, 492 Old Connecticut Path, Framingham, MA, 01701.

[15] Abowd, G., Bass, L., Kazman, R., Webb, M., "SAAM: A Method for Analyzing the Properties of Software Architecture," in Proceedings of the 16th International Conference on Software Engineering, Sorrento Italy, May 1994, pp. 81-90

[16] Garlan, D., Allen, R., Ockerbloom, J., "Architecture Mismatch: Why Reuse is so Hard", IEEE Software V12, #6, pp17-26, November 1995.

[17] Garlan, D. and Shaw, M., "An Introduction to Software Architecture," in Advances in Software Engineering and Knowledge Engineering, vol. I, World Scientific Publishing Company,1993

[18] Brown, A., Wallnau, K., "A framework for systematic evaluation of software technologies" to appear in the special issue of IEEE Software on assessment of software tools, September 1996.

[19] Brown, A., et. al., *Principles of CASE Tool Integration*, Oxford University Press, 1994, ISBN 0-19-509478-6.

[20] Thomas, I., Nejmeh, B., "Definitions of tool integration for environments," IEEE Software 9(3), pp. 29-35, March 1992.

[21] Wasserman, A., "Tool integration in software engineering environments," in F. Long, ed., *Software Engineering Environments, Lecture Notes in Computer Science 467*, pp. 138-150, Springer-Verlag, Berlin, Germany, 1990.

[22] Brown, A., Judd, R., Riddick, F., "Architectural issues in the design and implementation of an integrated toolkit for manufacturing engineering" submitted to the International Journal of Computer Integrated Manufacturing.

[23] Abowd, G., Bass, L., Howard, L., Northrup, L.,*Structural Modeling: An Application Framework and Development Process for Flight Simulators*, SEI Technical Report, CMU/SEI-93-TR-14, August, 1993, Software Engineering Institute, Carnegie-Mellon University, Pittsburgh, PA.

[24] Sha, L., Rajkumar, R., Gagliardi, M., A Software Architecture for Dependable and Evolvable Industrial Computing Systems, SEI Technical Report, CMU/SEI-95-TR-005, July 1995, Software Engineering Institute, Carnegie-Mellon University, Pittsburgh, PA.

[25] Royce, Walker, and Royce, Winston, "Software architecture: integrating process and technology" TRW Space and Defense, Quest, Summer 1991. Also see http://www.stars.reston.unisysgsg.com/arch-006.html.

[26] NIST, "Next Generation Computing Resources: Reference Model for Project Support Environments (Version 2.0)", NIST Special Publication 500-213, November 1993

[27] Wakeman, L. and Jowett, J., "PCTE: The Standards for Open Repositories", Prentice-Hall, 1993.

[28] Frankel, R., "Introduction to the ToolTalk Service", Sun Microsystems Inc., Mountain View, CA., 1991.

[29] Ousterhout, J., "Tcl and the Tk Toolkit", Addison Wesley.

[30] Holand, I. and Bell, K., eds., *Finite Element Methods in Stress Analysis*, Tapir: Technical University of Norway, Trondheim, Norway, 1969.

[31] Barkmeyer, E., Hopp, Pratt, Rinaudot, SIMA Background Study, Technical Report NISTIR 5662, National Institute of Standards and Technology, 1995.

[32] Barkmeyer, E., SIIMA Reference Architecture Part I: Activity Models, NIST Technical Report (in publication).

[33] Schoof, L., Yarberry, V., Exodus II: A Finite Element Data Model, Sandia Report SAND92-2137-UC-705, Sept. 1994.

[34] Bremeau, C., Thomas, I., "A Schema Design Method for PCTE", in proceedings of the PCTE 1993 Conference, ISBN 0-95-10631-2-X.

123

Evolving Dependable Real Time Systems

Lui Sha, Ragunathan Rajkumar, and Michael Gagliardi

Software Engineering Institute
Carnegie Mellon University
Pittsburgh, PA, 15213, USA
{lrs, rr mjg}@sei.cmu.edu

Abstract

To keep systems affordable, there is a trend towards using open standard and commercial off the shelf (COTS) components in the development of dependable real time systems. However, the use of COTS also introduces the vendor driven upgrade problem that are relatively new to the dependable real time computing community.

If we refuse to accept the "new and improved" hardware and software components provided by vendors, then the hope that using COTS components will help keep the system modern via market forces will be dashed. If we decide to keep our systems modern, then we have to develop approaches that can introduce new hardware and software components into deployed systems safely, reliably and easily, in spite of the inevitable bugs in some of the new COTS components.

In this paper, we give an informal review of the Simplex Architecture, which has been developed to support safe and reliable online upgrade of dependable computing systems.

This paper is revision of the SEI technical report: A Software Architecture for Dependable and Evolvable Industrial Computing Systems. CMU/SEI-95-TR-005.

1. Introduction

The movement towards using open standard COTS components for dependable real time computing systems creates the challenge of how to manage rapid upgrades. Current system architectures do not tolerate errors in the insertion of a new technology or in the modification of a given system. If there is an error, the operation of the system will be adversely impacted. This will be a pervasive problem in industrial and defense systems requiring high availability, real time performance, and safety.

A paradigm shift is needed, from a focus on enabling technologies for completely new installations to one which is designed to mitigate the risk and cost of bringing new technology into functioning systems. Technology is needed to support *evolving systems*. Industry needs a computing infrastructure in which upgrades will be safe and predictable, with negligible down-time.

The Simplex Architecture is a software architecture based on COTS components. It has been developed to address the above concerns. The architecture was initially developed to support the safe online upgrade of feedback control and radar systems, regardless of whether there were faults in the modeling, design, and implementation of new software or computing hardware[1]. This paper provides an overview of this architecture. The rest of this paper provides an overview of the technology foundation of the Simplex Architecture. Section 2 gives an overview of the basic requirements of the Simplex Architecture. Section 3 gives a very brief overview of the technological foundation and Section 4 provides an overview of the software architecture. Finally, Section 5 gives the summary and conclusion.

2. Basic Requirements

From the viewpoint of a designer, an architecture specifies an envelope of alternative designs. Each of these designs will have its own characteristics and can meet the requirements. The design of the Simplex Architecture addresses three basic requirements. Firstly, *an architecture that is designed to support system evolution must itself be evolvable*. Trade-off decisions, such as flexibility vs. efficiency, change from application to application. Within an application, decision weights change as technology and user needs evolve. For example, in many early PC applications, e.g., spread sheets, most of the available computing resources were devoted to problem solving rather than user-interface needs. Today, a significant percentage of the computing power used by an application is devoted to graphical user interface. A trade-off decision can, at best, be optimal at some particular time and in a given environment. Thus, it is important to have the mechanisms to evolve both the application software as well as the Simplex Architecture itself.

Secondly, *application codes should be protected from changes to non-functional quality attributes and vice versa*. It is important to minimize the impact of changes on appli-

Reprinted from *Proc. IEEE Aerospace Applications Conf., 1996.*
Copyright © 1996 by The Institute of Electrical and Electronics Engineers, Inc. All rights reserved.

125

cation programs when the system evolves. Interfaces between components and subsystems must be defined in such a way that tradeoffs between non-functional quality attributes such as dependability and performance can change over time without the need for modifying application programs. For example, when a new software component is first introduced, it may need to be embedded in an application unit that has built-in safety checks and detailed operational monitoring. This may impact performance adversely. When the risk of a component failure decreases, some of the risk mitigation measures at runtime can be reduced accordingly. These changes should be made without any modification to the application program, since the semantic (functionality) of the application remains unchanged.

Thirdly, *the architecture must provide application independent utilities to meet timing constraints, to tolerate hardware and software failures, to monitor system status, to configure the system, and to provide users with templates and standardized transactions to manage changes in general and online changes in particular.* To support system evolution, we provide users with commonly used system utilities so that they can focus on the semantics of their applications.

3. Underlying Technologies

In order to allow changes to software modules during runtime, an advanced real time resource management technology is needed. In Simplex Architecture, real time process management primitives are built upon generalized rate monotonic theory[5]. In order to tolerate both hardware and software faults, to manage changes during development, and to support the evolution of dependable systems after their deployment, a new theoretical foundation is needed to allow for well formed diversity among redundant components. The theory of analytic redundancy provides us with such a foundation [6]. In the following, we give a brief review of these two subjects.

3.1 *Real Time Scheduling*

Generalized rate monotonic scheduling (GRMS) theory guarantees that the deadlines of tasks will be met, if the total CPU utilization is below some threshold and if certain rules are followed. GRMS is supported by major national standards including Ada95, POSIX real time extension, and IEEE Futurebus+. The following is a synopsis of generalized rate monotonic scheduling for uni-processors. For an overview of this theory for distributed systems, see [5]; for system developers who want detailed practical guidelines see [2]. The name "rate monotonic" scheduling comes from the fact that this algorithm gives higher priorities to tasks with higher frequencies.

A real time system typically consists of both periodic and aperiodic tasks. A periodic task $(_i$ is characterized by a worst-case computation time C_i and a period T_i. Unless mentioned otherwise, we assume that a periodic task must finish by the end of its period. Tasks are independent, if they do not need to synchronize with each other. By using either a simple polling procedure or a more advanced technique such as a sporadic server [7], the scheduling of aperiodic tasks can be treated within the rate monotonic framework. In each case C units of computation is allocated in a period of T for aperiodic activity. However, the management and replenishment of the capacity is different in each case. The scheduling of periodic tasks with synchronization requirements can be analyzed as follows [3].

Theorem 1: A set of n periodic tasks scheduled by the rate monotonic algorithm will always meet its deadlines, for all task phasings, if $\forall i, (n \geq i \geq 1)$

$$\frac{C}{T_1} + \frac{C_2}{T_2} + \dots + \frac{C_i + B_i}{T_i} \leq i(2^{1/i} - 1)$$

where B_i is the duration in which task i is blocked by lower-priority tasks. This blocking is also known as priority inversion. Priority inversion can occur when tasks have to synchronize. Priority inversion can be minimized by priority inheritance protocols [3]. The effect of this blocking can be modeled as though task i 's utilization is increased by an amount B_i/T_i. This theorem shows that the duration of priority inversion reduces *schedulability*, the degree of processor utilization at or below which all deadlines can be met.

The Simplex Architecture assumes that application tasks are scheduled according to the rules of GRMS and the operating system in use supports either the priority inheritance protocol or the priority ceiling protocol and is free of unbounded priority inversion in the management of shared resources. Both POSIX.1B OS specifications and Ada 95 runtime specifications incorporate priority inheritance protocols and satisfy this assumption.

3.2 The Basic Concept of Analytic Redundancy

Many industrial systems and defense systems have stringent reliability requirements. The standard practice is to replicate software on redundant computers and to use the majority voting for the outputs. Unfortunately, replication provides no defense against design or implementation errors. Furthermore, voting schemes based on the replication approach suffer from the *upgrade paradox*. That is, if only a minority is upgraded, the change will have no effect on the resulting system, no matter how great the upgrade. On the other hand, if the majority is upgraded and there is a bug, the system will fail.

To allow for safe evolution of a dependable computing system, we must go beyond replication and allow for *well formed diversity* among members of a fault tolerant group. What is well formed diversity? There are three forms of redundancy: replication, functional redundancy, and analytic redundancy. Given identical input data streams, two functionally redundant systems will produce identical output data streams. Functional redundancy permits the use of different but mathematically equivalent algorithms. For example, many different programs can be written to solve a given set of linear equations. While functional redundancy permits internal diversity that is not visible at the input and output level, analytic redundancy permits diversity that is visible at the input and output level.

Two analytically redundant systems need not produce identical results. However, the diversity permitted by analytic redundancy is well formed in the sense that both of them satisfy some model. As an everyday example, the oxygen mask is analytically redundant to the pressurized air system of a high flying airplane in the sense that both of them can deliver the needed oxygen to keep passengers alive. The Taylor series expansion of a continuous function at the vicinity of a point is analytically redundant to the function if we only need a good approximation.

In the context of control applications, one may use a simple and well understood controller as the fallback controller for an advanced but yet to be fully proven controller. A good example is the secondary digital controller and the normal digital controller in Boeing 777 [8]. Generally, the advanced controller is expected to provide more functionality and to have a higher control performance, for example, the ability to follow a reference signal (command) faster and/or smoother. However, the trajectories of the advanced controller must be within the controllable states of the fallback controller. In other words, the state space of the advanced controller must be a subset of the fallback controller's controllable states, although they may have very different behaviors (state transition graphs) in response to a command. In the Boeing 777 example, to ensure that the normal digital controller will never bring the plane outside of the controllable states of the fall back secondary digital controller, the flight envelop of the normal digital controller is continuously monitored during the flight.

The notion of analytic redundancy is captured by a *system operation model*. In the context of plant control applications, a system operation model is designed to deal with *externally observable* events only. There is a set of consistency constraints on the input data streams to the state machines, and a set of consistency constraints on the output streams from the machines, and a set of consistency constraints on the state of the plant under control. That is, we permit well formed diversity on inputs, outputs and on how a plant is controlled.

Note that a system operation model does not include predicates on the internal states of controllers so that programs with different specifications and internal states can be used to satisfy the same model. On the other hand, we include the states of the plant into our model since the states of the plant must be observable in order to be controlled and the observed state transitions of the plant allow us to evaluate the controllers.

We assume that the plant states are observable and controllable. We partition the states of a plant into three classes, namely, operational states, mishap states, and hazardous states. Operational states are those required for the correct execution of the application. Mishap states are those states of the physical system that incur damages or injuries. Hazardous states are those that are neither operational states nor mishap states. Hazards are conditions that cause incorrect state transitions that may result in mishap states. A function is said to be critical if an incorrect implementation of it can generate hazards. When the state variable is continuous, the safety margin guarding a given set of mishap states is the minimal distance between the given mishap states and operational states. For example, the safety margin of falling off a cliff is the shortest distance to the edge. When the state variable is discrete, a useful definition of safety margin is the minimal number of hazardous states a system must go through before it reaches a mishap state when starting from an operational state. An everyday example of a discrete hazardous state is the "push down" state of a child proof cap of a medicine bottle. One may also assign weights to hazardous states and the distance becomes a weighted sum. The weights are used to model how strong is the barrier effect of various hazardous states.

In a system operation model, the constraints on the plant states are divided into two classes: safety specifications (constraints) and performance specifications. Safety specifications are predicates that exclude mishap states. The most common form of safety specifications are the specifications of the boundary conditions of the operational states, for example, the flight envelope of the Boeing 777 normal digital controller. Getting out of the boundary of operational states leads to the activation of safety actions, e.g., too large a current triggers the circuit breaker. The class of performance specifications (constraints) is usually stated in terms of response time, steady state errors and tracking errors. In controller design, another important consideration is stability and robustness with respect to perturbation to the plant control and variations in the parameters of the sensor, plant and actuators. Some of the controller design objectives can be in conflict. For example, a fast response time calls for higher gains but too high a gain may lead to instability and increased sensitivities to noise and system parameter variations. The different tradeoff decisions lead to the use of different control technologies.

Since plant states can be sampled by each of analytically redundant controllers independently, the general form of input constraints is simply a statement of the data sampling requirement for each controller. We can, of course, specify that identical inputs must be provided to all the controllers. However, this is generally not needed from the viewpoint of system observability. We will do so only if such specification is easy to meet and meaningful.

A system operation model also includes the optional specification of the correlations between the output of a reference controller and the output of the new controller. Even though the different control algorithms give different outputs, the outputs are often correlated. The correlation can be quite strong when the system state is far away from the set point since any reasonable algorithm will use a large force to push the system towards the set point. If a strong correlation between outputs exists (conditionally) for the given application, it can be used as an additional diagnostic tool to monitor the execution of the complex controller.

3.3 Model-Based Voting

To tolerate both hardware and software failures and to safely evolve dependable real time systems, the voting protocol must permit well formed diversity. In a multi-computer fault tolerant group, model based voting is a means to support well formed diversity. Instead of directly comparing the output values step by step, a computer that controls a device is monitored by others to see if it observes the system operation model. Model based voting allows us to introduce new hardware and software technologies into the system safely. New upgrades will be accepted as long as they improve functionality or performance while observing the system operation model. In addition to supporting system evolution, model based voting also allows us to tolerate combined hardware and software failures.

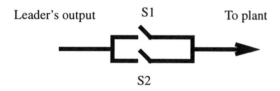

Leader's output   S1   To plant

S2

Switches S1 (2) controlled by voter 1 (2)

Figure 1. Voter

A fault tolerant group is a set of (analytically) redundant computing equipments designed to meet a set of fault tolerance requirements. Assuming that an analytically redundant backup controller exists and the operational boundary of the complex controller can be monitored in runtime, the basic requirement for a triplicated fault tolerant group using model based voting is as follows:

- tolerate an unlimited number of application design and implementation errors in complex controller software,
- tolerate active failures and malicious attempts within one computer,
- automatically reconfigure the system into a duplex standby system after one of the computers fails and
- support the safe online change of hardware, system software or application software.

These requirements can be fulfilled by a leadership protocol known as the Simple Leadership Protocol (SLP). While the detailed description and analysis of this protocol is too long for this paper, the basic idea is quite simple. Under a leadership protocol, a member of a fault tolerant group is selected as the leader who controls the plant. The rest are said to be (registered) voters. The leader is monitored by the voters. If the majority of the voters consider that the leader has violated the system operation model, the leader will be impeached and a new leader is selected from the voters. The basic logic of the voter hardware is the well known I/O interlock logic as illustrated in Figure 1.

SLP was described in detail and its properties were proven in [6]:

Theorem 2: In a triplicated fault tolerant group using SLP, if system operation model violation is detectable at time t, the leader will be impeached no later than $(t + 2T_{max})$, where T_{max} is the longest sampling period used in the fault tolerant group.

Remark: Theorem 2 does not assume that tasks in the three computers are synchronized. In fact, synchronizing the execution of the tasks in the three computers will not reduce the worst case delay of leader impeachment. Finally, the sampling frequencies used by members of the fault tolerant group need not be the same.

Theorem 3: Under SLP, the triplicated fault tolerant group can tolerate an unlimited number of application level software errors in the complex controller software.

Theorem 4: Under SLP, the system can tolerate active failures and malicious attempts confined within one computer of a triplicated fault tolerant group.

Theorem 5: Under SLP, upon the failure of the leader in a triplicated fault tolerant group, the system automatically reconfigures into a duplex system.

4. Overview of The Architecture

The Simplex Architecture is a family of high level application development frameworks (middle ware) that has been designed to support the online evolution of dependable real time computing systems. From the perspective of application developers, it is a collection of online software modification facilities, real time process management and communication facilities, and fault tolerant facilities. In addition, there is a set of application program interfaces (API) that users follow in order to get the benefits of easier and safer online software evolution.

4.1 Making Changes Safer

To ensure safety and an acceptable level of performance in spite of errors introduced during changes to application software, we need to ensure the timely execution of monitoring and fallback software and protect them from being corrupted. To this end, we need to defend against software faults that could compromise the execution of monitoring and fallback software. Simplex Architecture classifies the software hazards into three basic types. Hazards are conditions that can produce incorrect state transitions in a given system.

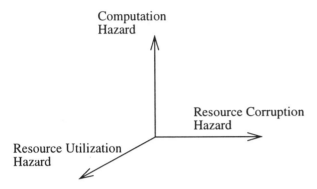

Figure 2. Error Space

The three types of software hazards are:

- Resource Utilization Hazards: for instance, a process overrunning a timing quota, or running out of memory. In Simplex, timing hazard is covered by the use of Generalized Rate Monotonic scheduling. All real time tasks are locked in the main memory. Demand paging, if supported, is allowed for non-real time tasks only.

- Resource Corruption Hazards: for instance, one subsystem accidentally trashing another subsystem's variables. Memory corruption is protected against by the use of separate address spaces provided by OS and supported by hardware. The communication between processes is conducted via a message passing protocol. Process pairs can share a partial address space for efficiency reasons as long as we can guarantee the critical data and codes cannot be corrupted.

- Computational Hazards: for instance, an error in an algorithm which causes a subsystem to produce incorrect, hazardous results. To guard against computational errors during changes, Simplex Architecture provides support for the use of analytic redundancy. Application developers need to provide the monitoring and fallback software in addition to the foreground application software. Simplex Architecture performs the real time process management, scheduling, communication and switching.

The hazards are shown in Figure 2.

4.2 Making Changes Easier

To support online software changes, we need to provide application developers a software packaging construction that can be modified and replaced online. The basic building block of the Simplex Architecture is the *replacement unit*, a process with a communication template that facilitates the replacement of one unit with another online. Replacement units are designed in such a way that they can be added, deleted, merged or split online by a set of standardized upgrade transactions. Using the replacement unit as the basic building block allows a uniform approach to support not only the evolution of the application architecture but also that of the Simplex Architecture itself. In fact, the replacement unit used in the architecture can itself be refined and upgraded online.

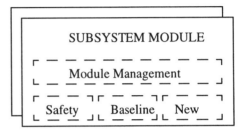

Figure 3.

The basic software unit that packages a distinct application function is the *subsystem unit*. A subsystem module is used to implement a distinct application function, for example, set point control, trajectory generation, motion coordination or the user interface. A subsystem module consists of specialized replacement units in the form of an application independent *module management unit* and several application units. A typical set of application units consists of the b*aseline unit* that runs the existing baseline software, a *new unit* that represents the intended upgrade for the existing software the *safety unit* which implements a safety controller (optional), system performance and safety monitoring functions. Device I/O functions can reside within the safety unit or in a separate application unit. However, it cannot reside within an application unit whose correctness is questionable, since device I/O is always critical to the control of the system.

The *module management unit* is a replacement unit with functions that are designed to carry out process management and the upgrade operations, for example, the creation and destruction of the *new unit*. Figure 3 illustrates a subsystem module with four specialized replacement units, the module management unit and three application units, namely the *safety unit*, the *baseline unit* and the *new unit*.

The communication needs between subsystem modules and units within a module is satisfied by the *real time publishers and subscribers* facility[4]. This facility is a variation and extension of the group communication facility in ISIS[9]. As a group communication facility, it allows information sources and sinks to dynamically join and leave a "newsgroup" in a uniformed way and thus provides a basis to carry out the replacement transaction. As a real time communication facility, it separates the non-real time operations related to the creation and destruction of communication links between replacement units from the real time operations such as the sending of real time sensor inputs and controller outputs, so that real time control communication will not be adversely impacted by the non-real time communication.

Each subsystem module also acts as a software fault-containment unit. As a rule, the *new unit* and the *baseline unit* are untrsuted and run in separate address spaces. The *safety unit* and *module management unit* can be optionally combined as two compile-time software modules in a single replacement unit for efficiency reasons. The separation between trusted and untrusted units provides protection against resource corruption hazards. Resource utilization hazards also need to be considered. For example, an application unit can burn more CPU cycles than expected because of some error condition. The protection against timing faults can be provided in one of two ways. First, one can keep track of the CPU cycles used by the application units and compare the count with an expected value. This requires OS support and consumes CPU in the form of some scheduling overhead. Secondly, one can assign to the safety units a higher priority than those of the application units. This approach can be implemented in an OS that supports fixed priority scheduling and the CPU cost is in the form of bounded priority inversion to all safety units[3]. One may use Theorem 1 to compute the impact of these two different approaches.

4.3 Upgrade Transaction and Application Unit State Transitions

The fundamental operation provided by the Simplex Architecture to support system evolution is the replacement transaction, where one replacement unit is replaced by another. During this replacement transaction, state information (e.g. those relating to controllers or filters) may need to be transferred from the *baseline unit* to the *new unit*. Alternatively, the *new unit* may capture the dynamic state information of physical systems through plant input data. Without state information, there may be undesirable transients in the behavior of the new replacement unit when it comes online. Hence, the replacement transaction of a single replacement unit is carried out in stages:

1. The *new unit* is created.

2. Plant input data and other state information, if any, are provided to the *new unit* when it is ready. The *new unit* begins computations based on the plant input data. The output of the unit is monitored but not used.

3. The upgrade transaction waits for the output of the *new unit* converges with that of the *baseline unit* according to a user provide criteria. Once the convergence is reached. The output of the baseline unit is turned off and the new unit is turned on.

A two-phase protocol can be used when multiple replacement units are to be replaced simultaneously. The first phase is to wait for all *the new units* to reach a steady state (step 3 above). The second phase is a distributed action that simultaneously switches on all the *new units* and switches off all the (old) *baseline units*. The granularity of "simultaneity" is subject to the accuracy of clock synchronization in a distributed system. If the switching of any unit is not successful, the system can automatically switch back to the output of *baseline units* and the replacement transaction is aborted.

Among the application units, only the *safety unit* is the trusted unit that is presumed to be correct. Every effort should be made to ensure that this assumption is indeed correct, since the system will fail if this is not true. When the *baseline unit* and the *new unit* are first introduced into the system, their status are marked as "fault-free" internally. If both the outputs from *baseline unit* and the *new unit* are ready and if the system is in an operational state, the output from the *new unit* is used. If the system under *new unit's* control violates the operational model, the system will mark the *new unit* as faulty and uses the safety controller's output until the system returns to the operational state. At this point, the system control will pass to the *baseline unit* unless it is marked as faulty as well. Users have the option to execute (retry) an application unit that is marked as faulty for a number of times specified by users. Faulty application units that run out of their retry counts can either be destroyed or be executed for diagnostic purpose. That is, their outputs will be recorded but not used. Application units that create resource utilization hazards or resource corruption hazards will always be destroyed since they could jeopardize the execution of other software modules.

Finally, if the *new unit* passes all the tests specified by users, users can copy the *new unit* to the *baseline unit*, restart the new *baseline unit* and then destroy the now redundant *new unit* through the commands provided by the user's interface. The system is now ready to be upgraded again.

4.4 System Configuration

Subsystem modules can be composed to support coordinated motions as illustrated in Figure 4. The application unit of the subsystem module at the higher level of motion control generates coordinated setpoints. The controllers of devices 1 and 2 are implemented respectively by the application units at two lower level subsystem modules. The communications between them are carried out by the real time publisher and subscription service described before.

Computers can be grouped into a triplicated fault tolerant group[1] that implements the SLP protocol reviewed in previous sections. Conceptually, the existence of multiple computers can be viewed as merely multiple physical address spaces instead of multiple logical address spaces provided by the operating system. For example, one can implement the *new unit* and *baseline unit* in one of the three computers and designate it as the leader while implementing only the safety unit in the other two. Many other variations in configurations are possible and straightforward. .

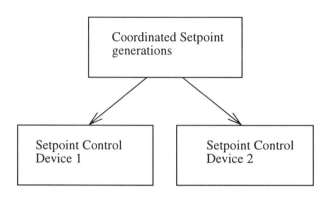

Figure 4. Application Configuration

The most important configuration decision is, however, the preference of how the leader is handled when an untrusted unit brings the system outside of the operational states. By definition, the other two registered voters will vote out the leader and select a new leader, even if the (old) leader has also detected this event and has started the recovery process successfully. Once the (old) leader recovers, it can re-join the group and be designated as the leader of the fall tolerant group again. The drawback of this simple approach is that when the leader is out, the hardware redundancy is reduced by one temporarily, even though it is a software fault.

An alternative is to let the leader restrict the operational state to a smaller subset and use this subset as its internal operational states. Thus, if the *baseline unit* or the *new unit* violates this restricted operational state boundary, it will be handled by the leader internally since the plant still in the normal operational states. The drawback of this approach is the reduction of the size of the possible operational states. This may or may not be an issue for a given application.

The configuration of subsystem modules are managed by a processor configuration manager (PCM) (one on each processor) which is in turn managed by a system configuration manager (SCM). Both PCM and SCM are replacement units with additional functions. The SCM interfaces with the user through a user-interface manager, another specialized replacement unit. Through this user-interface, an application system administrator defines the topology of the distributed system and the types of processors, networks, and operating systems in use. The administrator also defines the class of

interchangeable resources including processors, processes, and networks. In addition, the administrator defines the system state variables to be monitored.

5. Summary and Conclusion

Industrial and defense computing systems often have stringent safety, reliability and timing constraints. Failure in such systems can potentially have catastrophic consequences, and system downtimes can be expensive.

In this paper, we give a brief overview of the technology foundation of the Simplex Architecture. The architecture can be used to maintain the safety, reliability and real time constraints of industrial and defense computing systems, despite inevitable glitches when new technologies are introduced and integrated with existing equipment. The architecture is based on open system components, and supports the safe evolution of the application software architecture itself online. It will also support the safe online addition and removal of computing hardware and system software.

Two demonstration prototypes were built and are available for demonstration. The single computer prototype uses a personal computer that controls an inverted pendulum. The controller software can be modified on the fly. Members of the audience are invited to modify the control software online. Arbitrary bugs at the application level can be inserted by the audience. The demonstration shows that the control performance can only be improved but not degraded. The second prototype is a triplicated fault tolerant group which implements the Simple Leadership protocol. It permits the safe online modification of not only the application software but the hardware and system software. An improved minority can gain and improve the control performance. However, no hardware or software errors at that computer can degrade the control, including malicious attempts with root privileges at that computer. The triplicated fault tolerant group can also be reconfigured online into a duplex system or a uni-processor system and vice versa as needed. A third prototype for demonstrating the safe online upgrade of distributed control is being developed.

Currently, the SEI is actively working with industry partners and government agencies to mature this promising new technology.

Acknowledgments

This work is sponsored in part by the SEI and by the Office of Naval Research. The authors want to thank John Lehoczky, Jennifer Stephan, Marc Bodson and Danbing Seto for the discussion of control related issues, Neal Altman and Chuck Weinstock for the discussions on software engineering issues and John Leary for his review.

---

1. One may choose to have a higher degree of redundancy by a simple extension of the SLP.

131

6. References

[1]   Bodson, M., Lehoczky, J., Rajkumar, R., Sha, L., Stephen J and Smith, M., Control Reconfiguration in The Presence of Failure, Proceeding of the IEEE Conference on Decision and Control, 1993.

[2]   Klein, M., Ralya, T. Pollak, B., Obenza, R. and Harbour, M. G., A Practitioner's Handbook for Real Time Analysis, Kluwer Academic Publisher, 1993 .

[3]   Sha, L. and Goodenough, B., Real Time Scheduling Theory and Ada, IEEE Computer, Apr., 1993.

[4]   Rajkumar, R., Gagliardi, M. and Sha, L., *The Real Time Publisher/Subscriber IPC Model for Distributed Real Time Systems: Design and Implementation,* Proceedings of the 1st IEEE Real Time Technology and Applications Symposium, May 1995.

[5]   Sha, L., Rajkumar, R., and Sathaye, S., Generalized Rate Monotonic Scheduling Theory: A Framework of Developing Real Time Systems, IEEE Proceedings, Jan., 1994.

[6]   Sha, L., Gagliardi, M. and Rajkumar, R., Analytic Redundancy: A Foundation for Evolvable Dependable Systems, Proceedings of the 2nd ISSAT International Conference on Reliability, and Quality of Design, March 1995.

[7]   Sprunt, B., Sha, L. and Lehoczky, J., Aperiodic Task Scheduling for Hard Real Time Systems. The Journal of Real Time Systems (1):27-60, 1989.

[8]   Yeh, Y. C. (Bob), Dependability of the 777 Primary Flight Control System. Proceedings of DCCA Conference, 1995.

[9]   Birman, K. P., The Process Group Approach to Reliable Distributed Computing. TR-91-1216, CS Department, Cornell University, 1991.

Modernization of Software Maintenance Practices using Computer-Aided Sub-Processes (CASPs)

Alan W. Brown

Software Engineering Institute
Carnegie Mellon University
Pittsburgh, PA, 15213, USA
awb@sei.cmu.edu

Abstract

Software maintenance consumes significant portions of an organization's budget. Yet many organizations find it difficult to adopt new software maintenance practices (i.e., processes, methods, and tools) in a systematic, cost-effective way. In this paper we consider some of the problems of transitioning new practices into a software maintenance organization. We then look at the concept of Computer-Aided Sub-Processes (CASPs) and consider how they might be applied to effect technology transition. Previous experiences with CASPs are examined, and the lessons for software maintenance organizations are discussed.

1. Introduction

Software maintenance is a key activity for any large software-intensive system. In fact, the data from existing studies reveal that software maintenance activities consume the major share of the total budget in many large software-based organizations [3]. The reasons for the high cost of software maintenance are many and various. Key factors include:

- schedule pressures experienced during software development leading to an emphasis on functionality delivered rather than the long-term maintainability of the system;

- the incompleteness and poor quality of the documentation provided with many systems;

- the wide variety of tasks contained within the term "software maintenance", often classified as correction (e.g., bug fixes in operational code), adaption (e.g., re-hosting on a new machine), and enhancement (e.g., adding completely new system functionality).

These factors clearly have an essential impact on the difficulty of the software maintenance task. However, in this paper we concentrate on one further factor that is rarely explicitly addressed in this context. That is, the problem of documenting existing maintenance practices as the basis for facilitating technology refreshment in a software maintenance organization.

While it has been recognized that there is no substitute for experience in dealing with the many intellectual challenges that face software maintainers, often there is available technology to support the maintainer in many of their activities. However, typically an organization does not have the means to introduce the technology in a systematic, cost-effective way. There is massive inertia in such organizations. Undoubtedly some of the problem is resistance to change; however it is our belief that appropriate technology transition techniques, tuned to the needs of software maintenance organizations, can greatly improve the current state of affairs.

We highlight the technology transition problem above the many others primarily because it is an issue that we have recognized in a number of our customers, but for which we can find little practical help in the software engineering community. Ideally, we would like to adopt techniques found in existing software engineering literature based on current best practice. However, in addressing this problem we have not been able to identify best practices that satisfy the organizations' needs.

Many factors stand in the way of change. This includes the lack of return on investment data on methods and tools, lack of funding for maintenance, poor perception of maintenance as a career, etc. [4].However, our belief is that the key is to establish a way to package the new practices such that they support the wider organizational goals for measurable process improvement, yet provide practical documentation, advice, and tool support to engineers carrying out software maintenance activities.

In this paper we consider one approach to enabling technology transition through the development and application of Computer-Aided Sub-Processes (CASPs). Briefly stated, the CASP approach is to design and implement a technology transition package focused on supporting a well-defined piece of the complete software process (what we call a "sub-process"). This transition package can be used to document the often complex set of methods and tools currently in use during software maintenance, providing a set of practical

0-8186-7718-X/96 $5.00 © 1996 IEEE

products that assist software engineers in executing their tasks. This documentation can then be used as the basis for modernizing those practices.

The remainder of the paper is organized as follows. In Section 2 we describe the CASP approach, providing a detailed example in support of software requirements analysis. In Section 3 lessons learned from the application of the CASP approach to software development organizations are discussed. In Section 4 we consider how the CASP approach can be applied in software maintenance, describe characteristics of a typical software maintenance organization from the perspective of the pressures being exerted to improve those practices, and highlight issues that must be addressed in making the CASP approach successful in software maintenance. Conclusions and future directions for this work are highlighted in Section 5.

2. Computer-Aided Sub-Processes (CASPs)

Over the past 2 years we have been developing and applying a technology transition package within software development organizations. This package is based on the notion of identifying a fragment of the software engineering life-cycle (a so-called "sub-process") and developing a complete set of materials for supporting that sub-process within an organization. The CASP can then be use:

- to document existing practices;
- to identify opportunities for improving existing practices;
- as a vehicle for transition of new or improved practices into an organization.

Having selected an appropriate sub-process, a CASP explicitly defines the requirements of that sub-process, then creates a coherent operational package by defining the methods which implement the sub-process and the tools which support the methods. The contribution of the CASP approach is that it treats process, methods, and tools in a unified way so that all of the different classes of users can gain insight into what is being achieved, how it is being carried out, and what support is provided to assist in the task. In this sense, the documentation of a CASP acts as a blueprint that establishes a common understanding of the engineering approach to be followed, and ties together the future work of each of the different classes of users.

Figure 1 illustrates the multiple levels of description that provide the basis for the CASP approach. The CASP concept is based on the three circled levels of abstract services (i.e., sub-processes, methods, tools) illustrated in Figure 1, in a hierarchy of 6 levels.

At the highest of the three levels, the sub-process is described in a high level way, defining the major steps and major issues with respect to the practice of that sub-process within the organization (e.g., a few pages from existing company policy documents describing software requirements analysis). This can be supported by reference to recognized

standards such as the Department of Defense (DoD) software development standard MIL-STD-2167A. The format could be text or diagrams (e.g., data flow diagrams, IDEF0 diagrams, etc.). All required inputs and outputs for the sub-process must be identified.

At the next level, methods are employed to describe and enact the sub-processes. These could be established commercial methods (e.g., Jackson Structured Design (JSD), Hatley-Pirbhai, or Booch), a variation of a commercial method (e.g., a locally customized form of Hatley-Pirbhai), or a home-grown method specifically developed by this organization.

Similarly, at the tools level, support for the methods may be by commercial, customized commercial, or home-grown tools. In fact, in reality it is likely to be a combination of tools that come from each of these categories.

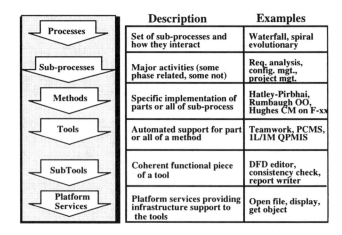

	Description	Examples
Processes	Set of sub-processes and how they interact	Waterfall, spiral evolutionary
Sub-processes	Major activities (some phase related, some not)	Req. analysis, config. mgt., project mgt.
Methods	Specific implementation of parts or all of sub-process	Hatley-Pirbhai, Rumbaugh OO, Hughes CM on F-xx
Tools	Automated support for part or all of a method	Teamwork, PCMS, 1L/1M QPMIS
SubTools	Coherent functional piece of a tool	DFD editor, consistency check, report writer
Platform Services	Platform services providing infrastructure support to the tools	Open file, display, get object

Figure 1. The Multi-Level CASP Hierarchy

Hence, at the heart of this hierarchy are three levels of services — sub-processes, methods and tools — that form a CASP. In this paper we concentrate on these three levels, with reference to the higher and lower levels only as necessary to provide additional context.

A specific sub-process is always the root of a given CASP. Frequently it is convenient to use a life cycle phase as the root sub-process for a CASP, for example, requirements analysis, design, data analysis, or subsystem integration. Other candidate sub-processes might span several life-cycle phases, e.g., configuration management, process enactment, and project management. For a sufficiently complex sub-process, it may be desirable to further subdivide it into child sub-processes to serve as roots for CASPs. The choice of which sub-processes to consider as CASPs is organization-specific — at one large development organization requirements analysis was chosen as the initial CASP due to its strategic importance to their current projects.

To describe the notion of a CASP in more detail we first consider an example of this requirements analysis CASP. This example, and the background to the CASP concept is further described in [6].

2.1 An Example CASP

We illustrate the CASP approach by considering a requirements analysis CASP that is in use in a large aerospace organization. The root of the CASP, as shown in Figure 2, is a process description that outlines the major steps involved in software requirements analysis as practiced within this organization. It may take the form of a recognized standard approach to this sub-process as found in a commercial or military standard, a home-grown approach as described in some appropriate notation (e.g., data flow diagrams, structured English, or IDEF0 notation), or a combination of these.

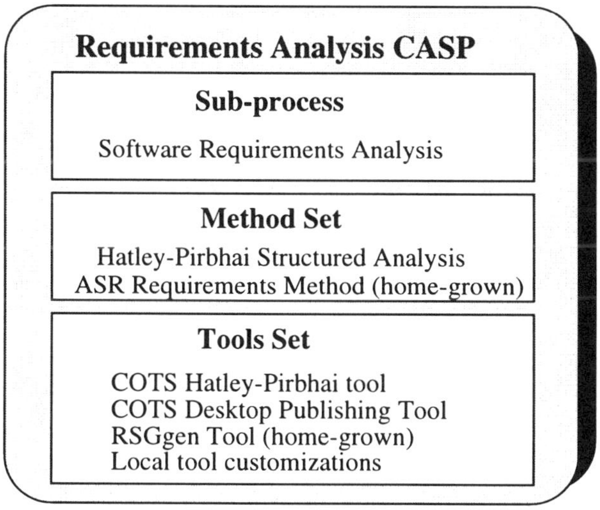

```
┌────────────────────────────────────────┐
│      Requirements Analysis CASP          │
│  ┌────────────────────────────────────┐ │
│  │           Sub-process              │ │
│  │  Software Requirements Analysis    │ │
│  └────────────────────────────────────┘ │
│  ┌────────────────────────────────────┐ │
│  │           Method Set               │ │
│  │  Hatley-Pirbhai Structured Analysis│ │
│  │  ASR Requirements Method (home-grown)││
│  └────────────────────────────────────┘ │
│  ┌────────────────────────────────────┐ │
│  │           Tools Set                │ │
│  │  COTS Hatley-Pirbhai tool          │ │
│  │  COTS Desktop Publishing Tool      │ │
│  │  RSGgen Tool (home-grown)          │ │
│  │  Local tool customizations         │ │
│  └────────────────────────────────────┘ │
└────────────────────────────────────────┘
```

Figure 2. Example Requirements Analysis CASP

In this example the software requirements analysis sub-process is implemented by a combination of two methods. The first method is the Hatley-Pirbhai (HP) structured analysis method, as defined in [5]. This describes the basic approach that will be used to perform requirements analysis. However, in order for a project to use the HP method to meet project needs, they will have to tailor and extend it. This results in the second method which consists of a set of project procedures describing exactly what steps and what conventions to follow for carrying out the HP method in this organization. Thus, the second method is dependent on (or uses) the first. The second method will also reflect the choice of tools at the next lower level, identifying particular features of the tools that must support the method. For example, the following rule from the method level reflects certain requirements from the tools that will support that method:

"Units are defined for each program input by entering the units e.g., 'furlongs per hour' in the attribute UNIT associated with each data dictionary definition."

Automated tools support methods to make it easier to capture data, manipulate data, verify data, and in some cases to generate data. A given method may or may not be supported by tools offering a range of support services for the methods defined. For example, it is possible to practice the HP method without any automated tool support. However, for projects of reasonable size, maintaining consistency among the data items would be nearly impossible. Hence, most sub-processes and methods on operational projects are supported by one or more tools offering a range of support services.

In Figure 2, four tools are identified: a commercial off-the-shelf (COTS) tool which supports the HP structured analysis method, a COTS desktop publishing tool that can be used to produce reports and documentation on the requirements analysis carried out, and a home-grown off-the-shelf (HOTS) (i.e., developed by another part of the organization) tool specifically written to help in automating the extraction of HP diagrams for inclusion in the documentation. In addition, the COTS tools have themselves been configured and customized for local needs (e.g., specific requirements analysis documentation templates have been created in accordance with organizational guidelines). These customizations of COTS tools (sometimes called enhanced COTS (ECOTS)) must also be recorded as part of the tool set used in the requirements analysis CASP.

3. Lessons from Existing Application of CASPs

The CASPs approach is in use in a number of projects as a technology transition vehicle for improving the adoption of new software engineering practices. Our approach to constructing CASPs in these projects was to choose an existing project and sub-process and then to concentrate on producing the appropriate documentation for a CASP. The result is a set of CASP documentation artifacts that provide the focal point for transition.

Table 1 summarizes that artifacts in the requirements analysis CASP at one particular project building a large embedded avionics application. It consists of a range of artifacts categorized under 12 sections, and amounting to many hundreds of pages of information. To ease use we also generated supplementary material for the CASP, mostly of an overview nature (e.g., an executive summary and a context diagram for each CASP).

While the application and evolution of the CASP approach is still on-going, we are already able to identify a number of key success factors for the approach, including:

- *The choice of areas for support.* It is vital that the sub-process chosen is well defined, critical to the organization, and provides a clear potential for impact. As a consequence we have found that this requires, at least initially, that the sub-processes are rather narrowly focused. We have also found that the energetic support of a local champion for that sub-process ensures that progress continues to be made even in the event of inevitable funding difficulties, management reorganizations, and changing priorities.

- *Appropriate resources available.* An obvious, but often overlooked, aspect is funding. To ensure that the CASP approach has impact it is necessary to have dedicated resources to the definition, documentation, application, and evolution of the CASP. Typically we have found that a small group of people must work closely with a project to tailor the CASP to the project's needs, advise on its application, and ensure that the CASP evolves as the project's needs evolve.

- *Well managed expectations.* Some initial problems with the use of CASPs were based on over-ambitious management expectations with respect to the ease with which new technology could be introduced across an organization. It should be emphasized that the CASP approach specifically targets individual technologies within a single project. while consistency across projects is encouraged through the re-use and adaptation of an existing CASP from one project to another, in current instantiations of the CASP approach this is achieved more opportunistically than systematically

In addition to these success factors there are a number of lessons that effect the ease of application of the CASPs approach, particularly with respect to how the CASP approach may be applied to a software maintenance organization. These lessons are highlighted below.

3.1 Smaller Tools

Trying to be conscientious about making the CASP complete, we were reminded that most projects use a wide variety of poorly documented and undocumented tools as filters, data translators, and so on. These are usually small homegrown (HOTS) tools or extensions (ECOTS) to COTS tools. The users manual for these may be contained in a memo, a text file, a scrap of paper, or only as part of a project's oral tradition. In some cases the tool is only known to its creator-user. We set an initial goal to at least get one page in the binder for each such tool.

A related problem is to decide what is and what is not a tool. For instance, suppose a toolsmith or requirements engineer writes a script file which can be executed to generate a report from another tool's database, e.g., a report script in RTM (a requirements management tool). Is the script a tool that should be documented as part of a CASP? In some cases the decision is clear. For example, it should be considered a tool when the report is delivered to the customer on a monthly basis as specified by contract. On the other hand, the script is not a tool if the report was only generated one time and its contents did not find their way into any enduring artifact. However, there are many gray areas in between requiring careful consideration.

3.2 Strong Relationship Between Methods and Tools

CASPs made a significant contribution by capturing information about the tools and methods in use on a project. However, what was surprising to the CASP developers was to see how closely inter-twined are the methods and tools aspects, and how necessary it is to capture these relationships. For instance, suppose that at some place in the methods documentation requirements engineers learn that they are required to provide a textual description for each data flow diagram (DFD). This is exactly where they want to see explicit instructions revealing that this means to use the requirements tool to attach a notation named 'description' to each DFD.

This blurring of methods and tools descriptions creates a dilemma because we want the documentation to be as useful to the engineers as possible, but if methods and tools descriptions are not separate, then it becomes more difficult to reuse the CASP in other contexts with different tools. At the moment, the best approach might be to encapsulate the tool references within the methods description. The need for the notation, where it will automatically get mapped into the requirements document, the required technical contents and format, etc., can all be discussed independent of any specific tool. The specifics of tool usage would then follow as a separate section. Separation can be made more clear by employing a unique font style for tool-specific text. Microsoft follows a similar approach in their Word 6 Reference Manual, encapsulating Word 6 differences between Windows and Macintosh users.

3.3 Electronic CASPs

Once the CASP approach began to take hold it became important to give easy access to CASP documentation to its users. This led to making all CASP documentation available on-line, allowing browsing, review, and printing of the documents. Initially, a straightforward approach was taken based on creating 12 separate folders (directories) containing the documents shown in Table 1.

There are several advantages to an electronic CASP. In particular, it becomes enormously easier to provide all interested parties access to the latest complete version of all sections. With a paper CASP, there is little hope that all copies would be even approximately in-step six months into a typical project.

The obvious evolution for the electronic CASP approach is toward the use of html documents and a netscape-based browsing capability. This provides advantages in terms of a flexible, easy to use front-end to the CASP, as well as the added advantage of providing a distribution mechanism for sharing CASP documentation across different machines at a variety of sites.

136

	Section Type	Description of Contents
1	Practice	Common Software Practice #12 (2pp) [Copy of company policy on software requirements analysis practice]
2	Relevant Standards	MIL-STD-2167A Requirements Specification DID (10pp) SEI Capability Maturity Model Key Practice Area #1 (10pp) [Standards adopted by the company that constrain and guide activities and work products]
3	COTS Methods	Hatley-Pirbhai Real-Time Structured Analysis (1pp) [Short description plus references to books, manuals, training courses, local experts, tutorials, etc.]
4	HOTS Methods	SRS Generation Guidelines IRS Generation Guidelines SRS Building Process Customer Software Development Plan, Appendix E (110pp) [Detailed procedures and conventions for methods used on this project]
5	COTS Tools	Teamwork Structured Analysis Tool (1pp) Interleaf Desktop Publishing Tool (1pp) Requirements and Traceability Management (RTM) Tool (1pp) Digital Interface Definition Tool (IDT) (1pp) SQL Systems PCMS Tool (1pp) Microsoft Excel (1pp) [Short overview with references and location of vendor user manuals, training materials, installation guides, local experts, etc.]
6	HOTS and ECOTS Tools	RSGgen, version 0.9 (70pp) attach_notes.exe, list_nites.exe, twk.com (11pp) [User manual for local filters and tools]
7	Platform	Digital VAX/VMS Version n.n (2pp) Apple Macintosh, System 7 (2pp) [Details of local installation and customization options providing the resources necessary for these tools]

Table 1. Documentation for a CASP

	Section Type	Description of Contents
8	Sub-process Inputs	System Requirements Specification (50pp) [Inputs needed to start this sub-process, and their relationships to maintain traceability with items in this sub-process]
9	Sub-process Outputs	RTM Requirements Database Hatley-Pirbhai Teamwork Model Software Requirements Specifications Interface Requirements Specifications
10	Metrics Collected	CSCI SRS Requirements Stability
11	Project Management Data	Requirements Analysis Progress (ACWP, BCWP, BCWS)
12	Process Management	PCMS (product life-cycle support)

Table 1. Documentation for a CASP

3.4 CASP Evolution

Early experience makes it clear that a CASP in use on one project is unlikely to be used without modification on a second project. The challenge then is to organize each CASP and to design CASP documents so that the portions that change are minimized. Our experience further shows that CASPs evolve on a project so that in any month some CASP documents will be added (e.g., a new regular report) and others will be modified. Controlling this evolution is essential in ensuring that all project members use the latest documented methods and tools. Hence, we are now addressing the issue of configuration management of the CASP artifacts themselves.

3.5 Summary

Use of the CASP approach in software development organizations has been found to be a valuable way to organize and document existing practices, and to provide a focal point for improving those practices. As can be expected, based on these experiences the approach has evolved significantly over the past 2 years with the result that:

- success criteria for appropriate selection of sub-processes to target for the CASP approach are better understood;

- the inter-relationships between methods and tools are given greater significance in a CASP, and more extensively addressed in CASP documentation;

- CASP documentation as a whole is more practical, accessible, and readable.

137

4. Applying the CASP Approach to a Software Maintenance Organization

Having matured the use of CASPs in the context of software development, we are now in a position to try the same approach in software maintenance. We believe that many of the ideas of the CASP approach are directly transferable. However, we are also aware that there are special considerations to be taken into account for successful application to software maintenance organizations.

In this section we first look at some of the pressures on software maintenance organizations that lead to the need for CASPs, and provide a context for considering the application of the CASP approach. Based on this background we then describe a number of special considerations that must be taken into account in applying the CASP approach to software maintenance. The section is concluded with a short summary.

4.1 Improvement Pressures in a Typical Software Maintenance Organization

Maintenance organizations are under pressure to bring current maintenance practices under greater control, and to adopt new, improved practices. This is driven by a number of factors:

- shrinking budgets, reductions in staff, and the need to increase individual productivity;
- advances in development practices, leading to delivery of software into maintenance that has been developed using object-oriented design methods and languages, embeds commercial off-the-shelf (COTS) software, and is designed with a client/server architecture;
- rapid evolution of the computing environment, leading to pressures to migrate existing systems onto faster, more modern hardware.

However, most software maintenance organizations are responsible for large quantities of operational code, developed over an extended period of time in a variety of languages, executing on a number of mainframe and mini-computer platforms, and interacting with established databases that have been optimized for performance over many years of use. As a result, each organization has built up a set of skills and practices that allow it to maintain existing systems even if these skills are highly dependent on a few individuals, and the practices often highly manual and subject to long turn-around times.

Hence, software maintenance organizations are in the uncomfortable position of balancing the pressure to adopt new practices with the need to maintain the existing skills and practices. We illustrate this tension by describing two typical scenarios drawn from our experiences with working with U.S. government software maintenance organizations.

Scenario 1: CASE Tool Infusion

One large government organization employs several hundred software maintenance engineers to maintain and enhance a wide range of operational software [1]. Much of this software is mission-critical, often with high availability and stringent response-time requirements. Over the past few years an internal effort has been taking place to standardize and automate a number of the existing maintenance practices. Three phases of this effort can be distinguished:

4. *Investigation of key maintenance practices.* In particular, the configuration management (CM) practices in use were examined, and the capabilities of available CM tools were analyzed. Some measure of standardization on a CM tool across the organization was achieved, although the rigor with which the tool is used in each project varies greatly.

5. *Examination of CASE tool integration technologies.* The aim was to try to tie together existing CM, design, test, and documentation tools to provide traceability between design, code and test artifacts. Despite great efforts, little progress has been made in this area. Many factors contributed to this failure, including the low level of CASE tool use in the organization, and the immaturity and volatility of the CASE tools and integration technologies employed.

6. *Measurement of CASE tool impact.* Many CASE tools had been purchased over the years, but it was difficult to estimate which tools were in use, and how they had effected software maintenance activities. There have been poor results thus far from attempts at gathering metrics data on tools use throughout the organization. The only reliable metric is the number of licenses for each tool available. Attention is now turned to qualitative assessment of areas in which the CASE tools have had noticeable impact.

In summary, we note that large amounts of money have been spent on a variety of CASE tools. Currently, tool use is sporadic, non-standard, and uncoordinated. Attempts to obtain quantitative data on the impact of the investment has largely been unsuccessful.

Scenario 2: Delivery of a New System into Maintenance

In another large government organization they are maintaining large amounts of real-time embedded command and control software. The majority of this software (and the hardware on which it operates) are at least 20 years old, and is written in a variety of languages such as JOVIAL, COBOL, and various assembly languages. Recognizing the increasing costs and lengthening turnaround time for new releases, the organization is in the midst of a large system modernization effort.

For over 5 years development efforts have been going on to replace one of the major systems being maintained. After a number of false starts, redirections, and redesigns the system is now planned to come into operation in 1997. At that point the maintenance organization is responsible for the on-going operation of this new system. They are concerned about this role because:

1. it is the first system they will maintain that is written in Ada;

2. unlike existing systems that use redundant hardware, this system employs a complex software fault tolerant scheme;

3. requirements and design documents are to be maintained using an unfamiliar commercial suite of CASE tools;

4. a management decision is to out-source maintenance to the commercial organization developing the software, and transition the maintenance role to internal staff over a number of years.

While these system characteristics represent a major challenge to the maintenance organization, the problems are increased when it is recognized that this is only one of a range of new systems that will become operational over the next few years. Other systems may or may not share these characteristics, compounding the software maintenance problem being faced.

In summary, we see that software modernization efforts bring new challenges to the software maintenance organization that make it essential for new processes, methods, and tools to be supported. This evolution of maintenance practices is a continual process as the existing software is replaced over time.

Implications for Maintenance

These two scenarios are typical of the issues being faced today in software maintenance organizations. They describe a number of challenges being faced in terms of modernization of the software maintenance practices being employed, and highlight key technology transition requirements for software maintenance organizations. To be effective, a software maintenance modernization effort must:

• address the combination of process, methods and tools in a cohesive way;

• be practical in nature in describing how a practice is applied;

• provide a way to assess the impact and cost-effectiveness of a practice;

• support continued improvement and enhancement of the practice over an extended period of time.

4.2 Commentary

Based on our experiences with the CASP approach in software development organizations, we are now beginning to investigate application of the CASP approach in software maintenance organizations. Results of our initial analyses are particularly favorable, pointing to the value of the CASP approach in managing and organizing the large amounts of information that is needed during software maintenance

activities, and providing a technology transition vehicle for modernization of software maintenance practices. Currently, we are focusing on 3 candidate sub-processes where CASPs may provide an ideal mechanism for modernization of existing practices:

• *Configuration Management (CM)*. A great concern to many maintenance organizations is the variety of activities involved in tracking system components, building a component from its sub-components, and so on. A CASP can act as a central resource for capturing information about CM practices and tools.

• *Software Testing*. There are many forms of software testing that take place during development and maintenance. Unfortunately, in many organizations testing procedures are ad hoc and highly variable across individuals and projects. The CASP approach provides a way to control these practices by recording the processes and tools that are use, and making them available across a project.

• *Program Understanding*. When problems repeatedly occur with a software system it is often necessary to assess that software for its quality, complexity, and structure. Currently program understanding is highly dependent on the skills of the software maintainer, who is supported by a collection of home grown and commercial tools. The CASP approach can act as a focal point for documenting the activities currently embodied in software maintainers, and for identifying how the tools are used to support those activities.

These areas have been selected due to their importance to the projects with which we are working, and the characteristics of the activities themselves: while consistency across projects and organizations is a major goal, currently each activity is typically carried out by a complex collection of automated and manual techniques involving locally developer scripts, filters, and techniques. In these areas it is often found that this variety of methods, techniques, tools, and scripts is an obstacle to efficiency and quality. Understanding and organizing this material is imperative if the practices are to be managed and improved

However, in applying the CASP approach to software maintenance we believe it is necessary to adjust the approach to the needs of maintainers. For these software maintenance CASPs we have identified a number of key aspects which must be directly addressed within the CASP.

First, we recognize the importance of explicitly defining a series of software maintenance scenarios within a CASP. Most maintenance activities are driven by key events that trigger activities to occur (e.g., a new system release, an bug report, etc.). It seems essential to use these events as an index into the CASP, and to organize much of the material around these events. For example, given the report of a critical failure in a mission-critical operational system, the CASP should facilitate determining the processes, methods, and tools required to respond to that event. This makes the CASP a focal point for maintainers who will use the CASP as the primary source of information on how to handle key maintenance events.

Second, it has been recognized within our particular maintenance organization that the CASP approach may be an ideal instrument to assist them with a significant educational problem they are facing in migrating a cadre of existing maintenance engineers to a new set of practices. While a range of educational materials is available or in development, the CASP approach is seen as a way to tie them to operational practices and to make the educational aspects much more relevant to the software maintainer. Use of electronic CASPs leads to possibilities of including computer-aided learning, simulation, and on-line training as part of a CASP. So, for example, part of the software testing CASP may be training to new software maintainers on how to create appropriate test cases for unit testing, with on-line examples and exercises for the maintainer to try.

Third, we are finding that a key issue in some software maintenance organizations is clearly to define the roles and responsibilities of different parts of the organization. This issue is particularly important were part or all of the maintenance activities are performed by sub-contractor organizations. In these cases it is essential that the CASP explicitly distinguishes who is responsible for performing an activity, who performs the task of overseeing that activity, and how disputes and disagreements are handled. For example, a change control board (CCB) is a common mechanism for prioritizing and problem reports and assigning them to various future releases of a system. Describing the CCB, its make up, roles, and authority could be a key aspect of a CM CASP.

4.3 Summary

In most organizations there is a clear need for the application of a systematic, cost-effective approach to documentation and improvement of software maintenance practices. While the CASP approach provides a significant opportunity to address this need, software maintenance presents a number of challenges to the use of the CASP approach. In our use of the CASP approach we are particularly focusing on 3 key challenges:

- re-orienting the CASP to be more event based through the incorporation of typical maintenance scenarios;

- expanding the CASP approach to adequately deal with the training needs of software maintainers;

- clearly distinguishing the different roles and responsibilities of those carrying out software maintenance tasks.

5. Conclusions and Future Work

In the current climate of shrinking budgets, rapid hardware evolution, and expanding end-user needs, modernization of software maintenance practices is essential in every software organization. However, infusion of new technologies is painfully slow, expensive, and unpredictable. Much of the reason for this is that technology transition is rarely simply a technology problem — many other social, economic, and political issues must also be overcome.

To directly address these problems the CASP approach provides a focal point for identifying and transitioning the wide variety of information that forms the processes, methods, and tools applicable to a software maintenance practice. In this way the CASP approach shares many of the characteristics of other more generic technology transition approaches (e.g., the "whole product" approach [2]) while being specifically tailored to the needs of software engineers.

Our experiences with the CASP approach in software development organizations has been very positive, supporting activities such as requirements analysis and software design. We are now applying the CASP approach to software maintenance organizations and adjusting the CASP approach to better suit the needs of software maintainers. We are in the early stages of applying CASPs to software maintenance, and many more lessons will be learned as the approach matures.

Acknowledgments

Much of the pioneering work on the definition and application of the CASP approach was carried out by Jock Rader of Hughes Aircraft Corp.

The SEI is sponsored by the U.S. Department of Defense.

6. References

[1] Brown A.W., Christie A.M. and Dart S.A., "A*n Examination of Software Maintenance Practices in a U.S. Government Organization*", Journal of Software Maintenance, V7, #4, pp223-238, Wiley, 1995.

[2] Fowler P. and Levine L., "A Conceptual Framework for Software Technology Transition, Technical Report, Software Engineering Institute, Pittsburgh, PA, CMU/SEI-93-TR-31, 1993.

[3] Guimaraes T., "*Managing Application Program Maintenance Expenditures*", CACM V26, #10, pp739 - 46, 1983.

[4] Layzell P.J. and Macaulay L., "An Investigation into Softare Maintenence — Perceptions and Practices", Proceedings of the Conference on Software Maintenance, pp130-140, IEEE, 1990.

[5] Rader J.A., "*Automatic Document Generation with CASE on a DoD Avionics Project*", Proceedings of the 10th Digital Avionics Systems Conference, Los Angeles, CA, October 1991.

[6] Rader J.A. and Brown A.W., "*Computer-Aided Sub-Processes (CASPs): A Practical Approach to the Use of CASE Technology to Support Process Improvement*", Proceedings of the Sixth International Workshop on Computer-Aided Software Engineering (CASE95), pp20-29, IEEE, 1995

IEEE COMPUTER SOCIETY
50 YEARS OF SERVICE •1946-1996

http://www.computer.org

Press Activities Board

Vice President:
Joseph Boykin
CLARiiON Advanced Storage Solutions
Coslin Drive
Southborough, MA 01772
(508) 480-7286
FAX (508) 480-7908
j.boykin@computer.org

Jon T. Butler, Naval Postgraduate School
James J. Farrell III, Motorola
Mohamed E. Fayad, University of Nevada
I. Mark Haas, Tandem Computers, Inc.
Ronald G. Hoelzeman, University of Pittsburgh
Gene F. Hoffnagle, IBM Corporation
John R. Nicol, GTE Laboratories
Yale N. Patt, University of Michigan
Benjamin W. Wah, University of Illinois
Ronald D. Williams, University of Virginia

Editor-in-Chief
Advances in Computer Science and Engineering Board
Jon T. Butler
Naval Postgraduate School
Dept. of Electrical and Computer Engineering
833 Dyer Road #437, Code EC/BU
Monterey, CA 93943-5121
Phone: 408-656-3299 FAX: 408-656-2760
butler@cs.nps.navy.mil

Editor-in-Chief
Practices for Computer Science and Engineering Board
Mohamed E. Fayad
Computer Science, MS/171
Bldg. LME, Room 308
University of Nevada
Reno, NV 89557
Phone: 702-784-4356 FAX: 702-784-1833
fayad@cs.unr.edu

IEEE Computer Society Executive Staff
T. Michael Elliott, Executive Director
H. True Seaborn, Publisher
Matthew S. Loeb, Assistant Publisher

IEEE Computer Society Press Publications

The world-renowned Computer Society Press publishes, promotes, and distributes a wide variety of authoritative computer science and engineering texts. These books are available in two formats: 100 percent original material by authors preeminent in their field who focus on relevant topics and cutting-edge research, and reprint collections consisting of carefully selected groups of previously published papers with accompanying original introductory and explanatory text.

Submission of proposals: For guidelines and information on CS Press books, send e-mail to cs.books@computer.org or write to the Acquisitions Editor, IEEE Computer Society Press, P.O. Box 3014, 10662 Los Vaqueros Circle, Los Alamitos, CA 90720-1314. Telephone +1 714-821-8380. FAX +1 714-761-1784.

IEEE Computer Society Press Proceedings

The Computer Society Press also produces and actively promotes the proceedings of more than 130 acclaimed international conferences each year in multimedia formats that include hard and softcover books, CD-ROMs, videos, and on-line publications.

For information on CS Press proceedings, send e-mail to cs.books@computer.org or write to Proceedings, IEEE Computer Society Press, P.O. Box 3014, 10662 Los Vaqueros Circle, Los Alamitos, CA 90720-1314. Telephone +1 714-821-8380. FAX +1 714-761-1784.

Additional information regarding the Computer Society, conferences and proceedings, CD-ROMs, videos, and books can also be accessed from our web site at www.computer.org.

6/11/96